MUSIC MAKERS

MUSIC MAKERS

A Guide to Singing in a Chorus or Choir
with a Short History of Choral Music

by
Gerald G. Hotchkiss

SUNSTONE
PRESS

SANTA FE

Sunstone books may be purchased for educational, business, or sales promotional use.
For information please write: Special Markets Department, Sunstone Press,
P.O. Box 2321, Santa Fe, New Mexico 87504-2321.

Library of Congress Cataloging-in-Publication Data:

Hotchkiss, Gerald G., 1930-
   Music makers : a guide to singing in a chorus or choir with a short
history of choral music / by Gerald G. Hotchkiss.
      p. cm.
   ISBN 0-86534-449-3 (softcover : alk. paper)
   1. Choral singing. 2. Voice culture. 3. Choral music. I. Title.

MT875.H83 2005
782.5—dc22
                          2005011762

Published in

WWW.SUNSTONEPRESS.COM

SUNSTONE PRESS / POST OFFICE BOX 2321 / SANTA FE, NM 87504-2321 /USA
(505) 988-4418 / ORDERS ONLY (800) 243-5644 / FAX (505) 988-1025

Dedicated to Robert Shaw,
whose advancement of choral singing is immeasurable.

CONTENTS

II: A GUIDE TO SINGING
IN A CHORUS OR CHOIR ---------- 31

PREFACE

This book was written for amateur singers like myself— men and women who love to sing together with others.

While preparing this book, I researched the history of vocal music and discovered a great deal that added not only to my knowledge of music in general but placed the songs I have sung in a new and much more enlightened perspective.

With that in mind, I have divided this book into two sections.

The first is a short history of choral music from its beginnings until today, noting its development, major influences, composers and great works. It may help you as a background to your singing, whether in a classical, religious, folk or popular mode.

The second is a complete guide to both singing itself and, in particular, singing in a group, whether it be a church choir, a symphony chorus, a madrigal octet, a folk concert or barbershop quartet.

Together, they are intended to advance your knowledge of choral music and enhance the joy of singing together.

This book is also the accumulation of what I have learned singing under many, many conductors, some of worldwide fame, others known only to a local audience. I do not list them here because leaving even one of them out would be less than complete. Each has added something to my joy and accomplishment in singing.

I

A HISTORY OF CHORAL MUSIC

I

EARLY HISTORY / 32,000 BC-500 AD

A bone flute was found in Central Europe dating back 28,000 to 32,000 years ago, proof to archaeologists, reporting in *National Geographic,* that the earliest Cro-Magnon people, now called Aurignacian from the French site where many of the stone and bone tools were discovered, had an aesthetic consciousness.

How old then, is singing? Surely older than the flute. Maybe older than language, itself. David Tame in *The Secret Power of Music* notes, "The universal vibratory energies (music) were called by the ancient Egyptians the Word of Words of their gods; to the Pythagorean of Greece they were the Music of the Spheres; and the ancient Chinese knew them to be the celestial energies of perfect harmony." It is not hard to suspect that, just as the early minstrels, the Jongleurs, of the middles ages, not only entertained, but were held in some esteem within the strict cultural confines of their society. The earliest singers were also held in awe, with music itself, a power believed to be a close link to the unknown cosmos.

Before written notation, our only sure source of knowledge about music is from pictures of instruments being played or the much earlier cache of bone flutes. Early literature would suggest that, unlike today, singing would have been limited to ceremonial rituals, holding a magical power affecting the lives of the musicians' society. Certainly it took on these characteristics in Greek, Chinese, Roman and Hebraic cultures.

Our Western ears owe much to the Greeks. The word "music," itself, comes from the Greek word *mousike*, meaning

any art presided over by the Muses. The Greeks also gave us "rhythm" and "hymn" and even "polyphony." Numbers, which much later influenced Johann Sebastian Bach, were mystical to Pythagoras, and mathematical ratios were used to organize music and later rhythm itself. In addition, the Greeks gave us notations for both instruments and the voice.

Early Christian music owes much to the Hebraic singing of psalms, as well as dancing and the playing of instruments, all mentioned in the Old Testament.

Today we separate our singing into three basic groups: religious, classical and secular or "popular." With the advent of Constantine's conversion to Christianity, uniting the religious and secular powers in one, music converged into a narrow focus on religion, culminating in the crowning of Charlemagne in 800, which consolidated Europe both politically and religiously.

Today we think of the Gregorian chants of the fifth century as the beginning of Western religious singing, just as the development of guilds and a feudal society, to counterbalance the power of the church, gave us our earliest secular songs. And throughout all this time, "folk" singing was there, continuing an oral tradition that predated all notated music.

- sy, His bur-then is light, His bur-then, His bur - then is light.

GREGORIAN CHANTS

The early church recognized the value of musical chanting to enhance the Divine Offices, such as Matins and Vespers, as well as the Mass. Most often we associate it with monophonic singing without accompaniment and usually sung with as little vibrato as possible. Chants have regained popularity in the past decade and are often added within contemporary complex choral works.

Near the end of the ninth century, voices and chants in intervals and octaves creating two, three and four part music were added, and from this start came possibly the greatest enhancement in the development of Western music.

RHYTHM

As every choral singer knows, rhythm or timing, is everything when people are singing together. It wasn't until the thirteenth century that musical notation and printing were developed. And the first notations were in threes, not twos as we note today. The threes, or triple measure, were a reflection of the Holy Trinity. Music still held that mystical godhead. By the next century, colored notes appeared to indicate a change

His yoke___ is ea -

in time value, and then around 1430, black notes indicated a shorter value than white notes, but by three-quarters rather than the one-half we use today. The first printed book of music appeared at the beginning of the fifteenth century in Venice and spread quickly throughout Europe.

POLYPHONY

Part singing, which is the simplest definition of choral work, developed from early folk songs and thus surely inspired the development of polyphonic chants. In the beginning, this singing involved three voices in the same register with a variety of rhythmic and melodic inspiration. This led to many types of modifications that culminated in the most important form of polyphonic singing in the thirteenth century, the motet.

THE MOTET

From the French *mot* meaning "word," the motet added secular words in Latin and vernacular to the chants usually sung in the tenor range and often by instruments, with voices adding words and harmonies. The popularity of the diverse and large repertoire of motets continues today.

- sy, His bur-then is light, His bur-then, His bur - then is light.

SECULAR SINGING

At the same time that church music was developing into polyphonic singing, minstrels roamed Europe. Jongleurs in France, Gauklers in Germany and Gleemen in England juggled and sang for the entertainment of the courts of their lands. In France and Germany, thousands of the songs of the troubadours and minnesingers have been preserved from the early twelfth century. Their poems and songs, preserving the customs and mores of the past, were now written down for posterity. A few centuries later in Germany, these musicians gained a middle class status as Meistersingers, master singers, with the famed singer, Hans Sachs, of the early sixteenth century immortalized in Richard Wagner's *Die Meistersinger von Nurnberg.*

THE CHORALE

As part of the Reformation, Martin Luther emphasized music in the worship service. Chorales, hymns, were employed to be sung by the congregation. Hassler and Praetorius are examples of early composers of this new form in Germany, and Jan Pieterszoon Sweelinck in Holland, and William Byrd and Orlando Gibbons in England.

THE MADRIGAL

The madrigal form that we enjoy today originated in Italy in the sixteenth century. Contrapuntal, emotional, placing an emphasis on the music fitting the words. Orlande de Lassus, Giovanni Giasomo Gastoldi, Carlo Gesualdo and the finest of them all, Claudio Monteverdi, created scores of madrigals emphasizing the Italian epigram. A typical epigram: "I die for your love; but, aha! my death frees me!" When these epigrammatical themes crossed the Alps into Germany, the madrigals took on a heavier tone: "I die and the blood leaves me, etc." and fortunately for those of us more in tune with the English madrigals, those early Germanic visceral themes were replaced with a more romantic genre: "Come, come again, sweet love," closer to the Italian whose form had reached England by the late 1500s. We sing many today, and John Dowland stands out as possibly the master of the English madrigal.

- sy, His bur-then is light, His bur-then, His bur - then is light.

THE BAROQUE PERIOD

In all of our musical heritage, the development of vocal music, both ecclesiastical and secular, during the seventeenth and early eighteenth centuries, stands above all else. From Monteverdi's *Orfeo* in 1607 to Bach's *Saint Matthew Passion* in 1729 to George Frederick Handel's *Messiah* in 1742 and the music of Andrea Gabrieli, Heinrich Schütz, Arcangelo Corelli, Jean Baptiste Lully, Henry Purcell, Antonio Vivaldi, Giovanni Battista Pergolesi, Jean Pillippe Rameau and Joseph Haydn, to name but a few of the great composers of this period, we owe such joy, inspiration, understanding and sublime comfort.

Now, we not only could sing in all parts and all rhythms and all meters and all intricacies, but are supported by instruments to introduce our voices, play as accompaniment or as another sound. We could be religious or classical or secular. We could be solo, ensemble or folk. We could sing and play and act and dance. History has given us the grand oratorios, the sublime Requiems and the great masses and passions, all of which are most often presented by amateur choruses the world over.

SOPRANO

His yoke___ is ea -

MUSIC TODAY FOR CHORUS OR CHOIR

The Opera

Most of us have sung some choruses from operas and many have tried an aria. But by and large, operatic singing is for the professionals, requiring not only a vast vocal range and strength of tone, but an understanding of many languages and all of the ramifications of phrasing, tonality and vocal development each requires. If we have any aspirations in that direction, chances are they may hinder rather than help our choral singing, since the operatic voice rarely fits into the overall sound wanted by an amateur choir. So many of us settle for the operetta, including that unique collection of parody of times and mores from England, "Gilbert & Sullivan."

Folk Songs

These wonderfully varied stories reflect different peoples of differing times and situations from low comedy to high inspiration. Whether Johannes Brahms' folk lieder, Appalachian Scotch/Irish ballads or Negro spirituals, as children, these folk songs introduced us to the love of singing.

- sy, His bur-then is   light,   His bur-then, His   bur - then is light

Their very simplicity often makes them more difficult for a chorus than an individual to sing well. But folk songs from time immemorial are ours, the amateurs, to sing.

Broadway and American Pop

The twentieth century gave the world the music of Irving Berlin, Jerome Kern, George Gershwin, Cole Porter, Richard Rogers, Frank Loesser, Frederick Loewe, Leonard Bernstein and Stephen Sondheim and the words of Oscar Hammerstein II, Lorenz Hart, Johnny Mercer, Alan Jay Lerner and Sammy Cahn.

Around the country in a hundred "Hollywood Bowls" and "Boston Pops," choruses have and are singing the great songs from Broadway and the American popular music world.

The Blues

Blues grew out of deeply rooted African music among blacks in the South. Its richness is both musically expressive and verbally emotional. For a chorus trained in classical modes, true blues requires the ability to shade notes. Structurally, the fifth and seventh of a chord are dropped a

half step to gain a blues sound. Beyond that, the words themselves often require a singer to slightly flatten a third, fifth or seventh note. Few choruses can even approximate the blues that a gospel choir can sing without much training.

Jazz

Another gift from African music was jazz. Vibrant complex rhythms laid on top of other rhythms brought jazz and swing into its popularity in America and then Europe. Western musical traditions were added, especially the use of many different instruments. Starting with Dixieland, boogie-woogie, swing and bebop, jazz continues to evolve in both popular and classical forms.

Rock (and roll)

Nothing has changed contemporary popular music like rock music. Its popularity is worldwide. Its focus on rhythm, adapted from the blues and country music, where in 4/4 time the second and fourth beat are emphasized and the guitar is usually the voice, it strings singing off key as well as on key. Rock started as an offshoot of blues and country

- - sy, His bur-then is   light,   His bur-then, His   bur - then is light.

music forms. Newer forms, rarely transcribed for choral presentation, include: heavy metal, punk, reggae, disco and rap.

"New" Music

One cannot venture into a description of twentieth century classical music without humility. We remember that in his time Bach was never first choice as a kapellmeister, that during his life Ludwig von Beethoven's most popular work was a brassy piece he did more for a joke than a serious opus. What can be said for today? Is it that the age of existentialism challenged the sacred, which was the backbone of classical music for more than two millennia. Did the new composers, like other artists in other media, feel a need to throw out the old precepts to find something entirely without precedence?

For singers, "new music" brought atonality, rhythms of immense variations, discordant voices challenging each part to hear its own and not other parts at the fear of losing one's own place.

Several "new" sounds were of obvious value. A much greater use of discordant voices leading away from nineteenth century sentimentality, best remembered in church hymns of that time—a major use of jazz tempos and rhythms, including rock, offering a bridge between classical and popular music. Much freer expressions of tonality introduced an age that would see both John Rutter's *Requiem* and Andrew Lloyd Webber's *Jesus Christ Superstar*.

Igor Stravinsky's *Le Sacre du Printemps* ushered in the new sounds. John Cage took them beyond description. Paul Hindemith maintained both classical and new forms. Aaron Copeland found the American idiom, and Bernstein challenged every singer to test his or her vocal precision in the Hebraic words and changing rhythmic patterns of his *Chichester Psalms*.

By and large, fewer composers have offered us the choral music enjoyed in the seventeenth and eighteen centuries. Major works of the twentieth century include: Stravinsky's *Symphony of Psalms*, Arthur Honegger's *King David*, Carl Orff's *Carmina Burana*, Francis Poulenc's *Gloria*, Benjamin Britten's *War Requiem* and Bernstein's *Chichester Psalms*, mentioned above.

- sy, His bur-then is light, His bur-then, His bur - then is light

The Great Choral Music

What are the great musical pieces for the chorus? Bill
Moyers once presented a two-hour program on PBS devoted
solely to the hymn, folk song, spiritual *Amazing Grace*. No
ecclesiastical music nears the popularity that the *Messiah*
enjoys in churches and concert halls the world over. These
four pieces are often regarded as the greats of classical choral
singing: Bach's *B Minor Mass*, Beethoven's *Missa Solemnis*,
Brahms' *German Requiem* and Handel's *Messiah*.

Requiems have a never-ending popularity for the chorus.
Wolfgang Amadeus Mozart's sublime Requiem was unfinished
at his death and completed by his assistant, Franz Süssmayr.
Hector Berlioz left Paris at the height of his popularity to find
in Rome small choirs of eighteen voices sometimes
augmented to thirty-two. He composed his Requiem for "eighty
women's voices, sixty tenors and seventy bases." And, "If
space permits the chorus may be doubled or tripled and the
orchestra proportionally increased." Giuseppe Verdi's operatic
Requiem was considered at first too secular for church usage.
And we haven't mentioned Gabriel Urbain Fauré's or Antonín
DvoYák's inspirational Requiems.

Many consider Brahms' *German Requiem* to be his most personal composition. He chose the text from both Testaments, and what glorious choices he made. He composed for the living rather than the dead, freeing the Requiem from a strict liturgical form. Fauré, a man of the world with an accomplished career serving a church in which he was a very doubting believer, wrote his Requiem shortly after his father's death, employing nontraditional text. Rutter's *Requiem* employed both Catholic liturgy and the seventeenth century *Book of Common Prayer*.

Remember they came to hear and see you.

II

A GUIDE TO SINGING
IN A CHORUS OR CHOIR

II

If you are like me, you've been singing for years without any vocal training other than warm-ups before a rehearsal. Sometimes your voice is in fine fettle and the high or low notes cascade from your lips with ease, while other times, nothing you do seems to help correct a faltering note or wobbly phrase.

I have searched the libraries and bookstores for a book to help me improve my singing, hoping some professional vocal music teacher had put his or her knowledge into print. There are a few, but they are too difficult, written more for the professional than the amateur like myself. That's why I decided to write this book for you and me, amateurs who love to sing, have a reasonable voice and would like to improve the tone and breadth of notes we might like to be ours. Even more to the point, I wanted to share many of the tricks and rules of group singing that great chorus directors have taught me.

Is there a perfect number of singers for a particular choral piece? I doubt it.

On May 5, 1991, as part of the celebration of the 100th Anniversary of Carnegie Hall in New York City, 2,800 singers, including seven separate choruses, gathered under the baton of Robert Shaw at 8:00 a.m., practicing a baker's dozen songs, from the simple *Old Hundredth* to Tomas Luis da Victoria's *O Vos Mones* and Mozart's *Ave Verum Corpus*.

They had never sung together before. Yet in the morning hours, they were singing quarter-tone pitch changes, not half-tones, as Shaw made one voice out of almost three thousand. And at 1:00 p.m., they gave their concert, tragically never recorded. Isaac Stern, the great violinist who almost single-handedly kept the great concert hall going, called it the crowning moment of the celebration.

Double-octets have sung Bach's *B-Minor Mass* to perfection.

For the amateur chorus, a smaller number is easier to blend but may demand sometimes too much of an individual part, especially when the four parts are divided into eight separate parts. For the church or temple choir, an additional issue arises: singers find inspiration in being part of a singing liturgy, but some, often older ones, may have difficulty with time and pitch. Do you deny them their joy for a more perfect blend, or do you embrace their enthusiasm and accept a few blemishes?

Possibly the biggest issue is not size but balance. For whatever reason, there always appears to be more sopranos and altos available than basses and, especially, tenors. So the numbers in the male parts may have more to do with the proper size of a chorus or choir than what it may be singing.

Whether in a church choir or a local chorus, a barbershop quartet or a madrigal octet, this little book can help you improve your vocal technique, your part singing and add to your contribution to the overall performance of your singing group.

Learn from these chapters and your rehearsals will sail along, giving your director more time to polish up the phrasing

and subtleties that advance your chorus or choir efforts from an average performance to an outstanding one.

SOME BASICS OF SINGING

There are all different types of voices. Some loud, some soft, some full of vibrato, others crisp like a boy soprano. And the music we sing asks for all of these. How do we create different sounds? I looked for books and asked different professional singers and voice teachers and discovered that it isn't that easy.

There is no one true path to singing, but rather many paths to the truth for your voice. Some of you will gain insight from knowing the physiology of the diaphragm, vocal chords and head, others from metaphors of feelings. But there are a few constants.

Trying *not* to sing helps. Singing high notes as if they were low notes and low notes as if they were high notes helps. Yawning before starting your first note helps. Letting the sound just come out rather than pushing it out helps. Making a round, vertically ovular mouth creates rich sounds versus angular smiling vertical mouths that create nasal harsh sounds.

His yoke____ is   ea -

It seems to be Zen—less is more, not trying is achieving, being relaxed while being intense. If this seems confusing to you, be my guest. I have sung successfully the wrong way all my life. But I may have an advantage over you. My voice is aging and not gracefully. All my bad and wrong habits are accentuating that downfall. So as difficult as it is to relearn how to sing, I know it is the only partial salvation I have left.

It means practicing breathing, the most self-conscious act I can think of—to consciously breathe deeply and support the breath from your diaphragm.

It means self-visualizing the air passing through your throat into your head.

It means consciously relaxing your jaw muscles. They tighten just at the thought.

It means hearing very different sounds coming out of your mouth from what you previously heard, not always sounding that great.

Some singers cup their ears to hear what they sound like. When I've tried that, I sound the same as when I don't and have found it a bit annoying when the singer next to me cups his or her ear (it's more men than women who do this) as if asking, "Who's on pitch?"

- sy, His bur-then is   light,   His bur-then, His   bur - then is light

I hope this introduction lets you know that in this chapter you and I are in the same boat. I am relating what others are telling me: we are beginners in a new world, relearning how to sing. I shall try to cover the variety of ideas told to me, some of which have worked for me, others have not. So you, too, will probably find some ideas useful and others not so useful.

THE PHYSIOLOGY OF SINGING

Below is a simple drawing of the passages that carry the air that is driven by your diaphragm through your vocal chords and into the shaded areas of your throat and head.

Here is what you need to visualize and do—think of the air passing to the back roof of your mouth into your head. With your jaw down and your throat open, like a yawn, let the air flow through the passages of your head, the higher and deeper the better.

His yoke___ is ea -

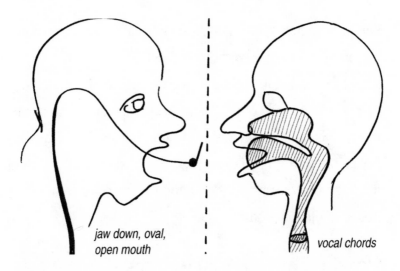

jaw down, oval, open mouth

vocal chords

Visualize your voice moving through your throat and head like this.

Actual passages through which you sing.

ROUND SOUND

Sing any vowel—eh, oh, ooh, eeh. Now as you sing that vowel, move your mouth and lips in various postures like a fish. Then change it to the laughing man at the carnival with the jaw loose and the mouth open and vertical, now open and horizontal. Listen to how different the vowel sounds. Try it with various vowels. You will soon recognize your nice

- sy, His bur-then is light,   His bur-then, His bur - then is light

sound, your rich sound. I call it your "round sound." Your lips are open and ovular—vertically round.

In your middle notes, your easy register, it will be easy to learn this round sound. But in your high and low registers, where singing is less secure, it will be harder. These are the places where you need to practice; and when you are learning a new piece, remember to keep the round sound for all your notes, not just the easy ones.

VOWELS AND CONSONANTS

Italian and Latin are easy to sing because they are full of vowels. English and German are harder because they are full of consonants. Singing is vowels. Musical instruments other than voices are only vowels and percussion. The consonants of voices create words and, unlike the other instruments of music, only our voices blend music with words. Two ideas blended into one thought, one emotion—the unique gift of singing.

An objective in singing is to maximize the vowels by careful use of the consonants. The minute we sing a consonant, music stops and only a word is formed. And some consonants, such as an r or an l, may close our vowels too

early. Fred Waring prepared words for his singers purposely omitting consonants, which impeded the musical sound and were unnecessary for the listeners' comprehension. Many r's can be omitted, "You awe the promised kiss of springtime." And when a consonant ends a word and the next word begins on a vowel, you may usually place that ending consonant on the next word, "You awe the promised ki sof springtime." There are times, however, when dropping an ending consonant or adding it to the next word changes either or both words incorrectly, so be alert to this.

I have been told that we Americans do not pronounce our vowels correctly. Maybe that's why we love to hear English actors and actresses. In any case, certain vowels, especially o and e, may be given very different sounds. Church Latin now asks for a soft e, an eh, rather than ah. S(eh)culorum not s(ay)culorum, for example. And your director may prefer a broader o that sounds like ah, rather than oh, such as gl(ah)ria, rather than gl(oh)ria.

The s consonant, particularly at the end of a phrase, can be troublesome for a choir. Your director will need careful watching so that everybody closes the vowel to an s at the same time, and in some cases, he or she may prefer just a few voices sounding the s at all. T at the end of a word also

- sy, His bur-then is light, His bur-then, His bur - then is light

needs close watching, sometimes sounded at the outside of your mouth, a strong te, and sometimes inside on the upper palate, a quieter cross between a te and a de.

An allowance some directors give sopranos and nobody else occurs on the very high notes, where vowels may tend to close the round sound. They are allowed to sing whatever vowel most comfortably allows them to sing the high notes. If all the other voices are singing the written vowel, the audience will hear it, and the very high notes will create beautiful music with no notice of a different vowel.

When a word includes a diphthong, two adjoining vowels such as in the word "lie," your director will usually ask you to hold the first vowel until the very end with just a whisper of the second. Suppose the word was on a four beat whole note. You would sing:

li	i	i	i	i	i	i	e.
one	and	two	and	three	and	four	and

I have found words beginning with wh and th especially awkward. Depending on the song, your director will probably help you decide whether to work on a strong oohwha or a meek wo. Often a director may ask you to begin the wh or th

His yoke___ is ea -

slightly before a beat so that the vowel comes out right on the beat.

Vowels on the high notes usually need extra care so that they aren't too loud. In most songs, sopranos and tenors are well advised to sing their middle and lower registers stronger than their higher registers, and nothing spoils a musical phrase more than loud high notes out of proportion to the rest of a phrase. Basses and altos need to insure that their lower notes keep "rounded" tones, when it may be tempting to close the mouth and thus close the vowel.

THE "WHOLE"

Somewhere in a notebook, F. Scott Fitzgerald admonished the would-be writer to find that one sentence or paragraph in the short story that he or she loved most, was most exquisite, and strike it out. Because it deterred from the whole, it was out of place. So it can be with a musical piece. Your director will interpret the whole and work the chorus through all its passages to create a balanced complete work. This often means that you will be asked to sing less loudly than the music states. Your fortissimos may be modified to enhance an overall passage. Or because your section is

- sy, His bur-then is light, His bur-then, His bur - then is light

stronger than another, you are asked to be quieter. Whether it be your section in a choir or a chorus in a larger work, it is written to enhance, advance, complement, contrast, expand or complete other parts taken together to make a whole.

When you have heard a great musical work, your excitement is first drawn to the totality of the performance and maybe then to individual moments. Since we sing together, many voices as one, so our chorus is often one part of that larger whole, and we can rejoice in what we bring and what the other soloists and orchestras bring to make that whole.

Down with the music and your chin, please.

YOUR VOICE

Chances are you know what voice you are. You are a soprano, an alto, a tenor or a bass. Go to a piano and find the notes that you can sing comfortably.

A soprano will be reasonably comfortable between middle C and A above the next C. An alto between G below middle C and E flat above the next C. A tenor between C below middle C and G above middle C. A bass between F below the C below middle C and D above middle C.

There are, of course, further differentiations. The coloratura soprano has the highest range even above the lyric soprano, the normal soprano voice. The mezzo soprano enjoys the same range of the lyric, but with a deeper, lower range. There is also the dramatic soprano with a more powerful voice, usually deeper but less fluid. The contralto is the lowest alto, with a richer, warmer and, unfortunately, rarer tone.

The highest male voice is the rarest, the tenor, lyric and melodious, or dramatic and more robust. The baritone is the most common male voice, a few with a range that may equal the tenor, but with a richer, deeper sound and some with the resonance and richness in the lower ranges of a bass.

- sy, His bur-then is light, His bur-then, His bur - then is light

The bass is the lowest voice, and their rich sounds build the foundation of every chorus.

It is my observation that sopranos have the most difficulty with rhythm because they too often hold high notes too long and usually sing the melody, requiring less technical thinking. Altos have beautiful voices, which they sing with timidity, partly because so often their parts are fill-in chords and they are unsure of the difficult notes. Tenors usually support their voices better than others because they cannot sing the high notes without that support, but they tend to rush running passages and need to soften their high notes that can become shrill. Basses love their sound and might be lazy; when they flat, the chorus is in deep trouble.

Most choruses are short of men. Consequently, the men often do less practice than the women. So if you are a man, don't let your scarcity give you any special rights and privileges.

BREATHING

Breathing starts with posture. Whether standing or sitting, or even lying down, as opera singers sometimes are required to do on stage, your posture is the beginning step of good

breathing. Sit near the end of your chair so that you could not slouch down if you tried to. Stand with your legs slightly bent, feet apart, shoulders back and arms relaxed.

In fact, if you are not relaxed and in good posture, you cannot sing properly, and you'll surely be tired vocally and physically well before a rehearsal is over.

The support of your notes is air, and that support needs to come from the bottom of your diaphragm, not the top of your lungs. Take a deep breath. Ask yourself, "Where did it come from?" If it came from your lungs, lifting your chest, it wasn't a deep breath, it just felt like one. Try breathing from the bottom of your diaphragm first. It will feel strange. It is strange. But if you practice this strange breathing for days and weeks and months, you will build the essential support for good singing. It is still unnatural to me, yet when I breath properly, my singing is relaxed, my notes clearer, even high ones easier.

Duke Ellington, on hearing Marian McPartland play the piano, said, "It's wonderful, Marion, but why so many notes?" So it is with proper deep breathing. You need not use more breath than your notes will require. The air supporting your singing will be just enough, neither too little nor too much. In fact, try it lying on your back. Lying down relaxes you, and if

- sy, His bur-then is light, His bur-then, His bur - then is light

47

you practice deep breaths while lying down, you will find it easier when standing up.

THE PASSAGE

Where does that air go? Up from the bottom of your diaphragm, supported by proper posture, your diaphragm muscles send it through your vocal chords in your larynx, the voice box, so to speak, then behind your tongue at the base of your throat to the rear of your mouth, reflecting off the soft palate at the roof of your mouth, with most of it going out your mouth, but some of it traveling further through your nasal passages, with vibrations going even further into your forehead and cranium.

In tennis, the power of a serve comes from the completeness of the racquet being down behind the back and coming up through a full arc, hitting the ball at the top of the arc and following through out, not down. Visualizing your sound coming from your diaphragm up through the back of your head, arcing out, not down, will help you sing and build the highest notes.

All of this is visualization. Try to see and feel your voice in its passage through your head. While you are singing out

of your mouth, think of the air filling your head, resounding through all the bones of your skull and some even coming through your nose. Imagine that the whole of your head is supporting your tone, supporting your high notes, enriching, softening, enlarging, minimizing.

Here's another comment about round sounds. Your mouth should open in an oval with the long part vertical, never in a smiley horizontal face unless the intention is to be brazen and nasal and harsh. Practice singing an ah with an oval mouth, then change it to an eh and then an e, keeping that oval. It is the e's that usually break down our oval mouths, so remember and practice to keep that oval for all the vowels.

VIBRATO

Vibrato is a natural part of the voice, and for most of your choral singing, your natural vibrato will be correct. But everyone's vibrato is different, so your director may wish you to minimize yours if it is too much. In some pieces of music, Gregorian Chants for example, you may be asked to sing a "pure" tone, like that of a boy's choir. This is very difficult for me, as my vibrato is too fast anyway. I try to find the pure tone by singing to the back of my upper mouth with no forced

- sy, His bur-then is light, His bur-then, His bur - then is light

air. If I am relaxed, this is easy, but often I am not relaxed enough and it is quite difficult, so I sing as quietly as possible with as much energy as possible without pushing.

TAKING BREATHS

Take breaths when you need them, but never at the obvious middle of a phrase when it is clear that the whole phrase must sound sustained. Mark places that are not where others are likely to take a breath. If you take it in the middle of a long note, leave and come in again quietly. Remember, one of the joys of singing together is that each of us can catch a breath separately, so that the whole goes on without interruption. If you try to sustain a passage beyond your breath needs, you'll likely sing flat or lose tempo. Sometimes, however, you've got more air than you realize, and it can be exhilarating to complete a passage with full voice and then take that breath that you were dying to take before.

Take silent breaths. If a chorus goes ahh! before a passage, that noisy breath becomes part of the piece, certainly not intended by the composer and truly abhorred by the conductor. Your breathing must be silent and early enough for you to relax before singing.

SINGING SOFTLY

When you sing pianissimo (softly), you need all the air support you can muster. You need all the energy you can muster. You need all the intensity you can muster. Nothing is as exciting as a chorus singing very quietly with great focus, where each part has a moment of movement so exquisitely heard while other parts are in the background and the intensity rises because it is so quiet.

RHYTHM

Choral singing involves words, pitch and rhythm. In order of importance, it involves rhythm, rhythm, rhythm. Perfect pitch, beautiful vowels make for naught if the rhythm is off.

Every singer, whether or not he or she can read music easily, can read the beats of each note: whole, half, quarter, eighth or sixteenth. And every singer can read the "time" expressed next to the clef sign: 4/4, 3/4, etc. The rhythm is the "beat" as expressed by the director saying, "one and a two and a three and a four." Often the composer has written how fast or slow the rhythm will be in beats per minute, but

- sy, His bur-then is   light,   His bur-then, His   bur - then is light

the singer needn't concern himself with that, since the director will establish the tempo of any song or section of song.

What separates the singer with a good sense of the beat from the average is learning and hearing the dynamic "inner beat" that lies behind the actual length of a note to be sung. It is this inner beat, a silent drummer, that sustains each note, that helps one make each "cutoff" crisp, each new note right on time and keeps each extended note full of energy, whether sung loudly or quietly, especially when sung quietly.

In a song with four beats to a measure, there are always eight or more inner beats (one and two and three and four and) (one and a two and a three and a four and a). Learn to sing the rhythm.

Do I hear a waltz?

His yoke___ is   ea -

I Got Rhythm

4/4 time

one and (rest)   two and three   and four and
                 I   GOT

one and two   and three and four and
    RHY   THM,

one and (rest)   two and three   and four and
                 I   GOT

one and two   and three and four and
    MU   SIC,

one and (rest)   two and three   and four and
                 I   GOT

one and two   and three   and four   and
    MY   MAN–   WHO   COULD

one and   two and   three   and   four and
ASK   FOR   AN-   Y   THING

one and two and three and   four and (rest)
    MORE ?

Your voice is singing, "I got rhythm, I got music, I got my man—Who could ask for anything more?" Your inner beat is drumming one and two and three and four and one and

- sy, His bur-then is light, His bur-then, His bur - then is light.

two and three and four and, etc. Not only does it make the syncopation easier, it makes each of the quarter and eighth notes crisper, and the final sustained three-quarter note gains energy as your inside ear hears the drummer beating, one and two and three and.

A common problem in choral singing is the tendency of singers to drift off on sustained notes at the end of a phrase. In George Gershwin's song about rhythm, the maintaining of that inner beat through the sustained word "more" is essential to its rhythm and liveliness.

This becomes all the more useful and essential when you sing songs with varying beats. Bernstein uses them aplenty. In *Chichester Psalms*, the chorus starts in 6/4 for one measure, 3/4 the next, 3/8 the next, 5/4 the next, 5/8 the next, 6/4 the next, then 3/4, 5/4, 7/4. Even the most professional singer must count the inner beats to hear the jazzy one/two, one/two, one/two/three, one/two.

Although there are exceptions, most phrases in music have standard places to cut off. If the final note of a phrase is followed by a rest, the singer holds that note right to the rest and stops on the up-beat of the rest. If, on the other hand, the final note of the phrase is followed immediately by the first note of a new phrase, the singer "cheats" the final note of the

preceding phrase, so that he or she can begin the new note right on time with energy. If one doesn't take a quarter or eighth rest, the new phrase always begins late with less than its needed intensity and precision.

Singing Bach, Handel and other baroque music, where there are runs and long phrases of short notes, the singer needs to hear the important beats and usually stress them slightly more than the others. Rather than giving each note equal value, da, da, da, da, da, da, the singer sings DA, da, da, DA, da da, or da DA, da, da DA, da. All music has dance to it. If you feel the dance, you will hear the beat and you will perceive the notes to be stressed.

The most common fault in chorus singing is slowing down on pianissimo passages. Unless the music indicates a retard, singing softly should never include singing slower. In fact, it is often the intensity of the rhythm maintained through the soft, quiet passages that creates its intensity. Here again, listening to the inner beat will strengthen the pianissimo passages.

Sopranos need to take special care in singing high notes so they do not hold them longer than their value. In building to support those notes, it can be difficult to "give them up" on time. For all voices, when notes run through

sy, His bur-then is light, His bur-then, His bur - then is light where your voice "changes," be careful to maintain the beat. Often the vocal change leaves you slightly unsure of the next note, and dwelling on its pitch can make you miss a beat. Remember, rhythm first, notes second.

You will know when your rhythm is truly good. The conductor or director will take liberties with the written notes. He or she will shorten eighth notes, sustain certain phrases and begin to interpret his or her understanding of what the composer intended, which perhaps was never perfectly written down. But that cannot happen until each member of the chorus feels the beat so surely that he or she can slow it down, speed it up and always keep it in sync.

There is only one beat that is correct in choral singing—the beat of the conductor. You must feel it, and the only way you can do so is to watch him or her. On key phrases, for either the whole group or your part, you must watch for the introduction and always watch the conductor out of the corner of your eye while looking at the music.

There is only one voice in a chorus—the whole chorus, and you can only attain that if you can hear the other parts, especially when you are not singing. Too often a part that is silent will come in late upon reentry. If you listen and count

the inner beats of the other parts that are singing, you will always be in the music and your part will come in on time.

During rehearsals, it is tempting to rest while other parts are practicing, whisper to an associate or take it easy. Don't. Talking is always unacceptable.

If the director asks if there are any difficult places, never hesitate to raise your hand. You aren't alone, and what is difficult for you is often difficult for others.

READING MUSIC

Sometimes singers in a choir or chorus cannot read music or only partially read a score. How do you learn your part? Like some others, you might have learned the way most of us first learn, by ear. A doctor friend of mine would begin our first rehearsals by singing many wrong notes but always in the right chord, and slowly he switched to the right notes as he sat with others of us and heard them. By the sixth rehearsal, he had all the notes right and sang them beautifully with his clear and sure voice.

There may be some members of a chorus who are to some degree unsure of their ability to sight read. As they get to know their parts, they may sing more assuredly, but even

- sy, His bur-then is   light,   His bur-then, His   bur - then is light

in the concert, some can be a bit timid on the difficult parts of the score. Hopefully, there are always one or two singers who lead, but also, hopefully, they do not have to lead by singing alone or too loudly. You may not become nor want to become that leader, but you can become a stronger supporter.

As I wrote this section, it became clear to me that it is very difficult to teach sight reading in a book. Reading this will help you, but I suspect you will need to learn to read with friends and an instructor. You may want to ask your director if a sight reading class could be arranged, or if that isn't possible, get a member of the chorus to help those wishing to be better sight readers.

Many of us have learned the scales: do, re, me, fa, sol, la, ti, do. Probably back in grammar school, and too many years have passed since you have had need of them. The octave between one do and another do contains twelve half steps (thirteen if you include both do's). We call them: do, di, re, ri, me, fa, fi, sol, si, la, li, ti, do. The octave also contains whole steps, and the scales we learned as children contain both: do-re-me are two whole steps; me-fa is a half step; fa-sol-la-ti are three whole steps; and ti-do is a half step.

You can hear a whole step or a half step. With practice you can even visualize them. Take the easiest song your chorus is practicing. Since you are learning to read the music, forget about the words and just concentrate on the notes themselves.

The first thing you will need to learn are the notations, the notes, that are written on the lines or in the spaces on the two clefs used to describe music.

Soprano, alto and tenor parts are notated on the upper or G clef; basses and occasionally tenors are notated on the lower or C clef. These two clefs and the spaces in between them tell you where your notes are, and they are all the notes of the scale.

Do   Re   Me   Fa   Sol   La   Ti   Do
Both are in the same key of C, one octave apart. Sopranos and altos sing in the upper clef, basses in the lower clef; temors sing in both clefs.

- sy, His bur-then is   light,   His bur-then, His   bur - then is light

Second, you will need to see what "key" the music is written in. That will tell you where do is. Learning what key a piece of music is written in is easy.

If there are no sharps or flats notating the key, it is the key of C. Were you to play its scale on the piano, you would use only the white keys. It is the easiest to learn. For all other keys, you need to learn the two verses somebody made up to help us.

For sharps: *Good Deeds Are Ever Bearing Fruits.* One sharp is G, two is D, three is A, etc. If the music is written in three sharps, it is in the key of A. You look for the A on your clef, and that is do.

For flats: *Farmer Brown Eats Apples Down Good.* One flat is F, two is B, three is E, etc. If the music is written in two flats, it is the key of B. You look for the B on your clef, and that is do.

At this point, you may be saying to yourself, "He must be crazy to think I can learn all this mumbo jumbo." Please stay with me, and you will discover a happy ending. Just to make you feel better, Irving Berlin, the most prolific composer of popular music ever, hated all these different keys. He played his music only in the key of F sharp, which you have learned is six sharps, using all the black keys on the piano. But he

60

instinctively knew that F sharp wasn't the right key for all his music. So he had a piano made with gears added that could change the notes. He continued to play all those black keys, but the gears switched them to others, depending on what actual key he wanted to use—usually C, B flat or E flat, the most popular keys, because they fit the vocal ranges of most voices.

Let's go back and review. Each line or space on the scale represents a note, such as A or D sharp or B flat. All you need to do is find what key the music is written in and where that key is, because that is your do on the scale.

You know that between do and re is a whole step; between re and me is a whole step. Thus, if the first two notes are do and me, you sing two whole steps. Let's just sing the scale.

                                        DO
                                    TI
                                LA
                            SOL
                        FA
                    ME
                RE
            DO

-sy, His bur-then is   light,   His bur-then, His   bur - then is light

You also will notice that there are other notes between many of these, but don't concern yourself with them until you feel very comfortable with the basic notes of the scale. When they occur in your part, for the beginning, just circle them and remember that they require a half step up or down from your basic scale notes.

And also remember that you have an added gift that many good readers may not. If you have learned to sing by ear, you have a very good "ear."

Use that ear because it will instinctively give you most of your notes. In listening to others in your part and singers in the other parts, you will already know about where your note is, even before learning to sight read. Sight reading is an extension of your basic knowledge. It is not a replacement.

WORDS

No other musical group has the flexibility of intonation, pitch and subtlety of expression than the totality of choral singing offers. But the essential and most important difference between a symphony or string quartet and a chorus is the words.

The words are of primary importance. The music is an extension, an inspiration derived from the words.

A favorite story of urban folklore notes that Mrs. Richard Rogers and Mrs. Oscar Hammerstein were lunching at the Palm Court of the Plaza Hotel in New York one weekday, when they were approached by a lady who remarked, "Oh, Mrs. Rogers, I so love your husband's songs. My favorite is *Some Enchanted Evening.*" To which Mrs. Hammerstein replied, "Excuse me, but *my* husband wrote *Some Enchanted Evening;* Mrs. Rogers' husband wrote 'da de-da, de-da-da.'"

The words tell a story, express an emotion and describe a scene. Often, we sing in the original language because translations never quite fit the original. When that language is foreign to us, it is essential that we read and understand a translation, so that we can approximate the intention of the words as if they were native to us.

Sometimes, when we sing hymns in Latin, Hebrew or other languages, we forget that they, too, are words put to music. The phrasing is just as exact as in our own native tongue. Just as we say, "words, comma, put to music," not "words put, comma, to music," we need help from our conductor or knowledgeable chorus member to phrase correctly in the language we are singing.

- sy, His bur-then is light, His bur-then, His bur - then is light

Often, there is a story behind a particular song or chorale, and a good director will relate it to help illuminate the context behind the words, to explain why the music sets the words as it does.

Some composers, like Monteverdi, make the words and music one, and it would be difficult to lose their integrity. Others, unfortunately, are not as unified, and a director must make the choices between an intelligent verbal passage and an intelligent vocal passage.

The stirring French national anthem, *Marseillaise,* composed by Rouget de L'Isle, is a wonderful example of words and music as one. *The Star-Spangled Banner*'s composer is omitted in Webster's Collegiate Dictionary, possibly to save embarrassment for a singsong ditty so badly suited to its words that pop singers maul it with applause at baseball and football games.

The phrasing of words is a key to choral singing. Frank Sinatra developed the ability to hold phrases for six and eight bars by swimming underwater and silently saying phrases as if he were singing. And we have no better example of the importance of words than his or Ella Fitzgerald's clear diction and perfect phrasing.

WORDS AND MUSIC–
OR–MUSIC AND WORDS

Which comes first, the words or the music? This chicken and egg proposition has two correct answers–both. Certainly in popular music, librettists and composers have often interchanged who started something. The Richard Rogers' *Victory at Sea* music came before its use in a musical with the words by Oscar Hammerstein II following. Parts of Handel's *Messiah* were taken from earlier scores, as was quite common among composers in those days. So there, too, the words came later. But more often than not, the words come first, obviously, in setting poetry to music, but also in opera, madrigals, folk songs and blues.

The conductor may favor words over music or music over words, depending on his or her interpretation of the work. Beautiful melodic passages often demand phrasing of notes over words that don't always command the right emphasis of phrase. In other cases, the sheer poetry of the words demands that they take precedence. German lieder incorporates both. Monteverdi madrigals demand both. Negro spirituals are both.

-sy, His bur-then is light, His bur-then, His bur - then is light.

For the singer, two issues often come into play. One, diction, a clear enunciation of a word. Wh's and th's starting a sentence need to be spit out before the downbeat. Otherwise, the vowel, the first actual musical sound coming out of your voice, will be late, and nothing is as noticeable as a late entrance. The g sound can clam up your mouth with your tongue sticking to its roof (just try it) and, again, forcing a late entrance. Many choruses use a k sound rather than g—*Klory to God* for instance. The audience, particularly listening to well-known choruses, will hear a g.

Never mind her clinker, you'll get your turn.

His yoke___ is   ea -

Two, a good, round improper sound, rather than a proper ugly sound. In the upper registers of sopranos and occasionally tenors, a lovely vowel, however improper, is better than a rasping or throat tightening proper vowel. Basses are tempted to fill their chests with a deep basso profundo voice, as they register lower notes, when a lighter sound is appropriate and supports the other voices.

"Words, words, words," Elisa Doolittle cried out in *My Fair Lady.*

When singing German, it is always consonants, consonants, consonants—spitting out the gutturally rich beginning of so many German words, getting to the vowel on the beat, which means the consonants sneak in ahead of time.

For American voices, the trick is to get your words in the front of your mouth right next to your teeth. You may not have time to say anything in the back of your throat. Italian, Spanish, Portuguese and Latin are so much easier. The vowels are everything. French has its own peculiar mystique, with vowels on the tip of your tongue.

Whatever the language, part of your private practice should be with the words, especially when there are fast

- sy, His bur-then is light, His bur-then, His bur - then is light

phrases where you will never have time to look at the music, the words and the conductor all at once.

Cheating

There will be times when you find you cannot do it all. So cheat. Decide what you can do. Skip a quick word if you find you are always late on the important down beat or stressed word. Drop s endings if you are late. The others in the chorus will make up for your silence. If you lose a high note or a low note, let it float by silently and come back in within your comfort zone. But don't cheat out of timidity. How many chorus members don't come in right at the start of a piece out of uncertainty, "Let George do it!" That's a no-no. Count the beats before you sing, take a breath well before the downbeat and sing it out right on time—with George.

PRACTICE

Let's start with a confession. None of us practices between rehearsals as much as we should, and many of us never practice. So what can you do about it?

His yoke___ is ea - - - - - - -

First, ask yourself why. Maybe you have trouble sight reading and you don't have a piano and you question how you could practice. There are many things to practice besides the notes. There are the words. You can practice the words in time without notes. Or there are tricky rhythms, syncopations. You can practice these. If you arrive at each rehearsal with the words and the tricky rhythms down pat, you will be the star of any section.

Second, be realistic. You don't need to require of yourself an allotment of time that is unrealistic. Two 20-minute practices between each rehearsal will be a big help. You may even have trouble finding that much time. But there will be times when you know practice can really make a big difference before the next rehearsal.

Third, ask for part rehearsals outside, as well as during, rehearsals. If your section has more problems than others, ask a section leader or somebody with a piano to practice together. Some problems cannot be solved individually. They need the whole section.

Fourth, remember you aren't the only one who needs the practice or who feels a little guilty when he or she hasn't practiced.

- sy, His bur-then is light, His bur-then, His bur - then is light

REHEARSALS

Non-singers don't really understand that singing in choirs and choruses requires a lot of rehearsals. For every performance, there have been dozens and more rehearsals. A fortunate few groups enjoy spacious places with tuned pianos ready to abet the twenty or eighty rehearsing singers. But for many of us, cramped schoolrooms, awkward sanctuaries and slightly heated halls, accompanied by badly tuned pianos, are often the stuff of rehearsal support.

Who needs to watch the conductor when you can slouch so comfortably.

No matter. Ours to make the most of what we are given. And that is what this chapter addresses: how to make the most of rehearsals.

1. Talking. Do it before and after, not during.

2. Listening. Especially when your part is *not* being addressed. Nine times out of ten, whatever the director is addressing to another part also applies to yours in another section of the piece. Why waste rehearsal time making him or her repeat the whole message when your part comes up. Or, after addressing one part, the director wishes the whole chorus to sing, and not having listened, those other parts haven't a clue where they are in the piece. Had you listened, you would know.

3. Watching. How many times has a director motioned to cut or stop singing and dozens continue on for measure upon measure, until they notice there seems to be less than a full group of voices singing. This just wastes precious rehearsal time. So, *watch all the time.*

4. Posture. Sit up, preferably near the front of your chair. This will support your torso and prevent

slouching. If you slouch, you will give less energy than your part requires, and your pitch may waver.

5. Always be involved in the music. Especially when your part is not singing. You might note that your part has seven measures with no singing, and you blithely sit back and look around the room. Then suddenly, your part enters the piece, and your entry is late. Often, that entry is the most important moment in the music. So more minutes of rehearsal time are lost repeating the passages up to your entry, when your section, now finally awake, sings right on time!

6. Entries. Try not to depend on another section for your entry. Then, if a section is late or misses their entry, you don't compound the error. That means, of course, counting time. I find marking in pencil on the music, 1, 2, 3 or whatever beats before my entry, helps me be on time, whether or not another section was there to help me. If I do it in rehearsals, it comes naturally in the performance.

7. Stops. Only the director can make a chorus or choir stop as one voice. If you're not watching, it just cannot happen. Sometimes the stop is right on the

end of a beat, sometimes held over to the start of the next. Often, there is no retard, and the dynamic of the passage is in the moment of stopping. There may be a retard with different parts moving separately until the final note, which may be held longer than you anticipated. Stopping and starting are always important, so watch the director.

8. Paper clips. We skip all over the place in rehearsals, singing parts of pieces, and rarely rehearse a major work in its performance order. If you clip the separate sections, you'll find where the director wants you to be quicker and save time.

9. Marking. Presume your memory is faulty. Mark lightly in pencil all the directions your director makes. Much time is wasted every rehearsal going over the same notes on diminuendos, on dropping r's, on cutting notes shorter than annotated so that a new passage can begin with more emphasis, on changes of rhythm, whatever. From your first rehearsal on, mark it all in your music.

THE AGING VOICE

Surprise, surprise! Like every other muscle in our bodies, our vocal chords need exercise. As a friend once noted to me, "After fifty, it's all maintenance." The elasticity in our bodies we once took for granted, like an old rubber band, now does not bounce back as quickly. If stretching our legs is needed to keep our backs in shape, exercising our vocal chords is equally needed to keep our voices in shape.

The problem is not just a routine of warming up the voice, but often where to do it. Our spouses or roommates may not enjoy twenty minutes of our warbling every other day, and singing in the shower isn't exactly what we have in mind. If you are driving alone in a car, this may be an ideal place to practice. Or when everyone else leaves the house, grab a few minutes.

What to do? Each of us can make up our own routine. A good beginning is to copy your director's warm-up exercises. You don't even need a piano to start a simple scale: do, re, me, fa, sol, fa, me, re, do. Sing ah's and hums and eh's and oh's. Practice round tones. Move your voice from an eh to an ah without widening your mouth into a nasal blast—keeping your mouth opening the same for all the vowels.

As you sing scales or whatever intervals you choose, and as you go up the scale by half notes, try to keep your vocal chords relaxed as you gain higher tones. Don't "push" the voice to gain a higher note. Or on descending scales, remember to keep the lower notes high. We tend to flat descending notes if we don't "think" high. And as you reach very low notes, try to sing them as relaxed high notes. Similarly to the high ones, pushing the voice spoils the tone.

Whether you sing mah, me, mo or tra, la, la, the important thing is to exercise your vocal chords regularly and enjoy the rewards of how much better you feel and sing at rehearsals, as well as concerts.

YOUR FELLOW SINGERS

You are a member of a choir or chorus. Why not be the nicest, most supportive, helpful member. Here's how:

1. Be on time.
2. Warm up your voice by singing on your way to rehearsal.
3. Get there early sometimes to help move the chairs, etc.

- sy, His bur-then is light, His bur-then, His bur - then is light

4. Gossip and chat before the rehearsal starts, not during it.

5. When a note is given for pitch, do not hum your part.

6. Don't stomp your foot or pat your hand to the rhythm.

7. When your part isn't singing, pay attention to the music and don't chat with your neighbor.

8. If a neighbor makes a mistake, don't give him or her a dirty look.

9. If another singer needs help, offer it kindly.

10. Have your music in the right order for each rehearsal.

11. Mark up your music (lightly in pencil if it isn't yours) so you don't repeat errors.

12. Don't be afraid of making mistakes in rehearsal, such as holding back from an entrance lest you be too early or not singing a tough note lest it be wrong.

13. Compliment somebody you think is singing well.

14. Compliment another part that has handled something well.

15. Laugh and enjoy each rehearsal.

16. Loosen up.

Save your gyrations for the barbershop quartet.

FINDING A VOCAL COACH

This may be the most difficult part of choral singing. Ask fellow singers, choir directors, choral conductors and soloists for their recommendations. Sometimes, but not always, a coach who has your same voice (soprano, alto, tenor, bass) may be best.

-sy, His bur-then is light, His bur-then, His bur - then is light

Let your teacher know your own goals. Do you want to solo? Do you want to expand your vocal range? Do you want to sing particular types of songs?

Don't be afraid to change teachers if you aren't getting what you feel you need. Every voice is different, and every person has his or her own special needs and, just as importantly, special goals.

Some clues. If the teacher doesn't start with posture and breathing, with the need to relax and the desire to sing naturally, find one that does. You should enjoy the work of singing, and your teacher should help you enjoy it. Find out how much practice he or she asks of you and make sure it is realistic to your other demands. Where can you practice? Get help there, too.

SINGING GROUPS

If you haven't sung in many diverse singing groups, you may find a new type both challenging and rewarding. Here are a few of the many types of groups you may wish to join.

The Barbershop Quartet

This is usually a male group, but there are also female quartets. The style is "close singing," which is harmony that shades notes, usually with one or two voices moving around the whole notes held by the other two or three. The enjoyment of quartet music is in the intimacy of the singers, the opportunity of playing around with harmony, improvisation and usually not taking anything too seriously.

The Octet

Colleges and universities are the centers of numerous singing groups, usually octets, who offer popular ballads, college songs and, often, original humorous parodies of college life. The advantage of the octet over the quartet is the doubling of each voice or sometimes harmonies for eight separate voices. Octets also can sing a broad classical repertoire, and there are several professional singing groups famous for their breadth of music. The King Singers are an excellent example.

- sy, His bur-then is   light,   His bur-then, His   bur - then is light.

Madrigals

Singing madrigals offers you a wide variety of music, requiring both a challenge in the music and in the interpretation of the words. The epigrams that make up most madrigals are clever plays on words. Consequently, the words are just as important as the music. These are period pieces from a different time and place, yet worthy of listening to in every age.

Chamber Music

For much of America, there is no local symphony. Chamber music offers a smaller opportunity to expand the size of a chorus and music written for smaller groups. For the singer, it is an opportunity to sing with instruments accompanying the voices. Because the number of singers is smaller and the singing an integral part of the orchestral arrangements, your sight reading and musical ability will be tested. Much of Bach and Handel and Mozart is written for the chamber orchestra and chorus. Oratorios fit into this category, although they also can command a full orchestra.

Large Choruses

We are now talking about sixty or more singers with at least a dozen members in each part. They will be accompanied by chamber orchestras, as well as full orchestras, with the opportunity to sing the big choral works of Bach and Beethoven and Gustav Mahler. Because there are many singers, smaller voices, less accomplished singers, may find it challenging but worth the effort. My own personal negative about large groups, but certainly not in importance compared to the rewards of singing the great pieces, is hearing all the other parts. In rehearsals and too often in the actual performance, it is hard to hear all the other voices. When the sopranos and altos and tenors and basses are grouped together as sections, with the full orchestra in front of everybody, one can sing in proper rhythm watching the conductor, but not always in vocal balance. That is why the conductor so often will signal one part to tone down or another to sing more fully. (I don't say louder, because that often means a loss of vocal beauty.)

The best of all times, but too seldom enjoyed, is when a large chorus really knows its music and the individual parts are mixed up, so you are singing next to men and women

- sy, His bur-then is light, His bur-then, His bur - then is light

from other voices, not depending on a strong voice from your own section, but harmonizing in perfect balance with the others. You know when your part is dominant, when it is secondary and you all blend to the subtle changes in tonality, in rhythm, in phrasing a passage your conductor can create. That should always be your goal.

In most cases, large choruses practice with a practice director who will spend most of his or her time on notes, rhythm, timing and diction. You will be whipped into shape for the conductor to add phrasing, dynamics, meaning and balance with the orchestra.

Hide and seek in the back row.

When your concert is a great success and you are especially pleased with that conductor, remember your practice director who put all the hours shaping you for the concert's conductor. It reminds me of a question I once asked a fine winemaker, "Which is more important, the grapes or the winemaker?" "Eighty-five percent is in the grapes, and the other fifteen percent is in the winemaking," he responded. The grapes are your rehearsals, tended by your practice director. Then and only then can the maestro add his or her fifteen percent and get all the credit.

Opera Choruses

Friends of mine have been extras at the opera, carrying spears or whatever. But the choruses are made up of professionals, many, young voices on their way to larger parts and, for the rare few, the major roles.

Gilbert & Sullivan

Whether you are *Twenty Love-Sick Maidens We* or *Rising Early in the Morning,* you are part of the music of Arthur Seymour Sullivan and the words of William Schwenck

-sy, His bur-then is light, His bur-then, His bur - then is light

Gilbert—unique in the repertoire of English-speaking music. In cities large and small, in high schools and colleges, Gilbert & Sullivan is being performed somewhere every week of the year. My older brother began singing Gilbert & Sullivan in college and joined a group wherever he lived for the rest of his life. He reminded me that, while I was singing in my choirs and choruses with the music in front of me, he was not only singing without music, learning many, many refrains, but also dancing and cavorting on stage. If you like to do that and find the audacious words of the genius Gilbert and the sometimes banal ditties of the overrated (in his time) Sullivan a joy and challenge, you are in for treats wherever you reside.

Broadway Musicals

Our native *oeuvre*, although other nations have tried a few times to copy it. If Gilbert & Sullivan is too nineteenth century for you, Broadway offers twentieth and now twenty-first century ballads and patter songs, dancing and cavorting in the South or Siam, New York or Oklahoma, in top hats or rags. Any one of the top composers has written enough choruses to present *An Evening of . . .* Depending on your

84

SOPRANO

His yoke___ is   ea -

interests and talents, you might audition for a full musical in costumes and sets or a concert of Broadway musicals.

Other Groups

Your town may offer a hybrid. A singing group that does a little of everything from folk songs to cantatas. It has no set number of voices and may have as its core mission just the love of singing. These groups usually are more social and have singers of varying degrees of musical knowledge and ability. If there is not one where you live, and it is just what you would like, think about starting one yourself. Find a few voices who sing in church and temple choirs, a good pianist to accompany you, maybe a director from one of the schools, someplace to practice and send out the word.

TO CONDUCTORS AND DIRECTORS

This book was written for the many amateurs who sing under your direction. So it is only fair to suggest a few things that might improve our ability to perform up to your hopes and aspirations.

- sy, His bur-then is   light,   His bur-then, His   bur - then is light

1. In front of the group, never point to an individual who has made a mistake. It not only embarrasses the person but intimidates the whole chorus to the point that a section may be late entering a piece because each singer is fearful of making a mistake.

2. If you start a rehearsal with a piece or section in which the sopranos or tenors have too many high notes, you may lose those sections for the night. Amateur voices need a lot of warming up.

3. Don't be afraid of challenging us. Be demanding but with humor.

4. We may be able to chew gum and ride a bicycle, but not much more at one time. So limit your suggestions to two or three things at any one time.

5. Demand that we pencil in key instructions on diction, phrasing, cut offs, entrances.

6. Depending on the weather, we tire at different times. So be aware when we may need a short break.

7. If you are the actual conductor, please let the rehearsal director early on know any idiosyncrasies you plan, so we don't practice in some other style or sing parts too slowly or too quickly for your tempo.

Well, here you are, standing with feet apart, legs slightly bent, shoulders back, relaxed. Your music—that you have carefully annotated, spotting difficult places, key rests, when you must look at the conductor—is below your face and high enough to see it and your conductor. Your mouth is oval for a round sound. You've taken some deep breaths quietly.

Let your eyes smile, that oval mouth give just a hint of a smirk, your body a sense of confidence and, with all your fellow choristers, your choir, sing your heart out together.

- sy, His bur-then is light, His bur-then, His bur - then is light

If it's you or the kettle drum, you lose.

III

THE AUTHOR AND SINGING

III

Friends have asked me, "Have you always sung?" and as far back as I can remember, the answer is, "Yes." Like many others, I began singing in our church choir when I was nine or ten years old. In one piece of music, four of us were asked to be an antiphonal chorus in the front balcony, away from the rest of the choir. The director asked reflectively, "How will you get your note?" I answered, "I have it." Rather annoyed, he asked me what it was, and I sang the note, which

91

he then went to the piano and played. I was blessed with perfect pitch, and I presumed everybody heard the notes they read on a music score. My father had and my son has a musical asset much more important—a perfect sense of rhythm. I have learned to improve my timing by always counting the rhythm and reminding myself to slow down—like some tenors, I speed up on runs.

The first classical music we were taught in grammar school were two songs, *Barcarolle* from Jacque Offenbach's *Contes d'Hoffmann* and *Anitra's Dance* from Edvard Hagerup Grieg's *Peer Gynt.* I've always wondered what music teacher decided on those two as a beginner's introduction.

My first solo was in seventh grade in junior high school, *Shortnin' Bread.* I shall never forget the distraught face of Miss Florence McQueeny, who was directing the chorus, when nothing came out of my mouth on the first verse. In my terror, I pushed my stomach inside out trying to get some sound, any sound, to come out, to no avail. After the chorus came in, I finally got a grip and sang the ensuing versus. Later, I had the lead in *Sunbonnet Sue.* There was a moment when I was required to say, "Sue, I love you." Lest someone think it was a fact, I pulled a three-by-five card out of my pocket, looked the audience in the eye and read the line.

In high school, a few of us were chosen to be part of a young adults' chorus to sing Wagner's *Tannhauser* at the old Metropolitan Opera House on 39th Street in New York City. I loved learning all the choruses, as well as the tenor solo parts, and then a New England basketball tournament took precedence over the opera. That was my lost chance to sing on the Met's stage.

In my youth, very few young people took voice lessons, and they certainly did not include Puritan families like mine. The arts were not considered a serious undertaking, and in my opinion, were it not for the influx of artists and musicians into New York City and elsewhere, escaping from Eastern and Western Europe in the 1930s and early 1940s, the United States would not have had the development of great musicians we enjoy today.

Also like other youngsters, I took piano lessons, which I hated. When I had not practiced, my teacher would warm me that he would tell my parents, and then for the next two weeks, I would toil at Karl Czerny's and Muzio Clementi's exercises. In my senior year in high school, I convinced my mother I was not and did not plan to be a concert pianist and wanted to take lessons from a Yale professor who was teaching her piano "faking," which is playing popular tunes with just

- sy, His bur-then is light, His bur-then, His bur - then is light.

the vocal line and the chords as references. Eddie Sarinak taught me more in one year than so many others had tried in vain for years. He showed me that there was no difference in notation between Mozart's *Piano Concerto in C Major* and any popular tune: C, G7th, F, G7th, C. Nobody had ever mentioned chordal structure to me before, and knowing how music was created made practice a joy. I wish every grammar school would teach how music is created, rather than just songs.

As a freshman at Yale, I tried out for the Freshman Glee Club and the Battell Chapel Choir. Fortunately, that day I sang a high A with a purity I rarely had. And so, I was one of about three or four freshmen to make the choir. In the Freshman Glee Club, I sang a Monteverdi duet, *Zefiro Torna*, with cello and harpsichord accompaniment. I had never heard of Monteverdi, knew no Italian and hadn't a clue who Ralph Kirkpatrick, the eminent harpsichordist, was. But the words and music were one. I felt each nuance and, even now, fifty-plus years later, can sing most of my part.

I wish I had know then what I now know about Bach and his never being a first choice to be a kapellmeister. It would have lightened the greatest disappointment my early life encountered. As one of two leading tenors in the Freshman

and Apollo Glee Clubs (the junior varsity), I took it as a matter of fact that I would make the Yale Glee Club my junior year. It was not to be. I was told by Fenno Heath, the Apollo director and later a great developer of the Yale Glee Club, that I didn't make it because Marshall (Barty) Bartholomew, Yale's most famous glee club director, said that when I sang I was sharp. With perfect pitch, the accusation floored me, and it didn't help when half the Apollo Glee Club members came to me to ask how on earth I hadn't made the Yale Glee Club. Later, much later, I learned the truth. Two freshmen, taking voice lessons from Barty, were chosen for the few places for underclassmen. Actually, what I really wanted to be was a Whiffenpoof. Since as a high school boy not in a fraternity, I didn't know any Whiffenpoofs, I hoped to get to know them as a glee club member in my junior year. So that was out, too.

In 1951, a friend, Alden Hammond, started the New Haven Choral, and we gave an inspired all Cole Porter concert in the Yale Bowl with soloists from the Metropolitan Opera. The director was Russell Davenport, the leading Broadway director at that time. I sang the tenor solos at the rehearsals, and then the Met's tenor arrived for the dress rehearsal.

- sy, His bur-then is light, His bur-then, His bur - then is light

Graduating from college in 1952 meant immediately entering the military service. Rather than being drafted, I joined the Marines and later spent fourteen months in Korea. As platoon leader, after six months, I was moved from my platoon back to the battalion, where I served as S-2, the intelligence officer, for eight months. It was there that I decided to start a choir, commandeered a field organ and gathered about twelve to sixteen young enlisted men for the choir. My playing left a lot to be desired, but much more fun was learning the emotional Southern Baptist songs my Yankee Congregationalist hymnal never included. A highlight was our choir singing the *Navy Hymn* for an admiral and a general from I Corps.

Even in combat, music is a part of life. Our battalion commander, Lieutenant Colonel Carl Hoffman, went to Drake University and played the cornet. In World War Two in the Far East, he lost his cornet on Saipan. Later in a hospital, after being wounded on Tinian, he recovered the brass trumpet slightly dented.

We decided to enter an I Corps barbershop quartet contest. Colonel Hoffman had never heard barbershop quartet music, so I wrote out four or five songs and sang the lead to him, from which he created the most original harmonies. Like

His yoke___ is ea -

so many alto parts, the baritone in a barbershop quartet is the most difficult part, since it usually just fills in a chord with no melody and has nothing interesting to sing. So I sang that part. The second tenor was the lead, and the first tenor sang a third or fifth above, with the bass, Colonel Hoffman, building the bottom of each chord. We won the I Corps contest less because of our singing than the wonderfully original harmonies Colonel Hoffman arranged.

My next sojourn into singing was joining the Collegiate Choral in New York City, a 100-voice chorus made up of professional and amateur singers who gave a six-day recital at Carnegie Hall each year. I arrived to audition with several obviously professional women in front of me. Outside the audition room, I could hear arias from well-known operas before I was asked in. First, I was given music to test my sight reading, which was and is my strength. Then to my surprise, I was asked to sing my song. "What do you mean?" I responded. "The song you've learned to present to us." Totally unprepared for this, I was asked to return when I had my piece. "Can't I just sing something you've got here?" I inquired. To their chagrin, they let me leaf through some music and choose one that looked nicely within my range—just a high G.

- sy, His bur-then is light, His bur-then, His bur - then is light.

97

Someone played the piano, and I sang the unknown song and passed.

Many people don't have a clue how much it really costs to present great choruses like the Collegiate. In 1957, after all the tickets were sold out for all six performances, to pay for the hall, orchestra and publicity, we singers had to raise an additional $60,000.

Singing is, in so many ways, different from other forms of musical expression. Recently, I watched the face of Pincus Zuckerman, the famed violinist. He played with little movement of his body, while his face, his eyes, his brows and every muscle described the feelings he wished his violin to create. Because all of these facial movements may affect a singer's tone, the body being the instrument itself, it is often the case that a singer's face may appear quite different from the projected feelings his or her voice conveys. Chorus members are asked to look happy, to physically demonstrate the meaning of the words in their stage presence, but individual passages may display varying expressions on each singer's face as he or she creates a sound.

Just as the weather can affect an instrument, it can also affect a whole choir. I can recall rehearsals where everybody

seemed to have less energy, sections were flat and the hours seemed like drudgery. Other times they were pure joy.

My stepfather was a great tennis player, extraordinarily graceful. When he turned fifty and could not play with that grace, he quit tennis for golf. I have often thought about that, because the closest thing I have had to that sense of expertise has been my voice and ability to read music so well. As I have aged, the voice has lost its surety. The high notes are not always there. A vibrato has increased. Part of me wanted to quit singing when I knew how poorly my efforts were compared to my youth. But another part said, "So what? You're no opera star. Enjoy what you have." Of course, I long to be able to sing as I once did, but there are times when for a day I'm rather good and for the others I still contribute, especially in the early rehearsals when my sight reading really supports the tenor section. When a high G or A isn't there, I relish younger singers coming through.

And I remind myself that I am blessed with a tenor voice, the least in supply, allowing me a few more years to sing in good choruses.

- sy, His bur-then is light, His bur-then, His bur - then is light

BOOKS FOR FURTHER STUDY

I do not call this a bibliography, because my interest here is in offering the reader a few books I have found helpful in understanding both the history of music as well as its choral foundations.

Paul Henry Lang's *Music in Western Civilization* (W.W. Norton & Company) is a tome of 1,000 plus pages covering everything except music after 1940 with a very classical European bias.

David Tame's *The Secret Power of Music* (Destiny Books, Rochester, Vermont) is 300 pages covering early music, China, India, Twentieth Century jazz and blues, as well as the physics of the Ohm, and a joy to read throughout.

HarperCollins Outline series, *History of Western Music* by Hugh M. Miller and Dale Cockrell, does a wonderful synopsis of its subject including rock and rap in 300 pages— good for Trivial Pursuit if not for any true depth of knowledge or understanding.

Two lecture series stand out as books: Leonard Bernstein's 1973 six talks at Harvard, *The Unanswered Question* (Harvard University Press), and Roger Scruton's

1992, 1993 and 1994 lectures at Boston University, *The Aesthetics of Music* (Oxford University). Musts if you really want to know the essence of music.

John Cage's *Silence*, lectures and writings, may help explain how his music developed (Wesleyan University Press).

There are, of course, numerous books on individual composers, but for the singer, one is especially worthwhile reading: *The Songs of Johannes Brahms* by Eric Sams (Yale University Press).

"For there is a music wherever there is a harmony, order, or proportion; and thus far we may maintain the music of the spheres."
Religio Medici
Sir Thomas Browne

"I hear America singing, the varied carols I hear."
I Hear America Singing
Walt Whitman

- sy, His bur-then is   light,   His bur-then, His   bur - then is light

"Make a joyful noise unto God, all the earth:
Sing forth the glory of his name."
Psalm 66

"Oh clap your hands, all ye peoples;
Shout unto God with the voice of triumph."
Psalm 47

"He is made one with nature: there is heard
His voice in all her music, from the moan
Of thunder, to the song of night's sweet bird."
Adonais
Percy Bysshe Shelley

"If Music and sweet Poetry agree,
As they must needs (the Sister and the Brother)
Then must the love be great, 'twixt thee and me,
"Because thou lov'st the one and I the other.
Sonnet
Richard Barnsfield

"Music, when soft voices die

Vibrates in the memory"

When Soft Voices

Percy Bysshe Shelley

"We are the music makers.

We are the dreamers of dreams."

Ode: We are the music makers

Arthur William Edgar O'Shaughnessy

"If music be the food of love, play on;

Give me excess of it."

Twelfth Night

William Shakespeare

"It is from the blues that all that may be called American

music derives its most distinctive characteristic."

Black Manhattan

James Weldon Johnson

"Music must take rank as the highest form of the fine arts—as the one which, more than any other, ministers to human welfare."
On the Origin and Function of Music
Herbert Spencer

"Musick is the thing of the world that I love most."
Samuel Pepys

SOPRANO

His yoke___ is   ea -

Gerald G. Hotchkiss has sung in Christian and Jewish choirs, choruses, in octets, quartets, duets, barbershop, madrigals and Broadway reviews under many of the finest conductors in the United States as an amateur for more than sixty years.

-sy, His bur-then is   light,   His bur-then, His   bur - then is light

NOTES

SOPRANO

Hal - - le - lu - jah!

SOPRANO

His yoke____ is ea - - - - - - -

NOTES

Hal - - le - lu - jah!

-sy, His bur-then is   light,   His bur-then, His bur - then is light

THE MODERNIZATION OF IRAN
1921–1941

The Modernization

of Iran

1921-1941

AMIN BANANI

STANFORD UNIVERSITY PRESS
STANFORD, CALIFORNIA

Stanford University Press
Stanford, California
© 1961 by the Board of Trustees of the
Leland Stanford Junior University
Printed in the United States of America
ISBN 0-8047-0050-8
Original edition 1961
Last figure below indicates year of this printing:
86   85   84   83   82   81   80   79   78   77

To
MY PARENTS

PREFACE

This study is concerned with the legislative and statutory reforms promulgated in Iran during the regime of Reza Shah
Pahlavi. It is focused upon critical areas of social organization,
for which more analytical data than has hitherto been available
in the English language is provided. It may serve as a guide for
preliminary studies of Westernization in other Middle Eastern
societies, or as an initial appraisal of the actual effects of modernization in contemporary Iran.

The book is based primarily upon Persian sources. Apart
from official records such as the record of parliamentary legislation, contemporary sources for the reign of Reza Shah are
scanty and inadequate, in part owing to government censorship.
In the 1940's, by contrast, a great many books were written
about the Reza Shah period; unhappily, few of them are reliable.

The works of several Western scholars have been extremely
useful in suggesting certain areas of inquiry; but I have not relied upon these secondary sources for any factual information,
except in a few cases in which no primary source was available
to me. In this respect I wish to acknowledge my debt to Mr.
L. P. Elwell-Sutton, whose *Modern Iran* (first issued in 1941
and now published by Routledge and Kegan Paul) remains a
most useful general review. I also interviewed a number of
leading figures in Iranian public life who had responsible roles
in the events of this study. They prefer to remain anonymous,
and no direct reference to their views is made here. My own
early education in Iran and later observations there have been
helpful.

The Persian collections of the Hoover Institution at Stanford University, the New York Public Library, the Library of Congress, and the British Museum have all been useful to me. The Hoover collection, small as it is, was particularly valuable for its concentration on the period of this study.

An explanation of the method of transliteration used in the book is necessary. Like many other methods, it is not free from compromises and discrepancies, but it is fairly simple and should enable the reader who is not familiar with the language to pronounce the words with reasonable accuracy. Cumbersome diacritical signs have been eliminated whenever possible. Certain departures from the method are made in the case of words that have become familiar in English in a different transliteration. There are many Arabic words in the Persian language; when the context justifies transliteration according to the Arabic method (e.g., *shari'ah*), that method has been used. For the convenience of the reader a translation of the titles of Persian works is given both in the Notes and in the Bibliography. When deemed helpful, these translations are descriptive rather than literal.

The terms Persia and Iran are used more or less interchangeably. When referring to specific groups of Muslim religious functionaries, their Arabic designations (e.g., *mujtahid, mulla,* and *'ulama*) are used in transliteration. But when references are general and inclusive, the English terms clergy and clerical are used for convenience.

It remains to offer my gratitude to my respected friend, Professor Wayne S. Vucinich of Stanford, who was generous with his time and encouragement. He read the manuscript in various stages of preparation and made valuable suggestions for its improvement. Professor Firuz Kazemzadeh of Yale read and criticized many parts of the manuscript, and I am happy to have the opportunity to thank him. Over the years he and I have discussed at length questions pertaining to the interaction of civilizations, and this work has benefited from those discussions. To the faculty research fund of Reed College I am indebted for assistance in the final preparation of the manuscript. The Consulate General of Iran in San Francisco kindly provided the photographs in this volume. No formal expression of indebtedness will be adequate to convey my wife's share in this book. She has edited and typed the manuscript in its early drafts. She has been my severest critic and kindest inspiration.

A. B.

Reed College
December 1960

PUBLISHER'S NOTE

The four pages of photographs that appeared in the original edition were omitted in the 1977 reprinting.

CONTENTS

THE MODERNIZATION OF IRAN
1921–1941

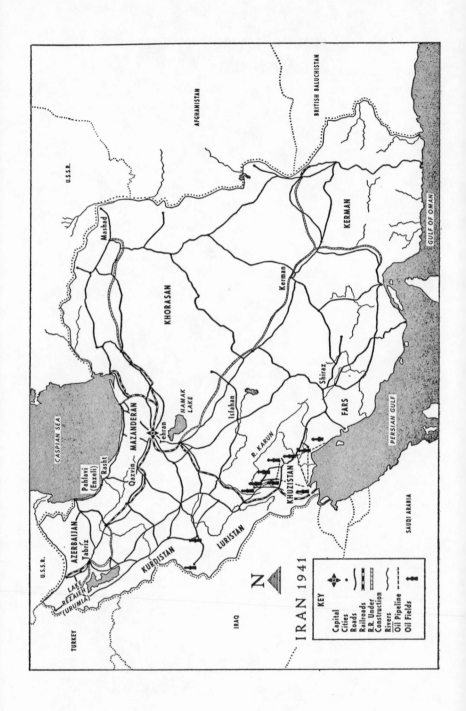

INTRODUCTION

In a world in which nations are rushed into increasing inter-dependence by the rapid growth of science and technology, the impact of one civilization upon another is of utmost significance. The physical conditions that once kept nations apart and caused the growth of different cultures have disappeared in our century. Moral and cultural values, social ideals, and, above all, scientific knowledge have come to be shared; and the result has most often been a state of flux and tension.

It would of course be fallacious to suggest that the inter-action of cultures is an exclusively modern phenomenon. Throughout history societies seemingly independent of one another, and indeed often mutually hostile, have been deeply in each other's debt. An outstanding example can be found in the Middle Ages, when the Western Christian world was engaged in a bitter struggle with the Islamic East; and yet the flow of commerce and the bonds of spiritual and intellectual endeavor held the two together. What is peculiar to our time is not the fusion of cultures but the intensity of the process, and its virtual singleness of direction.

The dynamics of this process are provided by science and technology, and since in the past five centuries it has been the West that has pioneered and excelled in these fields while at the same time coming to exercise a preponderant share of world power, one speaks today not of the interplay of civilizations, but of the impact of the West on the rest of the world. (I use the term "West" to refer to the civilization of those western European nations who also populated and civilized the western hemisphere.)

Science and technology remain the most conspicuous and the most important agents of Western influence. They are also the most desired fruits of the impact of West on East; no one objects to a more comfortable way of life. But with the improved standard of living there has often come a new challenge to the otherworldly traditions of the older societies. An even more immediate clash occurs when the infectious nationalism of the West takes root elsewhere, and especially when the preponderant share of world power exercised by the West evokes jealousy, hatred, and national egoism in the rest of the world.

In the light of these considerations, does the impact of the West threaten a complete distortion of values and disruption of societies? Or does it augur a greater area of human understanding, a larger body of common ideals, and therefore a greater possibility for social harmony and political federation? This is one of the most important questions of our time. I do not pretend to answer it. But its universality has been what chiefly prompted me to undertake this study.

In her assimilation of Western influences, Asia poses more problems than other parts of the world. Because of her old and varied civilizations, her vast multitudes, her deep religious traditions, and her history of abuse at the hands of the Western powers, she has been the area at once the most receptive and the most resistant to Western influence. The southwestern corner of Asia, in particular, affords a rewarding study of the problems created by contact with the West, for as the part of Asia closest to Europe, it has had the longest record of intercourse with the West.

Apart from the newborn nation of Israel and a number of nonsovereign and unassimilated peoples such as the Armenians, the Kurds, and the Chaldeans, three main ethnic and cultural groups inhabit this area: the Iranians, the Arabs, and the Turks. The Turks are the youngest of the three and the closest to Europe, and it is generally agreed that these factors have made them the most open to Western influences. The Arab world presents a totally different picture. Its civilization, older than Turkey's, is so completely a product of its religion that the influence of the West upon it must always first be seen in terms of the reaction of Islam to Western civilization.[1]

Of the three civilizations Iran is the oldest. Although in her present culture the dominant formative agent is Islam, some elements of what was a uniquely Iranian civilization in pre-Islamic days have persisted. Her language, mythology, and historical identity all preserve something of the past, and therefore her reaction to the impact of the West is an extremely complex one.

A complete review of Iran's association with the West and of the impact of the West upon Iranian society and culture is far beyond the scope of this study. Although certain background material will be given, the main purpose is to focus attention upon a relatively short period in the modern history of Iran, the years 1921–41.

This period, which marked the rise to power and the reign of Reza Shah Pahlavi, was one of cataclysmic change. The European influences that had been filtering into Iran since the sixteenth century finally gained ascendancy, and the country underwent a phase of intense Westernization. Most manifestations of Western influence in Iran today date from the time of Reza Shah. Certainly many physical aspects of Westernism are the product of that short period.

Paradoxically, these years produced also the greatest degree of xenophobia in Iran. This xenophobia did not express itself in open conflict with the West, but rather in suspicion and resentment. It was a period of rapid borrowing from Europe as well as of fierce assertion of a national spirit. The two processes were simultaneous and related.

The impact of the West, so marked during the reign of Reza Shah, did not diminish after his abdication in 1941. The pace of physical construction and development was considerably slackened, but the intellectual and ideological aspects of Western civilization, which had been forcibly kept out during the Reza Shah era, now flooded the country. The problems of Western impact have taken on a different emphasis since 1941, and I have not attempted to discuss the events of these later years.

The dimensions of this work, therefore, are not mere arbitrary dates of a ruler. They represent a compact period of great significance in the modern history of Iran, a period that not only changed the whole physical appearance of the country but also stirred, awakened, and confused the minds of the people. Here is one of the rare occasions when chronology cooperates with the historian to set apart a short period worthy of individual study.

The first three chapters of the book give the historical background needed for an understanding of the Westernization of Iran. The remaining four chapters may be called an institutional study; they deal with Western impact upon the army, civil administration, public health, the judiciary, education, and the national economy. These are the fields in which active and official modernization was pursued and in which it is possible to rely on documentary evidence. Changes in the intellectual atmosphere, in the religious climate, and in family relations are touched upon only indirectly insofar as they relate to institutional factors. Certain other aspects of Westernization, such as changes in the status of women and Western influence upon the arts, have had to be excluded altogether, but I hope in time to write a sequel to this work, covering these subjects. Only a beginning is attempted here.

The method of presentation I have chosen is one of topical examination against a chronological background. It may seem at times that the background of political events and diplomatic relations with the West is overemphasized. But the emphasis is legitimate, for these events and relations made a deep impression upon the people of Iran and have done much to form their opinions about the West.

Chapter One

HISTORICAL ANTECEDENTS

Iran's long history of contact with the West began with the appearance of the Persians on the eastern coast of the Aegean and in the neighborhood of the Hellenic world (546 B.C.). This contact increased, until in 331 B.C. Alexander the Great invaded Iran, and the first real fusion of civilizations began to take effect. Throughout the Parthian period (250 B.C.–A.D. 226) and Sasanian period (A.D. 226–652) the mutual exchange continued. At this time Iran had so great an impact upon the West that the flow of ideas was from East to West, as indeed is witnessed by the rapid spread of Manicheanism and Mithraism in Europe. Then for a short period after the Muslim conquest of Iran (A.D. 633–52) direct contact with the West was lost.[1]

When the interplay of cultures was renewed, it was through the medium of Islamic civilization, and on a broad front from Spain to the Levant. The Crusades witnessed the last great flow of civilization from East to West. After that a series of catastrophic invasions by the hordes of Central Asia engaged the energies of the East and snuffed out the vigor of its culture. At this point East and West began to grow apart. For while the West was entering upon the Renaissance, the age of discovery and science, the East was plunged into isolation, stagnation, and fatalism.

The re-establishment of the Persian Empire under the Safavids (1500–1736), and the revival of Persian culture in the sixteenth and seventeenth centuries, meant renewed contact with Europe.[2] Political and military events provided the first sparks. The Ottoman Turks were not only the most constant threat to

Europe, but also the greatest deterrent to the consolidation of Safavid power in Persia; that Persia and the West should meet on this mutual ground was inevitable. The Holy See sent emissaries to the court of the Shah to inquire if the Turk could be kept preoccupied in the East. The great Shah Abbas (1587–1629) imported cannon founders and military organizers from Europe. It was also during his reign that the Sherley brothers acted first as unofficial and then as official ambassadors between England and Persia. Soon an unending caravan of ambassadors and merchants from England, France, Austria, Spain, the Holy See, and various German states began to arrive in Persia. They enlightened, amused, and sometimes shocked the Persians who came into contact with them; and they in turn were enlightened, amused, and shocked by the Persians. The reports of these ambassadors, as well as the colorful presence of their Persian counterparts in the courts of Europe, began to fire people's imagination. In Spain they followed the adventures of the Don Juan of Persia; in England Shakespeare and Ben Jonson were writing about the "Grande Sophy."

But the renaissance of Persian power and culture lasted less than two hundred years, and by the beginning of the eighteenth century the Safavid Empire was rapidly disintegrating. The meteoric rise of Nadir Shah (1736–47) momentarily checked the ruin. But during these years Iran was too preoccupied with her own affairs to maintain any contact with Europe. Europe, on the other hand, was finding more and more to interest her in the East.

THE GROWTH OF WESTERN INFLUENCE UNDER THE QAJARS

In 1794 a malevolent eunuch named Agha Muhammad Khan established suzerainty over Iran. Thus was founded the Qajar dynasty, which lasted one hundred and thirty fateful years. It was during this period that Western influences penetrated beyond ambassadorial and court circles and began to be felt in the life of the nation.[8]

The increased influence of the West in the nineteenth century followed European political and commercial expansion. The growth of Russian power from the beginning of the eighteenth century had been accompanied by an unconcealed drive for expansion. To the west Sweden was dwarfed and Poland liquidated. To the east a drive began that was to culminate, a century later, in the heart of Central Asia and the Manchurian shores of the Pacific. To the south were Turkey and Iran, and the rival interests of the British in Afghanistan, India, Tibet, and China.

The stage for conflict between Iran and Russia had been set before the rise of the Qajar dynasty. The Christian monarch of Georgia, a traditional vassal of the Shahs of Iran during their periods of power and ascendancy, had taken advantage of the anarchy before the success of the Qajars, and had pledged allegiance to the Tsar of Russia, requesting protection, which was willingly accorded. The vengeful Agha Muhammad Khan, therefore, set out on a punitive campaign against the Georgians, which culminated in 1795 in a dreadful sack of Tiflis. But Georgia remained within the pale of Russian influence.[4]

Into this scene entered Napoleon, who sent his ambassador to the court of the Shah with a fantastic scheme. Napoleon offered to restore to Iran her territories in the Caucasus in return for: (1) a Turko-Persian alliance to harass Russia from the rear, and (2) an overland route to the rich sub-continent of India to enable Napoleon to drive out the British. Had Russia and England not been quick to counter his move, Napoleon might have achieved some measure of success, but as it was his machinations came to nothing.

Although in this case England and Russia were comrades-in-arms against Bonaparte, their interests in Iran were clearly opposed. Russia made no effort to conceal her designs on Iran. From the mid-eighteenth century she had been engaged in aggressive expansion toward the Iranian borders, and the two countries were in open conflict from 1804–13. The war ended

disastrously for Iran, and the treaties of Gulistan and Turkmanchai in 1813 and 1828 permanently ended her claims to
provinces in the Caucasus and established Russia's control over
them.[5]

After 1828 a frontier between Russia and Iran did exist, but
for the most part it was of geographic significance only. For
nearly a century after Turkmanchai the oppressive power of
Russia was a stern reality in Iran. Extraterritoriality and various other concessions and privileges were wrested from her, and
the court in Tehran was powerless to take action even in internal
affairs without the approval of the Russian ambassador. Russian troops would cross the border without ceremony if diplomatic pressure was not sufficient. Had it not been for Britain's
skill in maintaining the balance of power in Iran even her nomi-
nal sovereignty could not have lasted long. But beyond Iran
lay India, and this meant that Britain had to do everything to
keep Russia away.[6]

The resurgence of economic imperialism at the end of the
nineteenth century and, most fateful to Iran, the discovery of
oil intensified the rivalry between Britain and Russia, which
resulted in the Anglo-Russian agreement of 1907. In order to
preserve peace and freedom for the rest of the world, the two
powers decided to make a sacrificial offering of Iran. They divided the country into respective spheres of influence in which
they gave each other carte blanche. A buffer strip in the middle
was left to the dubious sovereignty of the Shah. This agreement was not formally annulled until the end of the First World
War.

Against this background of political events an ever increasing stream of ideological, social, and intellectual influences
flowed into Iran from the West. In the first decade of the nineteenth century the first small group of Iranian students was
sent to Europe by Crown Prince Abbas Mirza (d. 1833) to study
military arts. In 1851 the first European-style college was
founded in Tehran. In 1858 telegraph lines reached Iran. Two

years later the first Masonic lodge was founded. In 1865 the
first girls' school was opened. In 1871 cabinet government with
an established procedure was formed.[7] By the turn of the century educated Iranians were thoroughly familiar with European ways, and they were highly sensitive to events in the West.

The twin movements of nationalism and constitutionalism
in Iran were both sparked by events in the West. The Iranian
constitutional movement, which ended in the political revolt
that shook the aged and stagnant Qajar autocracy in 1906, fed
directly upon the Russian Revolution of 1905. The influence of
this revolution seeped into Iran through the Caucasus; for after
the failure of their attempt in Russia, some of the leaders of
the revolution in Transcaucasia migrated to Iran, where they
founded newspapers and agitated for a liberal revolution.[8]

Similarly, the greatest influence on Iranian nationalism was
the Russo-Japanese war of 1904–5, which indeed had far-reaching effects on the rise of nationalism throughout Asia. The implications of the triumph of an Asiatic people over a European
power were not lost upon the new patriots of Iran. Jubilant
epic poems were written to celebrate the Japanese victory. The
war and the subsequent revolution in Russia also gave a fresh
meaning to the writings of such men as Malkom Khan (the
founder of Freemasonry in Iran), Mirza 'Ali Khan Amin ed-
Dowle, Jamal ed-Din Afghani, and Mirza Yusef Khan Mostashar
ed-Dowle Tabrizi. They had been voicing liberal, progressive,
and patriotic ideas for some thirty years, and their writings now
began to take effect.[9]

The reports and interpretations of the Russo-Japanese War
and of the Russian revolution of 1905, both in the Persian press
and in periodicals outside Iran, provided yet another stimulus
for political awakening. Most prominent among these papers
were *Akhtar* in Constantinople, *Habl-ol-Matin* in Calcutta, and
Sorayya and *Parvaresh* in Cairo.[10]

Thus nationalism and constitutionalism in Iran both received their impetus from outside events. In effect, the two

movements were often indistinguishable. Patriots and constitutionalists were generally one and the same. Indeed a constitution was thought by the patriots to be the solution to all
problems of national backwardness. But when viewed with the
purpose of assessing the extent of Western impact on Iran, a
sharp difference appears between the two. The time and the
nature of the national awakening were determined by events in
the West, but the spirit of nationalism itself was not inconsistent
with the traditions of Iranian history. The idea of a constitutional government, on the other hand, was a thoroughly Western
importation, and in principle ran counter to the fiber of political thought implicit in Islam.

The growth of this new nationalism was influenced by the
West in two ways: it was a reaction to Western power politics
in Iran, and it was an emulation of Western patriotism as a supreme virtue. This pattern of resentment and avid imitation,
while paradoxical, is a true key to the problems of Western impact on the East.

THE ROLE OF WESTERN POWER POLITICS

The story of Western power politics in Iran is not directly
within the scope of this work; but it played so decisive a role
in molding Iranian attitudes toward the West, and in providing
the spark for Iranian nationalism, that at least an outline is
necessary. In the years concerned, power politics, in the true
sense of the phrase, was practiced in Iran only by Russia and
Britain. Other nations either did not have any direct interest
in Iran, or Russia and Britain did not allow them to have such
interests.

The best aspect of Russia's policy in Iran is that it has always been entirely frank. Her military imperialism, followed
by economic imperialism, made little pretense about its aims in
Iran, namely, to annex and exploit whatever it could. During
the period of military setbacks and Russian expansion in the
Caucasus in the early nineteenth century, nationalism in the

modern sense was nonexistent in Iran. Any opposition was religious in nature. Once the overwhelming force of Russia was felt, the reaction among Iranians was one of fear and resignation. There was no irredentism.

Russia's open intervention and oppressive policies in the period of constitutional agitation marked the beginning of real anti-Russian feeling in Iran. The Anglo-Russian agreement of 1907, which divided Iran into spheres of influence, and the events that followed—the supporting of the Shah in revoking the Constitution, the role of the Russian-commanded forces in the closing of the Majlis, and the ruthless policies of the Russians in dealing with the constitutionalists in Azerbaijan—awoke genuine nationalistic feeling among the Iranians.[11] Other Western importations which were making their appearance at the turn of the century—printing presses and telegraph lines, newspapers and political cartooning—helped to fan the fire of this new feeling.

On the surface, the Revolution of 1917 brought a major change in Russian policy toward Iran. The Iranians, who had traditionally regarded Russia as a greedy neighbor bent on exploiting them, were greatly surprised, confused, and elated by the sweeping generosity of the treaty concluded in 1921 with all its sweet-sounding sentiments of anti-imperialism. This treaty seemed like the confirmation of the resolutions of the Baku Conference held in 1920, when the promise of Communism was spelled by Zinoviev, Radek, and Bela Kun to 1,800 delegates from the colonial and semi-colonial "East." Not the struggle of the industrial proletariat against their class exploiters, but the struggle of national movements against their foreign masters was the theme of this Conference.[12]

Soviet activities, however, soon restored an atmosphere of reality, for diplomatic practices remained unchanged. Shortly after the consolidation of Communist power in Russia, Soviet agents in Iran resumed the familiar tactics of pressure and bribery. There were no educated masses in Iran at that time, and therefore any popular discontent that existed had to be nurtured and encouraged by the Soviets without regard to its ideological implications.* The economy of northern Iran, moreover, was so tightly geared to Russian trade (it was in fact controlled by Russia) that it gave the Soviets an ideal lever for exerting influence and pressure in Iran as a whole.

British policy in Iran also influenced the growth of nationalism. Much has been made by Iranians of the subtlety of British policy, as opposed to the more blatant methods of the Russians; but on closer scrutiny one often finds British practices to have been similar to Russian. The basic difference seems to be in aim: whereas Russia's ultimate aim was annexation and territorial expansion, Britain's aim was to maintain her power over Iran but not to resort to openly aggressive measures unless all other avenues were closed.

The British ambassador in Iran in the mid-1920's once told an American journalist that British policy in Iran had always been the same, only the measures of diplomacy had changed. Basically the policy was governed by two motives, one strategic, the other economic. Strategically it was directed at first against Napoleon and subsequently against Russia, and its aim was the protection of India. In the second half of the nineteenth century commercial factors were added, being epitomized in the oil concessions in the south.[13]

The first phase of British policy in Iran, lasting until 1907, was one of conflict with Russia. It meant constant competition with Russia for additional influence, prestige, and power. On the part of the British this took the form of rumor-mongering and propaganda, exerting pressure by an occasional naval or military show of force, and stirring up intrigue among southern tribal chiefs. But by far the most potent weapon used by the

* Although at first the ideological baggage of the Soviet policy was of no particular value in Iran, after the Westernizing efforts of Reza Shah and the spread of education it became a very strong force. Students and intelligentsia constituted the backbone of the Iranian Communist movement in the years that followed.

British was bribery—often paid individually to men of power and sometimes in the name of "government subsidy."

The fierce Anglo-Russian competition was a cause of world tension, and Britain, finding Germany already arraigned against her, sought to lessen the chances of war by appeasing Russia. With the Anglo-Russian agreement of 1907 the second phase of British policy in Iran was inaugurated—one of cooperation with Russia. For the Iranians this phase was even more disastrous, because it led to the virtual dismemberment of their country and to open domination. Although Russia's acts of exploitation during this period were more overt than Britain's, the rising temper of Iranian nationalism was directed equally against both countries. Indeed a large number of newly educated and articulate Iranians put the entire blame for the Anglo-Russian agreement on Sir Edward Grey, for it seemed to them that he had sacrificed the interests of Iran for the safety of Britain.[14]

The third phase was ushered in by the Russian Revolution of 1917. It meant a temporary withdrawal of Russia and a free hand for Britain. In 1919 she tried to consolidate and legalize her hegemony by means of a treaty with Iran. The extravagant terms of this treaty, however, and the methods used to get it signed, prevented its passage through the Majlis. All that was achieved, therefore, was increased distrust of Britain, for whatever her intentions had been to the Iranians the treaty appeared open and greedy imperialism.

With the rise of Reza Shah a new phase in British policy was precipitated—the so-called period of benevolent inaction. Open bribery and interference in domestic affairs (such as packing the Majlis) were put aside, but political pressure was still applied, as in the case of the oil dispute in 1932.

The interference of both Russia and Britain in Iranian affairs created strong nationalism and resentment. The British were often the chief target of this resentment, and there developed a myth of British subtlety and unscrupulousness. This led to a form of apathy and fatalism in public affairs. Iranians frequently feel that nothing can be accomplished without the approval of Britain and they blame her for frustrating their national ambitions. They feel that the odds are overwhelmingly against them.

NATIONALISM AND CONSTITUTIONALISM

Iranian nationalism did not spring entirely from reaction against Western imperialism. The increasing number of young Iranians who went to Europe were impressed with the manifestations of nationalism there. A majority of these students went to France where there was a strong atmosphere of chauvinism in the years that followed the Franco-Prussian War, and they came back imbued with glowing patriotism. The newly born Iranian press reverberated with their patriotic sentiments. The examples of Italy and Germany, and above all Japan, were held up to the people by the press. The spirit of nationalism had made so much possible for these nations; why not emulate them and accomplish the same in Iran?

This form of nationalism, however, brought with it an increasingly strong tendency toward secularism, with the result that the clergy, who had been among the instigators of resentment against Western imperialism and had shared that form of nationalism with other Iranians, now became very suspicious of Western-inspired nationalism.[15]

As we have noticed, there was much in the traditions of Iranian history to nurture the spirit of nationalism. A nation whose history had extended over 2,500 years undoubtedly had many memorials of glory which could serve as an inspiration for patriots. Of the might and accomplishments of the Iran of the Achaemenians and Sasanians there are bold records carved in rock. Few nations can boast as eloquent an expression of intense patriotism and proud nationalism as the *Shah-namé* of Ferdowsi, the epic poem of Iran, written in the tenth century A.D. A long history of *shi'ah* opposition to her *sunni* neighbors had prepared Iran for ready acceptance of modern nationalism.

A revival of the imperial glories of ancient Iran was the natural form for the new nationalist movement to take.

An inevitable ingredient of modern nationalism seems to be a feeling of superiority over other nations in general and one's neighbors in particular. In Iran a tacit sense of superiority over the other nations of the Middle East was not new, but it was strengthened by this revival of the past. Fortunately, however, a deep-rooted sense of humor prevented this feeling from assuming dangerous and grotesque proportions.

Finally, the role of the Muslim revivalists of the period should not be overlooked in a study of the growth of nationalism. The activities and writings of Jamal ed-Din Afghani had a great effect among the early nationalists in Iran. A certain amount of the spirit of *Dar al-Islam* versus *Dar al-Harb** was revived, but it was too out of place in the context of modern global power politics to have much meaning. But although nearly forgotten in Iran, the idea is far from dead in the Arab world.

If nationalism was the product both of Western influences and native Iranian patriotism, constitutionalism was almost wholly inspired by Western ideas. On the political plane there is no more striking evidence of the impact of the West on the East than the constitutional movements that swept through the Middle East at the turn of the century.

In principle Islam was conceived as a church-state—a true City of God on earth. The moral and spiritual teachings of Muhammad are tightly woven into a pattern of social justice and political order, and it was intended that the Koran, as the repository of the teachings of Muhammad, should remain the

---

* Muslim political thought of the early caliphate period was characterized by a bipolar world-view. The *Dar al-Islam* ("The Domain of Peace"), or the lands under Muslim rule, were implicitly in a continuous state of war with the *Dar al-Harb* ("The Domain of War"), or all the territories under non-Muslim rule. It was expected that eventually the entire world would be a "Domain of Peace."

foundation of Islamic society. For centuries this ideal was adhered to. In addition to the Koran, there were: *hadith* (the sayings and traditions) of Muhammad, and in the *shi'ah* communities the sayings and traditions of the *Imams* also, which were of secondary and supporting value; and the practices of *ijtihad* and *ijma'*, or processes of diligent conjecture and consensus, which were entirely subordinate to the supreme laws of the Koran.

There is no doubt that the political structure of Islamic society was conceived as a theocracy. For the smooth operation of this theocracy the Koran and the principles derived from it were considered self-sufficient. Any attempt, therefore, to introduce into states with a preponderantly Muslim population written constitutions patterned after those of the West, and complete with the separation of powers and a bill of rights, is a tacit recognition of the breakdown and anachronism of the socio-political structure of Islam. This is true even when that constitution—as, for example, the Iranian Constitution—recognizes Islam as the official religion of the state. Although the movement toward Western constitutionalism may be taken as a sign of the inadequacy of Islam, it is not in itself in any way a criticism of Islam; it is simply proof of the inability of Muslims to implement the Islamic message of social justice and political order in twentieth-century society. The same development had taken place in the Christian West a few centuries earlier. Into the vacuum created by the weakening of religious order came secular institutions and man-made guarantees of human rights.

In nineteenth-century Iran the departure from Islamic precepts was very evident. There were no legal limits to check the misrule of capricious monarchs. They were supported by a parasitical clergy who in turn were sustained by the rulers. The life and property of the entire nation were at the disposal of the Shah and a group of royal governors who used their tenure of office to enrich themselves. Under such conditions it was not unnatural that an increasing number of educated Iranians began to look to the West rather than to Islam for guidance and for a political system that would guarantee the rights of man.

The Iranian constitutional movement which was responsible for the revolution of 1906,[16] represents the height of Iranian admiration for and imitation of the West. "The main body of the Constitution of Iran, in fact, is a translation of the Belgian Constitution of 1830."[17] The Constitution establishes the nature of the government and the constitutional powers of the monarch, who rules "by the grace of God and the will of the people of Iran." The Constitution has a Supplement, which is in effect a bill of rights. It affords fruitful study for anyone interested in the fusion of Western and Islamic ideas and institutions. It tries to accept all the tenets of Western liberal democracy, based upon the seventeenth- and eighteenth-century concepts of natural law and the natural rights of man, but subject to a strict conformity with the *shari'ah* and approval of the *'ulama*. It sets out to establish a Western liberal democracy with secular institutions but without the basic prerequisite of such a system: the separation of church and state.

An illustration of this anomaly is enlightening. The Constitution states:

> *Article 1.* The official religion of Iran is Islam of the true sect of *Ja'fariah Ithna 'Ashariah* [orthodox *shi'ah*]. The Shah must protect and profess this faith.
>
> *Article 2.* The Majlis, which has been formed by the blessing of the *Imam 'Asr,* may God speed His appearance, and by the grace of His Majesty the Shah, and by the vigilance of the Islamic *'ulama,* may God increase their example, and by the Iranian nation, may at no time legislate laws that are contradictory to the sacred laws of Islam. . . . It is self-evident that it is the responsibility of the *'ulama* to determine and judge such contradictions. Therefore it is officially decreed that in each legislative session a board of no less than five men, comprised of *mujtahids* and devout *fuqaha,* who are also aware of the needs and exigencies of the time, . . . be nominated by the *'ulama.** The Majlis shall accept this board as full

---

* The vital concept of *Imam 'Asr* is peculiar to *shi'ism.* It implies that the twelfth *Imam,* although hidden from sight, is nevertheless the true and

members. It is their duty to study all the legislative pro-
posals, and if they find any that contradict the sacred
laws of Islam, they shall reject it. The decision of this
board in this respect is binding and final.* This provision of the Constitution is unalterable until the coming of the *Imam 'Asr,* may God speed His appearance.[18]

Then it guarantees the following civil rights:

Article 8. The people of Iran shall have equal rights before the laws of the state.

Article 9. The life, property, home, and honor of every individual are protected against all molestation. No one
shall be molested except by the order of and in the manner provided by the laws of the state.

Article 10. Except in cases of major crimes, no one shall be
summarily arrested without the written order of the
Justice of the Court† as provided by the law. The charges
against the arrested person must be declared to him
within twenty-four hours of his arrest.

Article 11. No one shall be denied the jurisdiction of the
court competent in his case and be referred to another
court.

Article 12. No sentence may be handed down and carried
out unless provided by law.

Article 13. The house and home of everyone is safe and protected. No one shall enter any domicile by force except
by the order of and in the manner provided by law.

Article 14. No Iranian may be exiled, refused residence, or
forced to reside in a particular place except where provided by law.

---

legitimate head of the *shi'ah* theocracy at all times. The *mujtahids* interpret the Faith and the Shah rules on His behalf only until such time as
He may see fit to reappear.

The term *'ulama,* literally translated the "learned," is generally used by
all Muslims to designate those divines who have made a study of theology.
Mujtahids are the highest dignitaries of the *shi'ah* sect. They provide a
continuity of authoritative religious legislation, based on a comprehensive
knowledge of the Koran and its traditions and arrived at by extreme diligence and endeavor. One becomes a *mujtahid* by receiving a *fatwa* (decree)
from another *mujtahid.*

* This provision for a supervisory board, although never altered, was
completely ignored by Reza Shah and is disregarded today.

† A civil court, as distinct from the religious courts of *shari'ah.* Civil
courts, however, were not yet in existence when the Constitution was
adopted. See pp. 68–69 below.

Article 15. No one's property may be expropriated except with legal warrants, and then only after settlement and payment of a just compensation.

Article 16. Confiscation of wealth and property as a form of punishment is forbidden unless required by law.

Article 17. Denial of access to one's property is forbidden unless required by law.

Article 22. Mail shall be exempt from confiscation and censorship except when provided by law.

Article 76. All trials shall be public unless they disturb order or offend morality. In such cases the court may rule for a closed trial.

Article 94. No taxes shall be levied except by law.

Article 97. Everyone shall be treated equally in matters pertaining to the payment of taxes.[19]

In regard to the rights and protection of aliens residing in Iran the Constitution states:

Article 6. The life and property of aliens residing in Iran are safeguarded and respected unless specified in the law of the state.

Article 24. Aliens may accept Iranian citizenship. Their naturalization and denaturalization will be provided for by a separate law.[20]

In contrast with the above liberal provisions are the following instances of Islamic restrictions:

Article 18. All sciences and crafts may be freely learned and taught except those that are forbidden by the *shari'ah*.

Article 20. All publications, with the exception of heretical books and literature harmful to Islam, can be freely circulated and censorship over them is forbidden.

Article 21. Assemblies and meetings that do not breed religious or secular strife and that do not disturb order are free in all parts of the country.

Article 58. No one shall become a minister of state unless he is a Muslim and a native citizen of Iran.[21]

The early attempts at Western-inspired reform were, like the Constitution itself, accompanied by Islamic restrictions. In the newly created administrative and judicial machinery such positions as notaries public,[22] military personnel,[23] and judges[24] were open to Muslims only.

POLITICAL PARTIES

When the naive illusion that the Constitution would cure all ills was shattered, the Iranians turned to another Western device—political parties—for political action and reform. In name as well as in platform these parties were often close copies of their European prototypes. In 1908 the first two parties were founded, under the names of Popular Democrats and Moderate Socialists. The Moderates, who were in the majority, were nominally Socialists (and were supported by the Russians), but the party represented the privileged class: the aristocracy, the rich merchants, and a few liberal clergy. They were in favor of gradual and moderate reform. The Democrats, the party befriended by the British, were a revolutionary party and were often accused by their opponents of heresy and atheism. Although the Democrats were a minority, they had considerable influence, for their ranks included the embryonic intelligentsia of the country: journalists, orators, and writers, all of whom attracted the young people and the emerging middle class. They also had the best newspapers in Iran, including *Iran-e Now* in Tehran, *Shafaq* in Tabriz, and *Now Bahar* in Mashhad. Their party platform included the following planks: (1) the separation of religion and politics; (2) compulsory military service; (3) the distribution of land among the peasants; (4) legislation to prevent hoarding practices; (5) compulsory education; (6) the formation of an agricultural bank; (7) a preference for indirect over direct taxation;* and (8) opposition to an Upper House as provided in the Constitution.[25]

During the First World War, when the British and the Russians were allies, the Democrats had looked to the Central Powers for support. But following the war the parties rearranged themselves to a certain extent, and in 1921 some elements from the old Democrat and Moderate parties formed a new Socialist party. Very soon, however, they divided into two

---

* Although this seemed a departure from the normal class interests of the party, it was a concession to reality; the Democrats were aware of the difficulties of collecting direct taxes from the rich.

factions: one group, composed of the younger socialists, definitely favored Communism and a policy of friendship with the the Soviets; the other group comprised the older members of the original parties who were suspicious of both Russia and Britain. In time the first group came to be called Socialist and the second Reformist. The Reformists gained a majority when the fourth session of the Majlis was opened in 1923 after a long wartime recess.[26]

Party lines and platforms, however, were never definite. Furthermore, they did not as yet bear a very precise relation to the political and social conditions of the country. They were simply reverberations of the great Russian Revolution. Soon the Socialists and the clergy clashed, and the Reformists expediently drew close to the clergy. Eventually Modarres, the leading figure among the politically minded clergy, assumed the leadership of the Reformists and turned the party into an instrument of reaction.

THE INTELLECTUAL FERMENT

Whereas the tangible effects of Westernization, both technical and ideological, scarcely reached the masses, they created a real revolution among the intellectuals. Modern sociologists are becoming increasingly aware of the important role of the "elite" in highly advanced societies. In more primitive societies the elite exercise an even greater proportion of authority. The intellectual atmosphere in Persia at the end of the nineteenth century, which was so receptive to the ways of the West, was created by a very few people; yet their influence was very great. All the political and physical changes were taking place against a background of intense intellectual curiosity and avid desire for Westernization.

These pioneer intellectuals shared the following characteristics: they were intensely patriotic; they shared an abhorrence of arbitrary rule and wanted constitutional rights; and they generally stood for secularization, and a vociferous group among them were extremely anti-clerical. Although a strong current of

Islamic revivalist spirit, generated by Jamal ed-Din Afghani, did exist among the intelligentsia of the time, the spearhead of Westernism is to be found with the advocates of secularization. It is to this group, then, that we must look first.

The reactions of the early intellectuals to the West, and their intense desire for Westernization, were often extremely naive, as the following editorial in the first privately owned newspaper published in Iran may indicate:

> Our purpose in founding this paper is to acquaint our fellow journalists in the West with the social and political problems of Iran. At the same time we welcome an exchange of ideas with them as to the solutions for these problems. From the contact of minds springs the lightning of truth. We wish to enlighten Iran by such lightning.
> Therefore, we wish the world of journalism in the West to accept this paper as a young but high-minded member. And we ask our European colleagues to enlighten us with their experience and knowledge, so that we may present these benefits to the Iranian nation.[27]

This was a bilingual paper in French and Persian, called *La Patrie-Vatan,* published in 1876. Clerical and court pressure, however, brought it to an abrupt end—its first issue was also its last.

The following editorial is from a Persian periodical published by a group of Iranians in Cairo. I should like to quote (and paraphrase) it at length because, in its Spencerian reasoning and anti-clerical tone, it is representative of the opinion of a large number of Iranian intellectuals and affords great insight into the vast influence of Western ideas:

> Our purpose in founding this periodical is to create a revolution in ideas, particularly in the ideas of the young who are still receptive to education. . . .
> In the first place, we should not be afraid of the word "revolution." Revolutions are the educators of mankind. Revolutions breed progress and advance civilization.

The editorial goes on to explain that in the past these revolutions were caused by the so-called prophets—or better yet—the prophets were moved by the needs of the time to cause the revolutions. Today, fortunately, there is no more need for prophets. And should any appear, it is better if they pass unrecognized. Today the revolution must come in the light of science and association with civilized nations, aided by rapid communication and transportation. The leaders of this revolution must be educated and rational men.

If a revolution is not created by the Iranians, the editorial continues, the forces of nature will saddle them with an oppressive foreign master who shall lead them to progress by force. Nature develops these strong masters, for this world is fit only for the strong. Furthermore, nature is right and just in favoring the strong. "Because if we do not wish to advance ourselves, we are not only harming ourselves, but we create an obstacle in the path of progress and civilization."

Millions of acres of the surface of this earth are occupied by the people of the East. What benefits do they return to the world of humanity to deserve this abundance? What service do they render in return for all the benefits they enjoy? People in other parts of the world are working hard and producing everything they need. *"The people of the East have been in debt to the science, learning, technology, and hard work of the Europeans for the past several centuries."* They benefit by the awe-inspiring inventions of the Europeans, and shall continue to do so. If they continue to benefit from the West and remain lazy, it would be only just for nature to suppress the debtor, the poor, the dishonest, and the pest. "We must end these days of ignorance! We must awaken and repay our debts, otherwise perdition is inevitable."

There is no question of the need for a change. There is much confusion as to how this change should come. Some so-called progressive *mullas* want a constitutional regime that is in accordance with the *shari'ah*. If they wish to base the government and the rights of people upon the Koran, *"they must realize that there is much of great importance in today's society that is unmentioned in the Koran."* There is no mention of elections, taxation, tariffs, the tenure of presidency, duties of ministers, and so on. What solutions do the *mullas* have to these problems? Do they wish to proceed according to the Islamic *feqh,* or do they propose to consult some *mujtahid* in Najaf? "We are totally opposed to such ideas, and for us a constitutional regime according to the *shari'ah* is utter nonsense."

Many of the European laws have been enacted with equity and in accordance with the needs of our time. They are the work of great jurists and are based on centuries of experience.

> We must adopt these gratefully and establish a "civil code" for ourselves. . . . We must also model our fundamental criminal, commercial, and other codes on European models. If we examine all the *feqh* and *hadith* books until doomsday, we shall never find any sensible answers to these problems. Likewise, if all the *mujtahids* were to put their heads together, their combined intelligence would be inadequate to cope with these matters. Therefore, we must respectfully approach the house of the "unclean and heathen" *farangi** and implore them to save us from our ignorance and misery. . . . *Mullas* and zealots will persecute us and call us irreligious, but the truth is that true Islam is not opposed to civilization.[28]

During the decade preceding the establishment of Pahlavi rule in Iran, anti-clericalism found strong expression among a group of poets and authors known as *motejadded* (innovators), whose works were popular among the middle classes. The best-known members of this group were Iraj Mirza, Farah, and Eshqi.[29] The methods that they proposed and that were, in fact, utilized in combatting the clergy were peculiarly Western. Freemasonry, for example, provided a nucleus for organized anti-clerical propaganda. [30]

An increasing number of younger intellectuals substituted nationalism for religious fanaticism. The changes that Reza Shah Pahlavi was able to bring about in so short a time in the social, political, and economic conditions of Iran were accomplished with the support of this group. If the reforms of Reza

* The popular term used to denote all Westerners.

Shah had an ideological content, it was this spirit of secular nationalism.

THE BABI-BAHA'I MOVEMENT

No discussion of the forces that shook Iranian society out of its long period of torpor and made it receptive to the impact of the West can ignore the part played by the Babi-Baha'i religious movement.

Originating in Persia in 1844, this movement attracted immediate attention because of its claim of fulfillment of *shi'ah* messianic expectations. It soon created a revolution in the climate of faith and ideas. Subjected to ruthless and open persecution both by the clergy and by the state from the very beginning, Babism soon asserted its independence and went far beyond the horizons of *shi'ah* Islam.[31] The novelty of its approach and the liberalism of its social teachings, as well as the brutality of its persecutors, aroused the interest and sympathy of European scholars and orientalists.[32] There was also a surprising wave of interest and curiosity in the press of Europe.[33] Many of the Persian intelligentsia who were looking to the West for enlightenment, and who were naturally sensitive to Western reactions to the conditions in Persia, were thus made aware of the incongruity of religious bigotry. Furthermore, European interest attracted the attention of these intellectuals to the progressive principles of the Babi-Baha'i movement. A Western observer has asserted that "There can be no doubt that the movement blossomed at an opportune moment for Persia and served to stem the rising tide of *shi'ah* bigotry, which was certainly in those days a definite bar to education and progress."[34]

A thorough examination of the Babi-Baha'i movement in all its aspects is beyond the limits of this study. It is necessary, however, to note its progressive social principles which, despite continued opposition, have played a definite part in preparing the people of Iran for modern social reforms. The basic purpose of the movement is to bring about the complete spiritual, moral, and political unity of mankind. In order to realize such a unity it advocates universal peace, world government, a world court, an international auxiliary language, equality of rights for both sexes, compulsory education, eradication of prejudices, and the agreement of science and religion.[35]

These ideals were novel and revolutionary in nineteenth-century Persia. At first glance they seem decidedly Western in origin and orientation. It must be borne in mind, however, that they were formulated and enunciated during the period 1844–92, when most of them were equally novel and radical in the West. It is also obvious that these principles are not directed at Persia or the East alone, but are intended to serve as the universal basis of a new synthesis.

For the past century there has existed in Iran a relatively large Baha'i community—indeed, Baha'is form the largest religious minority. By virtue of their progressive beliefs and their close contacts with coreligionists in other parts of the world, they present a markedly high degree of world consciousness. Further, their impact upon other Iranians is worthy of attention. They have pioneered in many social reforms and acted as agents of enlightenment. In advocating the emancipation of women, the spread of education, and the study of Western languages they have anticipated the influences coming from the West. Moreover, not only did the Baha'is advocate various reforms, but they had considerable success in getting their ideas accepted. An Italian observer in 1941 commented that "in the social field Baha'ism calls for . . . the abolition of polygamy, the restriction of divorce, and the abolition of veils for women. Indeed these principles today are part of the Iranian progressive movement and are triumphing with the national restoration brought about by Reza Khan."[36]

By attacking superstition and de-emphasizing the supernatural element, the Babi-Baha'i movement made the Persians more receptive to the scientific spirit of the West. No less a figure than a Persian *shi'ah mujtahid* states that: "It cannot be overlooked that the appearance of Baha'u'llah and his concepts of social evolution, denial of miracles, and progressive revelation, made a great impact on Iran. It can be safely asserted that after Baha'u'llah, the foundations of traditional religion were weakened in Iran."[37]

Chapter Two

THE RISE OF REZA SHAH

Iran in 1920, despite long and significant contact with Western civilization, was a totally Oriental nation. Neither Western technology nor Western ideology had as yet made any deep impact upon the country. This was particularly true of technological changes. Although the minds of the intelligentsia had been influenced strongly by the West, the face of Iran remained virtually unchanged.

THE SOCIAL SCENE

Society in 1920 was much the same as it had been a century earlier. There were some signs of Western influence among the small minority that constituted the upper class, but there were very few, and often none at all, among the vast majority of Iranians.

Moreover, the degree of Westernization among the members of the upper class was not uniform. Most of them did use a wide variety of European manufactured goods in their daily life, for example, clothing, toilet articles, paper, crockery, and glassware; but electricity in homes was a rarity even in the cities. A handful among the upper class had automobiles, but there were no paved roads anywhere in the country. On the other hand, it was not unusual for upper-class families to have at least one son who had been educated in Europe. These young men returned in Western clothing which, with some modifications, they continued to wear; most of them retained Western ideas and theories, particularly about politics. But their homes, their family relations, their marriages, and their personal habits and activities remained overwhelmingly Persian.

Among the merchant class the influence of the West was even slighter. The wealthier merchants formed an influential minority in Iranian society; their prestige and power, although not based on ownership of land, was almost equal to that of the aristocracy. But despite their commercial dealings with Europe, they displayed much less evidence of Westernization than the city-dwelling landed aristocracy. And the numerous small merchants, shopkeepers, artisans, craftsmen, and petty officials lived virtually untouched by Western ideas, although they did derive benefit from some material objects of Western manufacture, such as cheap cotton goods, kerosene lamps, and sugar.

The largest class in Iranian society, the peasantry, lived much as they had for centuries. Some villages by main roads had come in contact with outward signs of Western civilization; and a few items of Western origin had found their way into the homes of the more prosperous peasants. They had seen automobiles, perhaps even airplanes, but no traces of Western ideas could be found on their mental horizons. The large number of villages in inaccessible regions had even less contact with anything from outside. As for the tribal population of Iran (in 1920 nearly 15 per cent of the total), it remained completely untouched by modern advances of any kind.

It is to a small, heterogeneous, active, articulate, and constantly growing class that we must look for real evidence of a spreading and dynamic Westernism in Iran. A group that defied categorization, but that in reality was the nucleus of a modern middle class, it cut across all other sections of society. Many younger members of the upper class, a very large number of sons of the clergy and of young ex-clergymen (completely secular and often anti-clerical in their outlook), the sons of minor officials, and even a few sons of peasants composed the majority of this group. In Iranian society these young men formed the professional class—journalists, doctors, lawyers, teachers, army officers, and government officials. In 1920 they were a minority, but they were both the voice and the political conscience of Iran. They had made significant inroads into the medieval order of Iranian society and government. They had proven their capacity to assimilate Western civilization. They had put constitutional limits upon an old autocracy in the face of enormous obstacles. They had equalized opportunities to such a degree that any man of ability could occupy the highest offices. They had shown unparalleled eagerness for education and had established hundreds of schools since the granting of the Constitution in 1906. They had been responsible for the overnight growth of a remarkable free press that was not afraid to denounce injustice and tyranny whether at home or abroad. They were anxious to adopt wholesale the political, ethical, and busines codes of the most modern and progressive nations.[1]

But outspoken as this group was in its demands for change and progress, it lacked cohesion and effective leadership to translate its wishes into an organized plan of action. There was a feeling of fatalistic impotence in the face of the machinations—real and imaginary—of the Great Powers. Moreover, there was a pernicious pessimism (shared by a small but influential group of the aristocracy) about the ability and intelligence of the Iranian masses. Highly educated and thoroughly Westernized, they looked upon the great body of their countrymen with contemptuous disdain. This defeatist attitude, emanating as it often did from men in highly responsible places who were in a position to act, had a paralyzing effect on any program of action.

The Iran of 1920, in short, was beginning to give evidence of having been in contact with the West, but in terms of ideas not of technological achievements. The disparity led to intensified demands for improvement. At this propitious time the anarchic condition of the country brought about the rise of Reza Khan. He galvanized the political, social, and intellectual growth that had been slowly mounting for more than half a century, and that had been accelerated since 1906. Insensitive to the intellectual fineries of Westernism, he understood the chief reason Iran looked to the West—her need for material improvements and desire for action. During the next twenty years of his reign, then, the pendulum swung sharply in the opposite direction. Western ideologies were subjected to national modifications, while whole-hearted efforts were made to Westernize the face of Iran.

THE POLITICAL SCENE

The political events that led up to Reza Khan's rise to power have been adequately described by other writers;[2] here a brief account will suffice to put the *coup d'état* of 1921 in focus.

The reluctant grant of the Constitution by Mozaffar ed-Din Shah (1896–1907) in 1906, although cheered by the nation, had not led to any upsurge of popularity for the Qajar dynasty. And when Muhammad 'Ali Shah (1907–9) ascended the throne, memories of a century of misrule were soon fanned into intense revulsion against the Qajars. He surrounded himself with reactionary statesmen, and with the overt help of Russia (who upon concluding the Anglo-Russian Agreement of 1907 had embarked upon new and much more flagrant power politics in Iran), he sought to undo all the gains of the constitutional movement. With the aid of the Russian-led Cossack Brigade[3] the Shah cannonaded the Majlis and dispersed the deputies. But the liberal and nationalist forces, bolstered by tribal support and passively assisted by Britain, were able to restore the constitutional regime. The Shah escaped to Russia, and with his departure, the last truly autocratic Qajar ruler disappeared from the scene.[4] The net result of his short but violent reign was to make the Iranians more keenly appreciative of their newly won reforms and to deepen the general dislike and distrust of the Qajars.

When the last of the Qajars, Ahmad Shah (1909–25), a corpulent boy of 12, ascended the throne, the court remained the scene of much intrigue but no longer the seat of power. Liberal statesmen dominated the new Majlis, and successive cabinets tried their hand at reforms of a Western nature. A reliable picture of the political needs of Iran during this period and of her readiness for Western-inspired reforms may be obtained by studying the programs that the various cabinets of the period 1909–25 presented for approval to the Majlis.

Muhammad Vali Khan Sepahdar A'zam, the hero of the nationalist-liberal victory over Muhammad 'Ali Shah, was entrusted with the formation of the first of these cabinets. He recognized that the foremost task of his government must be the reestablishment of law and order in the country, and therefore proposed to devote the main portion of his budget to the reform of the regular army, the complete reorganization of the municipal police, and the formation of a new corps of security forces—a gendarmerie—to protect the roads and countryside. He also promised far-reaching reforms in the areas of finance, governmental organization and administration, the judiciary, and education. For the inception and execution of these reforms he proposed to "employ a number of foreign advisors . . . to create an order that is at once scientific and efficient as well as suited to the needs of the country."[5]

Mostowfi ol-Mamalek, who succeeded Sepahdar A'zam as Premier in 1910, presented the following program to the Majlis: (1) the employment of foreign advisors; urgent efforts were to be made to engage such assistance; (2) the reform of the police and, in particular, the security forces, in order to establish real security in the country; (3) the complete reorganization and modernization of the army; (4) the reform of the government finances; (5) the reform of the judiciary; and (6) reforms in education, including the dispatch of students to Europe.[6]

Sepahdar A'zam returned in 1911 to form his second cabinet. By then the breakdown of law and order was so complete that the Majlis granted him extraordinary powers that allowed him to deal with subversive and terroristic elements, to enforce emergency disciplinary measures in the army, and to curtail the activities of what he termed "irresponsible journalists." As constructive steps Sepahdar A'zam proposed: (1) the formation of mobile security forces; (2) financial reforms under the supervision of the newly arrived American mission; (3) the reform of the Ministry of Justice; (4) the reform of elementary and secondary schools and the foundation of a teachers' college in Tehran; (5) the encouragement of trade, the introduction of corporation laws, and the formation of chambers of commerce; and (6) the reform of municipalities.[7]

The years from 1909 to 1911, when Iran was governed by the cabinets of Sepahdar A'zam and Mostowfi ol-Mamalek, represent a pathetic period in her recent history. Naively hopeful that constitutionalism was the panacea for all the ills of their country, a small, enthusiastic group of liberal-minded statesmen had set out to reform Iran. Beset by opposition from the reactionary and privileged aristocracy and clergy and faced with the inertia of centuries of corruption and stagnation, they were also soon swept aside by the interference first of Russia and then of Britain.

The second cabinet of Sepahdar A'zam was, in fact, a last, brief attempt to defy the pressure from Russia and to maintain a semblance of true sovereignty. It lasted less than six months. For half of this time the government was engaged in putting down an attempted *coup d'état* by the deposed Muhammad 'Ali Shah. The final crisis arose over the employment of a group of American financial advisors headed by Morgan Shuster. The energetic activities of this group promised to put the finances of the country on a firm basis. Such an example might well lead to the importation of other advisors, resulting in the general improvement and strengthening of the country. At this point, however, a Russian ultimatum, followed by movement of Russian troops into Tabriz and in the direction of Tehran, brought about the fall of the cabinet and the dismissal of Shuster.[8]

The succeeding cabinet, formed by Samsam ol-Saltane, presented a program designed to forestall liberal and patriotic protests. It proposed, first, to revise the electoral law, and second, "to integrate domestic and foreign policy in order to secure the assistance of neighbors and the confidence of the people."[9]

In 1914 Mostowfi ol-Mamalek made an unsuccessful effort to form a second cabinet. It is interesting to note that in his program (which was rejected by the Majlis) he proposed: (1) the abolition of the old feudalistic system of pensions; (2) the speedy completion of the new codes of law; (3) the foundation of a secular law school to train personnel for the Ministry of Justice; (4) the establishment of several schools for girls; (5) the expansion of telegraph lines; and (6) new laws governing telegraphic communications.[10]

The final cabinet program, which was approved by the third session of the Majlis in 1914, was that of Moshir ed-Dowle. It proposed: (1) strict adherence to a policy of neutrality in foreign affairs; (2) the formation of commercial codes; (3) the enactment of bankruptcy laws; (4) the establishment of a teachers' college for women; (5) the adoption by all schools of a uniform curriculum and a uniform series of textbooks; (6) the gradual transformation of religious schools (*Maktab-Khane*) into regular elementary schools; and (7) the formation of chambers of commerce.[11]

The third session of the Majlis came to an end shortly after the outbreak of the First World War, which forced the Majlis into a long recess lasting until 1921. Although several cabinets were formed during the wartime period, the political situation in Iran bordered on anarchy. The exercise of governmental authority came to a virtual standstill. In the provinces the consulates of Russia and Britain and the British-owned telegraph offices* were the real seats of power. Various parts of the country were occupied by Russian, British, and Turkish troops. A German agent, Wassmuss, was active in southern Iran, organizing tribal resistance to Britain.[12] To supplant the Swedish-led Iranian gendarmerie and to counterbalance the Russian-commanded Persian Cossack Brigade, the British organized the South Persia Rifles. A group of nationalist statesmen, politicians, and journalists, influenced by German propa-

---

* Political refugees often used these offices as a place of sanctuary, much as they would a religious shrine.

ganda and distressed by the plight of their land, emigrated to Constantinople. Brigandage and tribal lawlessness were alarming. Highway robbery was universal; in fact, highwaymen often raided towns and, in the absence of any authority, sometimes remained, wrecking all economic activity.[13]

The Bolshevik Revolution and the subsequent evacuation of Russian forces from Iranian territory created a power void in Iran. The Iranian government tried to prevent the British from filling this vacuum, and a direct outcome of the Bolshevik Revolution was thus the marked hostility of the Iranians toward the British. Another direct result was a widespread outbreak of revolts. Kuchek Khan in Gilan and Khiyabani in Azerbaijan led revolts which bore signs of Bolshevik support. When the Soviets repudiated Tsarist privileges in Iran in January 1918, a new wave of popular and official Anglophobia spread through the country, resulting in a demand from Britain for a more friendly attitude. The demand was rejected by the Iranian government, and a crisis developed. The current government fell, and in July 1918 a new one was formed by Vosuq ed-Dowle, a known friend of the British. There followed two years of British political and diplomatic supremacy, highlighted by the Anglo-Persian Agreement of 1919, which provided for a virtual military and financial protectorate over Iran.

With no Majlis in session there was no official outlet for protest against the unpopular diplomacy of Vosuq ed-Dowle and his foreign minister Nosrat ed-Dowle Firuz. But rising popular discontent, the deterioration of internal security, and above all, the Soviet occupation of Gilan and resurgent Soviet diplomacy in general—now supported by a large number of articulate intellectuals in Iran—finally caused the fall of the government. The new cabinet refused to ratify the Anglo-Persian Agreement. When in November 1920 the Soviet government sent Iran an ultimatum demanding the evacuation of British troops, it was favorably received both by the government and by the public.

One of the first actions of the newly formed fourth session of the Majlis in 1921 was the repudiation of the Anglo-Persian

Agreement. In its stead, Iran agreed in February of that year to a treaty with Soviet Russia. The generous self-denial of the Soviet government—the repudiation of Tsarist privileges as well as the anti-imperialist blandishments of the treaty—made a profound impression on many Iranians. Russia's retention of the Caspian fisheries seemed but a trifle compared with the concessions she denounced. And the fateful article 6 of the treaty —permitting Soviet Russia to send troops into Iran if she considered her security endangered by the presence of a foreign power on Iranian soil—appeared at the time to some Iranians as a desirable lever against Britain.[14]

Such were the political events preceding the *coup d'état* of February 26, 1921, which brought Reza Khan to power. Although the original engineer of the *coup d'état* had been a young Iranian journalist, Sayed Ziya, it was accomplished with the aid of the Cossack Brigade, of which Reza Khan was the co-commander. When the people of Tehran woke up on the morning of February 26, 1921—only a few having heard a brief volley of shots in the early hours—they found the street walls plastered with directives. In bold letters they began, "I command." They were all signed by Reza Khan, Sardar Sepah, Commander-in-Chief of all the armed forces.[15] Sayed Ziya became Premier, but there was little doubt where the real power lay. From this moment began an era of relentless activity, which was generated by the determined and forceful Reza Khan, and which galvanized hundreds of his countrymen into action.

THE EXTENT OF EARLIER REFORMS

As we have seen, the various governments that were in power from 1909 to 1925 had proposed programs of far-reaching reforms. The tasks that Reza Khan set himself in those early years were the same as the avowed intentions of his predecessors; it was the degree of accomplishment that was different. It is therefore important to assess how much these predecessor governments had in fact accomplished.

In solving the most pressing problem of the country—the restoration of law and order and security—there had been no success. By 1921, in addition to brigandage and highway robbery, there was large-scale political and tribal revolt in the provinces of Gilan, Azerbaijan, Kurdistan, Luristan, Khuzistan, Fars, and Mokran. The reform and reorganization of the army had been neglected. The organization, the command, and the method of supply and payment of the regular army were chaotic. The only effective fighting forces were independent detachments, such as the Swedish-trained gendarmerie and the Russian-trained Cossack Brigade.

The task of administrative reform and governmental organization had also been left undone. In fact, in many cases it was impossible to enforce governmental authority at all, let alone to reform and reorganize it.

The only area in which the programs of the various governments had been partially realized was in the employment of foreign advisors to modernize certain phases of the national life. The majority of these advisors were imported in 1910 and the early part of 1911, before Russian pressure canceled further expansion of the program. During this brief period the Majlis approved a series of employment contracts for M. Mernard, a Belgian, as Supervisor of Customs, and twelve other Belgian customs officials. This group proceeded to introduce order and uniformity into the collection of customs duties, which were the government's chief source of revenue. Also at this time ten Swedish officers were employed to organize a gendarmerie, and twenty Swedish officers were employed to reform and asssist in the training of the regular army.

In 1911 an eleven-member American financial mission, under the direction of Morgan Shuster, was employed by the Ministry of Finance. The positions of "chief of the Treasury, public accountants for the Treasury, supervisor of the provincial treasuries, and chief of the newly formed income tax bureau (who was to draw up income tax laws and assess the property tax according to correct methods)" were all to be filled by members of the group. It was stipulated in the contracts of several of these men that in addition to their duties at the Ministry of Finance, they were to teach accounting and book-keeping at a state school. The salaries paid to these men ranged from $3,000 per annum plus transportation (for the lowest ranking member of the mission) to $10,000 per annum plus transportation (for Shuster). The life of the mission was short, however, and despite promise of success, Russian pressure forced the Americans to leave.[16]

The most significant appointment of a foreign advisor was the employment by the Ministry of Justice of Adolph Perni, a French jurist, to assist and advise on the preparation of a penal code. He completed his task by the end of 1911. In January 1912 the first penal code ever promulgated in Iran was submitted to the Majlis for approval. Consisting of 506 articles, this code was the first attempt to graft the Napoleonic Code upon the body of the *shari'ah* in Iran. "It was signed by three ranking *mujtahids,* who testified that it was acceptable by the standards of the *shari'ah* and that its new features did not violate the precepts of Islam."[17] It is significant that three leading *mujtahids* should not have objected to a French jurist preparing a code of laws for Iran. But far more significant was the implicit admission by the *mujtahids* that the body of the *shari'ah* was no longer adequate and that the legal concepts of the West might be added to Islamic precepts.

In 1911 a French advisor to the Ministry of the Interior and an American advisor to the Ministry of Post and Telegraph were employed. In the same year two other Frenchmen were engaged, one a professor of medicine and the other a teacher of physical sciences, who, in addition to teaching, was to operate a laboratory for analysis.[18]

This was the extent of modernization and Westernism effected by the governments that preceded the rise of Reza Khan. Moreover, despite their repeated promises, not a single government-sponsored student had been sent to Europe.

THE CHARACTER OF REZA SHAH

Little is known of the early life of Reza Khan, and for several reasons no real biography of this forceful man has been written.[19] He never encouraged people to delve into his past, presumably because there was nothing to fit the traditional mold of the noble savior. Furthermore, during his sixteen years on the throne very little was made public about his personal life. Even the date of his birth is unknown, for there was no registration of vital statistics in Iran until 1931. His official birthday was celebrated as March 16, 1878. He was born in the Caspian Sea province of Mazanderan, a region that remained the special object of his favor until the end of his reign. Biographical accounts that appeared early in his reign described his ancestry as being from the lower strata of the military class—his father was a sergeant of the cavalry. In later accounts the social standing of his family was elevated, and his father was raised to the rank of colonel. He himself began a military career at an early age, and not much is known of his life until he attained a position of command in the Cossack Brigade. He never received an adequate formal education, and his spelling was the subject of many anecdotes.

Reza Khan was tall, broad-shouldered, and possessed a natural air of authority. He was strong-willed and impatient, quick-tempered and uncouth; but he had to perfection the politician's talent for opportunism. Most of the qualities that alienated him from the refined, Europeanized, and often effeminate sections of society were the same that won him the support of the hero-worshipping lower classes. Although in the early, uncertain days of his career he showed that he knew how to play upon the religious emotions of the people, he was basically apathetic to religion and antagonistic toward the clergy. Moreover, once his power was consolidated, he acted with less caution, and he affronted the clergy and other religious elements on many occasions. His broad social reforms, such as the removal of the veil, were, of course, the subject of deep religious controversy. In his personal life, too, he would occasionally take advantage of an opportunity to offend the sensibilities of the clergy and the zealots. At trade fairs, for example, he made a point of sampling the local beer and commenting on its year-by-year improvement, and at the wedding reception of the Crown Prince he raised a toast to his son in champagne.[20]

He possessed a keen mind, an excellent memory, and an unusual ability to absorb information and briefings even if of a highly technical nature. He seldom made public speeches, but when occasion demanded he was always brief and to the point. Upon laying the foundation stone of the University of Tehran, the first university in Iran, he made the following speech: "The establishment of a university is something that the people of Iran should have done a long time ago. Now that it has been started, all efforts must be made for its speedy completion."[21]

His personal morals were above reproach. His conduct as a public figure, however, showed some serious faults, for as he grew in power, his desire to accumulate a fortune developed into a voracious greed, and he became very suspicious and ill-tempered.

THE SEIZURE OF POWER

Following the *coup d'état* of February 1921, Sayed Ziya tried to pursue a drastic and independent course of action. He made sweeping arrests and resorted to violent means of repression. Fearing unpopularity, Reza Khan arrested and exiled Sayed Ziya in April of the same year. He did not consider the time ripe for a complete assumption of power, and he therefore accepted the post of Minister of War in the cabinet formed by Qavam os-Saltane. The chief accomplishments of this government were the reorganization of the armed forces and the defeat of Kuchek Khan and his Bolshevik-inspired and Bolshevik-aided movement in Gilan. For these achievements Reza Khan alone was responsible, a fact which he did not fail to impress upon the people. One of the avowed policies of Qavam os-Saltane's government was employment of foreign advisors from non-neighboring countries only, a move directed against Russia and the British Empire.[22]

The fourth session of the Majlis was elected in the summer of 1921, the last Majlis to be elected without the complete control and supervision of the central government for more than two decades. Destined to witness profound changes not of its own making, it was a heterogeneous group that symbolized the futility of Iranian politics. Its membership was made up of a minority of well-meaning liberals and a majority of selfish, jealous, reactionary, and defeatist landlords and clergy, and it was dominated by Modarres of Isfahan, an egotistical *mulla* who had no aims beyond self-aggrandizement and the acquisition of power. For no other reason than to test his personal power he pitted himself against Reza Khan in political combat.

In 1922 Reza Khan was preoccupied with the primary task of suppressing revolts and restoring law, order, and governmental authority throughout Iran. In a series of successful campaigns with his reorganized and revitalized army, he put down political and tribal revolts in Azerbaijan, Luristan, Kurdistan, Fars, and Khorasan. He did not fail to derive the maximum political advantage from these military feats. Qavam os-Saltane was replaced by Mostowfi ol-Mamalek as Premier early in 1923.[23] Reza Khan kept the post of Minister of War, but by now he was acknowledged and popularly acclaimed as the chief power in the government.

In the two years that he had acted as Minister of War, Reza Khan had developed a deep-rooted distrust of and contempt for the Majlis. By nature he was not averse to high-handed action, to disregarding legal procedure and circumventing constitutional democracy. The opposition of a Modarres-led Majlis, and the intrigues of Modarres himself, served only to convince him of the soundness of his instincts. Thus in 1923, as the time for the election* of the fifth session of the Majlis approached, Reza Khan realized that if he were not once more to face a hostile Majlis, he must achieve a more complete control

* Elections of the Majlis are held every two years in the summer.

of the government. A plot against his life was discovered, supplying him with the necessary pretext to arrest the Prime Minister. In October 1923 Ahmad Shah appointed Reza Khan as Prime Minister and left for Europe, never to return to Iran.

Having now completed the preliminary steps to the assumption of total power, Reza Khan turned to the task of consolidating his position. He was strongly influenced by the events in neighboring Turkey, and he considered forming a republican government in Iran. The spring of 1924 accordingly witnessed a vigorous campaign for the establishment of a republic, and the enlightened segments of public opinion were prepared for its acceptance. However, the abolition of the Caliphate by the Turkish Republic coincided with this campaign and provided Modarres and other religious elements with their last potent weapon against Reza Khan. Quick and irrational arguments were advanced against a republican form of government. Ugly passions were aroused against Reza Khan by suggesting that he was a Babi and that he conspired to destroy Islam. But Reza Khan proved himself a master politician who could defeat his enemies at their own game.

On the morning of *Tasu'a*, the anniversary of the martyrdom of Imam Hussayn and the most elaborately commemorated event in *shi'ah* Islam, a strange procession appeared before the bazaar, the heart of orthodoxy and religious power in Tehran. Traditionally such processions include much flagellation, mortification of the flesh, wailing, and recitation; but this one was a comical combination of East and West. An army band, without caps, marched to a less than definitive version of Chopin's funeral march. At the head of the band marched Reza Khan Sardar Sepah, his bare head covered with straw. To convince any who needed further proof of his piety, he then made a pilgrimage to the *shi'ah* shrines in Najaf and Karbala. Thus once again Reza Khan triumphed. He had been obliged to abandon the republican project in order to gain this victory; but the last serious opposition was overcome.[24]

In December 1924, returning from a successful campaign against Sheikh Khazal in Khuzistan, Reza Khan received a hero's welcome in Tehran. On February 14, 1925, the fifth Majlis passed the following Act:

> The Majlis recognizes the supreme command of the country's defense and security forces as the special domain of Reza Khan Sardar Sepah. He shall exercise his command with complete authority, within the frame of the Constitution and the laws of the land. This command may not be removed without the approval of the Majlis.[25]

The next step was taken on October 31, 1925, when the Majlis passed the following Act:

> Majlis-e Showra-ye Melli, in the name of the welfare of the nation, declares the end of the Qajar Monarchy and bestows the provisional government, within the bounds of the Constitution and the laws of the land, to Reza Khan Pahlavi. The final form of the government shall be decided by a Constituent Assembly which shall convene for revision of Articles 36, 37, 38, and 40 of the Supplement to the Constitution.[26]

In December 1925 the Constituent Assembly, elected under the watchful eye of the government, met in Tehran and revised article 36 of the Supplement to the Constitution to read as follows:

> The Constitutional Monarchy of Iran is vested by the Constituent Assembly, on behalf of the nation, in the person of His Majesty, the Shahanshah Reza Shah Pahlavi, and shall remain in his male progeny generation after generation.[27]

Similarly articles 37, 38, and 40 were revised to bar any member of the Qajar dynasty from the throne, from the exercise of regency, and from marriages affecting the succession to the throne.[28]

Chapter Three

IN THE DIRECTION OF THE WEST

The changes brought about in Iran by Reza Shah were of sufficient magnitude to qualify as a revolution; yet the extent of this revolution has not been fully appreciated and is not easy to measure. The reasons for the difficulty are threefold: the changes were effected with the active, enthusiastic support of many and the tacit approval of a majority of Iranians, thereby minimizing the elements of resistance and struggle; the events in Iran were overshadowed by a drastic revolution in Russia and a radical upheaval in Turkey and therefore by comparison appeared mild; the Reza Shah movement lacked organized, deliberate media of expression, and the defined, well-formulated, and well-publicized ideology that has come to be considered the necessary baggage of any revolutionary movement.

Reza Shah wrote no *Mein Kampf*. Unlike Kemal Ataturk, whose reforms he emulated freely, he made no public utterances, wrote no articles, left no political testament, which, taken as a whole, could be considered his program or the ideological core of his revolution. We cannot speak of Pahlavism as we do of Kemalism. This can be explained by what appears to be a paradox. Reza Shah was not the leader of an organized, program-bearing, ideology-spouting revolutionary movement. He was, in fact, the product of the failure and futility of such movements in Iran. He embodied the impatience of men of action with the endless debates of the articulate reformers and revolutionaries. His nature, and the circumstances of his rise to power, did not make him sympathetic with idealistic theoreticians. He proceeded to immediate and practical goals.

This apparent lack of a formulated ideology has been

criticized by a number of Iranian intellectuals.[1] Various failures that became evident and reactions that set in after the abdication of Reza Shah in 1941 were attributed to this lack of formal principles and ideology. He was accused of proceeding too rapidly and ignoring the need for an ideological foundation.

A closer examination of the period reveals, however, that a definite ideological motivation was present in all the feverish activities of Reza Shah's regime. Although it cannot be located and studied in any one document or pronouncement, it can easily be deduced from his actions and the writings of his vociferous supporters. The inconsistencies, the failures, and the adverse reactions, therefore, cannot be attributed to the lack of an ideology, but to the premises of that ideology.

The ideals underlying the changes that took place in Iran from 1921 to 1941 were threefold: a complete dedication to the cult of nationalism-statism; a desire to assert this nationalism by a rapid adoption of the material advances of the West; and a breakdown of the traditional power of religion and a growing tendency toward secularism, which came as a result of the first two ideals. At the heart of these ideals, shared alike by the Iranian people and Reza Shah himself, was an intense nationalism—from it developed all other motivation.

These ideals represented the triumph of Western influence in Iran. She now entered an era in which Western influences, long felt but never before part of a coherent pattern, came to be of decisive importance. Although Iran was not completely Westernized, all the changes that took place were motivated by Western-inspired ideals. This distinction between complete emulation of and identification with the West, and adoption of Western-inspired ideals and activities, must be borne in mind at all times. It is a key to the understanding of the Iran of the Reza Shah era.

Nationalism as a legacy of the West had come to Iran

earlier.[2] Reza Shah was imbued with this spirit; it had come to him not from abstract contemplation of Western ideologies, but from distress and anger at the helplessness of backward Iran in the face of foreign intervention. Even his critics admitted that "he loved Iran, and that he saw his own greatness in the greatness of Iran."[3] To the end he remained an ardent nationalist, although, with accumulation of autocratic power, he fell victim to the temptation to identify his personal interests with those of his country.

Superficial observers have often dismissed Reza Shah as a not-so-successful follower of Kemal Ataturk. While in many respects he did model his reforms on those of Ataturk, he differed in one major aspect. The cultural heritage of Turkey was one of reflected glory. Therefore Ataturk sought to make a complete break with the past. Reza Shah, on the other hand, drew on the history of Iran as a source of inspiration. In this he was supported by popular sentiment, although it was not the Islamic past which was idolized, but the glories of pre-Islamic Iran.[4]

This assertion of Iranian nationalism did not imply a rejection of the tools and advantages of Western material civilization. On the contrary, they were eagerly adopted and utilized. But the aim of Reza Shah was that they "be absorbed into and become a part of Iranian national life, and . . . not be imposed upon it from outside . . . his object [was] to place in the hands of the Iranian people the economic and cultural tools to enable them to meet any western nation on equal terms. . . . European technology, law, economics and administration were thoroughly studied; but the new nationalized educational system was oriented towards the building up of Iranian self-confidence and self-sufficiency."[5]

The inevitable corollary of nationalism, reinforced by material progress, was secularism. Although the constitutional provisions proclaiming *shi'ah* Islam as the official state religion, and designating the Shah as Defender of the Faith, were never altered, in practice religion was circumscribed and undermined.

It will be seen how all the social reforms of Reza Shah dealt successive blows to the body of organized Islam and divested the clergy of their power. But he could not pursue a strong anti-clerical policy all at once, partly because of the power of the clergy in general, but particularly because of their monopoly in education. Therefore, a gradual program of mass education on national and nonreligious lines was pursued.[6] Although no frontal attacks were ever made on Islam, the new generation was taught to regard it as an alien faith imposed upon Iran by an inferior civilization. Nor was this spirit confined to the younger generation alone; among the intellectual elements of the older generation, too, all manifestations of religious unorthodoxy of a nationalist character were welcomed.

Although Reza Shah's reforms met with resistance from the clergy at every turn, he was soon able to intimidate his opponents into silent discontent. But his success in silencing this opposition should not be attributed to his force of character and energetic methods alone. He was inspired, encouraged, and supported by an articulate majority of the intelligentsia, and his actions were approved and applauded by a majority of the urban middle class—government officials, army officers, professional men, and students.

It is difficult to determine the exact point at which the healthy energy of patriotism turned into a malignant nationalism. But certainly in the early days of Reza Shah patriotic fervor had not as yet developed any chauvinistic tendencies. The idea of a nation meant unity within and not a haughty superiority over neighbors and outsiders. Newspapers, periodicals, the theater, poetry, and even popular ballads of the early 1920's were full of this spirit.

> Religion is a matter of heart and conscience. It should not serve political ends. For this purpose today we must embrace the idea of nation and patriotism. . . . The interests of the nation are above the interests of religion. They are more universal and more unifying. Everyone should be imbued with the spirit of nationalism. In this way we all stand together and our religions will not separate us.[7]

An increasing number of influential Iranians were becoming strong advocates of Westernization. The extent and nature of this trend become apparent if we consider a few of the men who served as the chief lieutenants or ideological supporters of Reza Shah. Among these were Taqizade, Kazemzade-Iranshahr, 'Ali Akbar Siyasi, 'Ali Dashti, Mostafa 'Adl, Amir A'lam, and Muhammad Sa'ed.[8]

Taqizade was born of a *mulla* family and was educated to be a *mulla*. When he was 15 he started to study French secretly. Upon the death of his father he renounced the clerical life and entered the American mission school in Tabriz. He was one of the leaders of the constitutional movement, an early organizer of the Majlis, and one of the founders of the Democratic party. In 1922 he went to Europe on a diplomatic mission and there married a German girl. Upon his return he served in several cabinets of the Reza Shah government, and later he represented Iran in the League of Nations and taught at the University of London.

Kazemzade-Iranshahr, also of clerical background, became a voluntary expatriate and lived in Germany and German Switzerland. Although living abroad, he exercised a powerful influence over the minds of his countrymen by his articles in the periodical *Iranshahr,* which he published in Berlin. It dealt with literary, philosophical, and historical subjects and had Westernized, nationalist, anti-clerical leanings. In later life Kazemzade-Iranshahr founded a pseudo-religious cult known as the Philosophy of Unity; he gathered a following of Swiss people in a village near Zurich and lost contact with Iran.[9]

'Ali Akbar Siyasi came from a middle-class family and studied in France. He served in several governments of the Reza Shah period and became Minister of Education as well as President of the University of Tehran. His book *La Perse au contact de l'Occident,* published in 1931, is a plea for Westernization in Iran, based on historical arguments.

'Ali Dashti was born in Karbala, the heart of *shi-ah* orthodoxy, of a *mulla* family. But he abandoned his clerical studies to become a journalist, and as the editor of *Shafaq-e Sorkh* ("The Red Dawn"), he disseminated pro-Soviet propaganda in the early 1920's. In 1927 he went to Moscow to participate in the Tenth Anniversary of the Red Revolution. He later altered his politics and became a perennial deputy in the Majlis. In the literary field he translated all the works of Anatole France into Persian, and was the author of *The Secret of Anglo-Saxon Superiority*, a book that extols and envies Anglo-Saxon qualities.

Mostafa 'Adl, considered the father of the modern judiciary system in Iran, came from a family of *mujtahids*. He was sent to Cairo to pursue Islamic studies at al-Azhar, but instead he entered a French school and later went to Paris to complete his studies. Upon returning to Iran, he first served in the Ministry of Foreign Affairs and then went to the Ministry of Justice, where he translated many European codes and incorporated them into the judiciary system of Iran.

Amir A'lam was born of an aristocratic family. He studied medicine in France and did much toward improving public health in Iran. He was the founder of the Red Lion and the Sun, an organization corresponding to the Red Cross. He was extremely civic-minded and fond of quoting Kant on the subject of duty.

Muhammad Sa'ed was of merchant stock, studied in Tiflis, St. Petersburg, and Zurich. He married a Latvian girl, and was one of the chief diplomats of the Reza Shah period.

These men are noteworthy not only because they were the chief advocates of Westernization in Iran, but because they played important roles in formulating the policies of the nation. The extent of Westernization is made abundantly clear when we consider the clerical background of most of these men. Indications of Westernization among some members of the aristocracy were not unusual. But the very fact that these sons of clergy rose to such positions of authority is, in itself, a most significant change that must be attributed to the impact of the West.

These Westernizers urged what in practice did not prove

easy: "a complete acceptance of the West and retainment of cultural and spiritual values of Iran in a purely national sense."[10] There were also wide differences of opinion over the method of Westernizing Iran. The most radical of the Westernizers went so far as to call for large immigration of Europeans into Iran, much as Catherine the Great had done in Russia nearly a century and a half earlier. Such immigration, it was argued, would bring about the dissemination of knowledge, the propagation of modern methods of living, and the introduction of European civilization into the life of the people.[11] But the majority of Westernizers wished to make a distinction between the useful application of Western technology and the blind adoption of Western customs. "We must learn their science, their technology, and emulate their sense of lawfulness, responsibility, and initiative. Otherwise, any ape can learn their dances."[12]

There were disagreements also concerning the best models for the Westernization of Iran. Kazemzade-Iranshahr was the spokesman for those who thought Germany and England should be the sources of inspiration for Iranians; he advised Iranian students to go to Germany and England and not to France,[13] because he thought the "Gallic qualities" were too similar to the Persian character. 'Ali Akbar Siyasi represented the opposite view, namely, that Iranians could never assimilate Anglo-Saxon institutions and ideas, whereas they had a natural affinity with the French, which they should cultivate to their advantage.

On the final point of the ideological content of the Reza Shah movement, anti-clericalism, there was considerable unanimity among the followers and supporters of Reza Shah. These men, most of whom had forsaken the ranks of the *'ulama,* recognized in the power of the clergy the strongest obstacle to progress.

One of the main spokesmen for anti-clerical opinion was 'Abdollah Razi, editor of the periodical *Rastakhiz* ("Resurrection"). Sometimes in signed and sometimes in anonymous articles, various members of the intelligentsia published their criticisms of the clergy in this magazine. A brief glance at a few of these articles indicates the strength of their authors' sentiments.

> The corruption existing in Iran is entirely the fault of the clergy. In dealing with them absolute and final steps must be taken. All [religious] practices must be stopped. It will not be as difficult as in Turkey, which was the seat of the Caliphate. The clergy must be fought with education and action. Education alone is not sufficient. A society similar to Freemasons may be the best weapon of anti-clerical propaganda.[14]

In an earlier issue of this same periodical is found a plea for freedom of belief and tolerance. The authority of the Koran is cited in support of this principle, and the author concludes that: "even the infidels must be left free and unmolested."[15] In a direct address to Reza Shah on the eve of his accession to the throne, *Rastakhiz* stated:

> Today we have acquired an army, and internal security has been established. But the root of our evil is not insecurity, it is the class of the clergy. If this root is not attacked soon all the gains of the army and the army itself will vanish. The best method of eradicating the clergy is to take away their means of livelihood. The *waqf* lands should be taken away and sold to poor peasants. There will be no popular opposition to such a measure, because it takes away from a few and gives to the many.[16]

Focusing on these objectives—national unity, Westernization, with the emphasis on material progress, and secularization —but lacking a definite plan or a timetable, Reza Shah was determined to change Iran from the moment of his rise to power in 1921, and he was now finding the support that he needed.

Chapter Four

THE ARMY, THE ADMINISTRATION, AND PUBLIC HEALTH

THE NEW ARMY

The history of Iran, crowded as it is with conquerors and campaigns, had never seen a standing national army. In fact, the idea of a single unified army was without precedent in Iranian history.[1] Ever since the Achaemenian times the country's rulers had felt safer with separate units of armed forces. This allowed them to play one band against another and prevented any concentration of power.

The armed forces of Iran at the end of the Qajar period consisted of the units of provincial and tribal levies, the palace guards, the Persian Cossack Brigade, the gendarmerie, and the South Persia Rifles. The provincial and tribal units were commanded by princes of the Qajar family and tribal chieftains. There existed a Ministry of War, but there was no effective centralization of power or established chain of command. There were no training programs, no order of battle, no table of arms, and no uniforms among the tribal units. These forces merely consisted of the able-bodied men of the tribe who were of military age and were normally occupied with their pastoral chores. Their military qualities were the natural by-products of their rugged lives. Their arms were usually seized from government forces. In times of emergency the government called upon these tribal forces to render military service, but they would respond only when to do so meant some immediate gain for themselves. The long-standing policy of the government was to neutralize the power of the tribes by playing them off one against the other; however, much of the armed conflict in the country involved various local engagements between governmental units and the tribal forces.

The provincial levies were drawn from tradesmen, artisans, and peasants, who carried on the duties of soldiery concurrently with their professions. They were paid small salaries and were expected to supply their own uniforms and, in some cases, their own horses. The military value of these units was very low; man for man, they were no match for the tribal forces.

The palace guards were a ceremonial regiment of full-time soldiers who, earlier in the nineteenth century, made up the core of the Qajar forces. They constituted the Shah's main weapon against rebellious princes. But at the turn of the century they had lost their favored position to the Cossack Brigade.

The Persian Cossack Brigade, originally a parade-ground cavalry unit of about five hundred men, was created in 1879 to satisfy the whim of Naser ed-Din Shah (1848–96).[2] It was organized by Russian officers and, despite its relatively small size, it came to be the most effective military unit in Iran. In the revolutionary days of 1905–11 it played "a most important role in Iranian politics as an effective instrument of Russian domination and a tool of the Shahs in their struggle against the people."[3] After the Russian Revolution of 1917, and the temporary eclipse of Russian influence in Iran, the command of the Cossack Brigade passed into Iranian hands. Reza Shah came into prominence through the ranks of this Brigade and used it as a stepping-stone in his rise to power.

The gendarmerie was an internal security force created by the new government after the deposition of Muhammad 'Ali Shah (1906–9) with the help of Swedish instructors and commanders. Throughout its turbulent life it was beset by political intrigue. Nevertheless, it provided modern training for a number of young Iranian nationalists. The new army that was organized by Reza Shah drew the majority of its officers and non-commissioned officers from the ranks of the gendarmerie.

The South Persia Rifles, organized in the southern province of Fars in 1916 by the British officer Sir Percy Sykes,[4] was primarily an instrument of British policy in Iran. It was created to combat the tribal forces stirred up by the German agent Wassmuss and the pro-German, Swedish-led gendarmerie. It was disbanded by Reza Shah in 1921.

The idea of modernizing the military forces had occurred to the Qajar rulers as early as 1812 and again in 1827, after two disastrous wars with Russia. 'Abbas Mirza, their heir apparent to Fath 'Ali Shah (1797–1835), had tried to initiate some military reforms, but court intrigue had prevented him from achieving anything.[5] During the reign of Naser ed-din Shah (1848–96), some Austrian officers were employed to reform the infantry and the artillery. The British, the Russians, and the Germans were also anxious to provide instruction and advice, although their primary goal was to keep each other out. But at no time was there a plan or an opportunity to create a unified, standing national army. Reza Shah was the first to recognize the strength of a unified army. He instinctively understood the lesson of European history—the emergence of a unified national state coincides with the development of a standing national army. Upon becoming Minister of War in 1921, he dissolved all independent military units and created the first unified and uniformed standing national army in Iran. It was the newly generated power of this army that elevated Reza Shah to the throne.

The first urgent task after the reorganization of 1921 was the creation of an adequate and competent officer corps. The hereditary officers and the princes of the Qajar family were shorn of their rank. Swedish-trained officers of the gendarmerie, as well as Reza Shah's former associates and noncommissioned officers from the Cossack Brigade, were given positions of command.

From the outset Reza Shah was determined to keep the new army free from foreign political influence. Although a large number of foreign advisors and technicians were hired for various administrative and technical projects during his reign, only a handful of Swedish officers were retained in the army. This does not mean, however, that Reza Shah was not aware of the need for Western assistance. A number of Tsarist officers who had taken refuge in Iran were prevailed upon to acquire Iranian nationality and to accept commissions in the army. (Most of these men were of non-Russian origin, either Georgians or Volga Germans.) The desirability of sending some cadets to Europe was also recognized, and steps were taken to select candidates. At the time, France enjoyed the reputation of having the best army in the world; and on June 10, 1922, the Majlis approved the request of the Minister of War and appropriated 671,600 French francs (plus 180,000 rials for transportation) to allow sixty candidates to be sent to French military academies.[6] For the next ten years successive groups of young men were sent to Europe for officer training.

As soon as Reza Shah could be certain of an adequate number of officers and noncommissioned officers, he proposed the enactment of a universal military training program.[7] On June 6, 1925, the Majlis passed the law of compulsory military conscription. This law provided that every male citizen should be drafted at the age of 21 for twenty-five years of military service. This period was to be divided as follows: two years in active duty, in uniform and under arms; four years in the active reserve; six years in the primary reserve; seven years in the secondary reserve; and finally six years in guard status.[8]

This law brought with it considerable social changes, all of which were an essential part of the over-all scheme of modernization and progress. During the two years of service, literacy classes were conducted, and attempts were made to provide rudimentary instruction in trades. The influence of urban life on the rural and tribal recruits proved so strong that upon completing their term of active duty they often remained in the towns. If they returned to their villages, they brought traces of the West with them: the sanitation facilities of the urban areas undoubtedly impressed them, and their uniform jackets and caps (which they were allowed to keep with the official insignia removed) were the first examples of Western clothing the villagers had seen. But more important than these superficial changes were the effects on the young men of exposure to the more secular, Western-influenced morals of the city.

There is no doubt that universal military training contributed considerably to the amalgamation of society, the rise of literacy, the urbanization of the young rural and tribal population, and the breakdown of provincial isolation. These advantages, however, were not appreciated by the population in general, who looked on compulsory military service as an evil to be avoided if possible. The annual visits of the draft boards to the villages and tribal areas were generally a dreaded occasion.

On February 15, 1936, a new law for the reorganization of the armed forces was enacted. It established new and purely Persian names for the ranks, revised the order of battle, regulated the basis of promotion, and established retirement pay, other pensions, and insurance for the military personnel.[9]

The universal military training law of 1925 was replaced on June 19, 1938, by a revised law. It provided reduced terms of service and a more rapid scale of promotion for graduates of secondary schools and universities.[10] Under article 16 of the old law, judges of the *shari'ah* courts, *'ulama,* students of theological schools, and the clergy of Zoroastrian, Christian, and Jewish faiths were exempt from military service. Article 62 of the new law made all clergy subject to two years of compulsory active duty, but exempted them from the subsequent reserve duties. On June 26, 1938, the promotion scale of the regular army was revised in favor of officers with a university education.[11]

In campaigns against the rebellious tribes, Reza Shah had learned to appreciate the value of two modern weapons: the armored car and the airplane. A number of armored cars were purchased, and a few German pilots flying Junkers aircraft were employed. In 1928 the first group of Iranians were sent to Russia for pilot training. Later, groups were sent to France. Aircraft were purchased at first from Russia and then from Britain.

The Iranian navy on the Persian Gulf came into being with two destroyers and four gunboats purchased from Italy in 1932. Iranian midshipmen were sent to the Italian naval academies at Livorno and Genoa.

The equipment of the army came from munition factories in Czechoslovakia, Sweden, and Germany. According to the official budget figures from 1921 to 1941 an annual average of 33.5 per cent of the total revenue was allocated for military purposes.[12] These figures, however, are not entirely reliable; the annual oil royalties, for example, were treated as a separate reserve fund not included in the budget. The larger portion of these royalties was spent on purchasing costly military equipment, such as ships, planes, coastal guns, tanks, and heavy trucks. Furthermore, the industrialization, transportation, and communication schemes of the country were undertaken to a large extent with military requirements in mind.[13]

Reza Shah's policy of giving priority to the needs of the army had some undesirable results. A definite privileged class was created, which often abused the individual and property rights of less fortunate members of society; and a distasteful arrogance on the part of the officers was condoned.

As a result of Reza Shah's efforts, a Westernized army of nearly 400,000 men could be mobilized by 1941. This army was capable of maintaining the absolute authority of the central government throughout Iran—a condition that had not existed in the country for centuries. As such the army was a political as well as a military force. But its size, strength, and equipment far exceeded what was necessary for maintaining internal order. On the other hand, the Allies' forcible entry into Iran in August 1941 showed that it was totally incapable of sustaining full-scale modern warfare against heavy odds. Therefore, the heavy investment of money, manpower, time, and resources, at the expense of other vital needs, may be considered an error of judgment. In the atmosphere of intense nationalism that had been created, however, such an error was well-nigh unavoidable.

ADMINISTRATIVE REFORMS

The anachronistic nature of Qajar Iran was most clearly reflected in the administration of her government. Arbitrary and entirely free from any legal restrictions, the government was nevertheless powerless in the discharge even of its normal functions. Nominally omnipotent, it was in fact virtually impotent. The causes of the government's inadequacy were twofold: it lacked the proper administrative institutions and organization, and it was dominated by a selfish ruling class. The administration of the Qajar period can best be characterized as a government by favorites. It was an oligarchy of the sons and relatives of the Shah, who looked upon office as a means for self-enrichment. As in any primitive economy, the most desirable form of wealth was ownership of land, and the ruling class devoted its energies to the acquisition of land. With the granting of the Constitution and creation of the Majlis, this class, together with a handful of provincial aristocrats and tribal chieftains, found a new lever for the exercise of power. They could now rule the people both in a civil, private manner—as they had always done by virtue of their ownership of land and their control over the livelihood of the peasants—and in a new political manner by controlling the government.[14]

The actual operation of the Qajar government was based on a system known as *madakhel* (indirect income)—an officially condoned form of graft and bribery. Every civil servant considered it his right to be bribed for carrying out his normal duties. Bribes were the necessary lubricant for the wheels of government. For any unusual favor additional payments were necessary.

The need for reorganization was generally recognized, and after 1906 the rudiments of a parliamentary government were established. A cabinet made up of the heads of ministries took the place of the loosely organized Council of Ministers, which had been little more than the Shah's private chancellery. As we have seen, foreign advisors were employed to reform and reorganize the finances of the country and the judiciary system; but the over-all task of reforming the administrative institutions and practices of the government was neglected.

The new Majlis elected in 1907 did in fact direct itself to the task of creating and stimulating local government. Laws for the establishment of provincial and municipal councils, closely patterned on the Russian *zemstvo,* were enacted. But, owing to the vicissitudes of the times, these councils were organized only in a few localities, to be dispersed shortly after they had been set up.

After Reza Shah attained power, his government was virtually a military dictatorship, and he himself became increasingly autocratic as time passed. Nevertheless, he felt that he must preserve at least the appearance of parliamentary democracy as prescribed by the Constitution, and in fact he put into operation some of the administrative provisions of the Constitution for the first time. He did this for two reasons: he did not wish to offend and alienate a large, vocal, and Westernized segment of the intelligentsia; and since the Constitution did provide a blueprint for a modern governmental apparatus, he found it useful to follow it.

The field of civil service required immediate attention. On December 12, 1922, the fourth Majlis enacted the first law regulating civil service in Iran. Based on Western models, this law established age, nationality, education, and character qualifications for prospective civil servants. It called for competitive entrance examinations, outlined a table of ranks, and provided a regular scale of promotion. It set penalties for corrupt practices and allowed for dismissal of incompetents. The most

Western features of this law (in that they agreed most nearly with Western concepts of social welfare) were embodied in articles 43 through 70, in which measures for the retirement and retirement pay of government employees were adopted.[15] In the ensuing decade it became evident that the increasing activities of the state and the growing size of the civil service called for special training in public administration. On February 17, 1932, the Ministry of the Interior was empowered to establish special classes for the training of civil servants. A law passed by the Majlis on the same date allowed preferential treatment in the promotion of the graduates of these classes.[16] According to a further law passed on January 14, 1933, the customary three months of trial service without pay was waived in the case of the graduates of the special classes.[17]

The traditional geographic and administrative division of the country into four *ayalats* and innumerable *valayats* was proving impractical from both the administrative and the economic points of view. Therefore, by the successive laws of November 7, 1937, and January 9, 1938, the *ayalats* were abolished, and in their place ten economically and geographically unified *ostans* were constituted—a far more logical arrangement.[18] The *ostans* were divided into several *shahrestans,* and the latter were subdivided into a number of *bakhsh.* The duties of the various local officials were defined. In keeping with the whole tenor of the Reza Shah reforms, the provincial government provided by these laws allowed for very little local initiative. Mayors, police officials, and other municipal officials were appointed by the Ministry of the Interior in Tehran.

Municipal government had received attention earlier. In October 1922, Tehran had hired an American advisor on city government and an American city-planning engineer.[19] The administration of the provincial municipalities, their sources of revenue, and their functions were reformed under the Law of Municipalities enacted on May 20, 1930, and the Charter of Municipal Councils enacted on May 27, 1930. These laws provided that all city revenues should be spent on local improvement schemes, an innovation that represented a not insignificant concession on the part of the central government.[20]

By 1941 the administrative machinery of the Iranian government had been vastly expanded. But the change was not merely quantitative. The personnel of the Reza Shah government bore little resemblance to the officials of the Qajar period. There were no longer princes of royal blood at the head of the various ministries, but educated men of middle-class origin; and the majority of civil servants were men of the middle class and, in some instances, of the lower classes. As a result of the deliberate glorification of the state, the men in government service enjoyed a high degree of social prestige. But the salaries of civil servants from the lowest to the highest rank were always at minimal levels. This fact, together with the force of age-old practice, made a modified continuation of the *madakhel* system inevitable. Graft and bribery remained a permanent fixture of government operations; all ranks, ministers as well as minor clerks, were involved. On December 20, 1936, following the discovery of large-scale embezzlements from the Ministry of Roads involving the Minister himself, the Majlis passed a bill setting severe penalties for the acceptance of bribes and the embezzlement of government funds.[21] But law had little effect on custom. From traffic police to governors and ministers it varied in magnitude only. Those who did not participate were often ostracized.

The adoption of Western practices was not always beneficial to Iran. A good example of the adverse effects that such imitation could have is seen in the custom of holding consultative conferences of top officials, known as "commission" meetings.

> In itself a very good practice, in Iran it has come to defeat its own purpose. There are on the average two "commission" meetings daily in every department. It gives the top officials the opportunity to drop their daily business and spend much time smoking, chatting, and drinking tea. Callers who have vital business with these officials must wait hours in the corridors or come another day.[22]

PUBLIC HEALTH MEASURES

Nothing is more likely to brand a country as backward than the lack of proper attention to matters of public health. The Iran of 1920 was certainly backward in this respect, and is only relatively less so today. It is interesting to compare the differences between East and West in the areas of sanitary facilities and medical knowledge in the tenth century with the differences that exist today. Much of the superiority of the Muslim East in the earlier period can be attributed to the religious teachings of Islam; and, paradoxically, religious superstition is often considered a chief reason for the prevalence of disease in the East today, although economic underdevelopment is certainly no less a factor.

The appalling lack of public health safeguards in the days before Reza Shah cannot be overemphasized. All enterprise in this field was left to the European and American missionary organizations. The first hospitals in the country were established by British and American missionaries in the 1830's. Such hospitals still exist in almost all the important cities of Iran. "At first, superstition and conservatism made these foreign hospitals suspect; but results had their effect, and it was found that the poorer classes were almost too ready to seek the benefits of good medicine and treatment."[23]

In the general awakening of social consciousness during the constitutional era, the government began to assume some responsibility in matters of public health. In 1907 a law was enacted which required the governors of the provinces to "pay strict attention to . . . public health and sanitation . . . and [to] act with utmost speed in the case of epidemics. . . . Physicians, nurses, medicine, and equipment must be dispatched to epidemic areas by the governor."[24] In 1910 the government took the first step toward introducing vaccination in Iran by setting aside "10 per cent of the tax on transportation . . . for improvements in public health and particularly for general and free vaccination against smallpox and diphtheria."[25] In 1911 the Majlis made the first of a series of abortive attempts to curb the use of opium by the imposition of a heavy tax on the drug. In the same year an ambitious scheme to regulate the practice of medicine, in particular to control the numerous quacks who had no medical training whatsoever, was approved by the Majlis. Licenses were necessary for all practitioners, requiring them to have graduated from a medical college. Certificates of medical knowledge from the American mission hospital in Tehran were accepted in lieu of a diploma. Finally in 1914, as an inducement to cleanliness, public baths were exempted from the payment of property tax.[26]

These measures were the extent of the government's efforts in the field of public health in the years preceding the Pahlavi regime. It must be remembered that none of these laws was fully implemented. Even if the various governments of the pre-Pahlavi period had had the authority to enforce these laws, the lack of physicians and of medical facilities would have been two great obstacles in their path. Upon learning that smallpox vaccines contained serums from human sources, the clergy waged an effective propaganda against vaccination and rendered the government's efforts useless. A reliable picture of the sanitary conditions of Iran, and the difficulties in the path of improvement at the beginning of Reza Shah's reign, may be obtained from a report prepared by the League of Nations in 1925:

> The beliefs of the people and the teachings of the religious instructors or *mullas,* as they are called, have not only an effect on the character of the people but also prevent the introduction of sanitary and other reforms. The opinions of the leaders of Moslem thought are important factors in all affairs of state. . . .
>
> Many of the customs of the people are interpretations of the Koran. The manner of killing the animals in the slaughterhouses, the washing of the dead, and their burial, are all performed in the manner laid down by the religious laws. The belief that all running water which is open to the air is good and safe for drinking is taught by the religion. Dissection or postmortem examination of bodies is forbidden.[27]

In 1922 out of a total of 4,287 deaths in Tehran only 30

were attributable to old age without any diseases and complications. In 1923 the figure was 41 out of 4,588; of this total 1,113 were infants under a year old. In 1924 there were only 905 physicians in the whole of Iran. Of this number only 253 possessed medical diplomas from accredited schools. The ratio was one doctor to every 11,000 people. This ratio is misleading, however, since out of the total 905 physicians, 323 practiced in Tehran, making the ratio in that city 1 : 680 and in the rest of the country 1 : 16,800.[28]

One of the earliest measures taken in the field of public health under Reza Shah was the creation of the Pasteur Institute in Tehran modeled on the Institut de Pasteur in Paris. The initiative for this step came from Nosrat ed-Dowle, Foreign Minister in the early 1920's. On June 21, 1923, the Majlis approved the employment of Dr. Joseph Mesnard, a member of the Institut de Pasteur, for a period of seven years. He was charged with the task of organizing and heading the Pasteur Institute of Tehran.[29] The Institute was divided into sections for human, animal, botanical, and industrial microbiology. It carried out laboratory analysis, prepared vaccines and serums, and administered inoculations. In 1925 the League of Nations considered it "the most efficient part of the Persian Sanitary Administration."[30] A Bureau of Pest Control was added to the Pasteur Institute in 1925 to manufacture serums for livestock. In 1929 all slaughter of livestock except at the municipal slaughterhouses was forbidden. In 1935 the Majlis passed a law that may be called a pure food act and that was particularly effective with respect to the meat supply.[31]

In 1927 and again in 1930 the government introduced exact procedure and high standards for the licensing of physicians.[32] By this time an adequate medical school existed in Tehran. Since a large number of its faculty members were French, and some of the instruction and many of the texts were in French, a knowledge of the French language was obligatory for entrance into the school. In 1925 anatomy was taught by diagrams, charts, and wax models, because dissection was not permitted by the clergy;[33] by 1930 no such cautiousness was necessary. The medical school was making increasingly valuable contributions, although most Iranian doctors were still trained abroad. By 1935 the ratio of doctors to the population had reached one doctor to every 4,000 people.[34]

Malaria, trachoma, and intestinal infections constituted endemic diseases in Iran. Efforts were made to drain the swamplands. Annual appropriations were left at the disposal of the Pasteur Institute to be used in the prevention of such diseases as malaria, rabies, typhus, diphtheria, and tetanus.[35] On June 1, 1941, a milestone was reached in the government's efforts to promote public health when the Majlis approved a law for the prevention and combating of infectious diseases. This law made the treatment of venereal diseases compulsory; made free medication available to needy patients; made willful, knowing, or negligent transfer of such diseases, as well as fraudulent promises of a cure, subject to punishment; and provided for periodic inspection and certification of brothels. It also required compulsory vaccination against smallpox at the ages of 2 months, and 7, 13, and 21 years, as well as additional vaccination in times of epidemics. Vaccination certificates were required of all children yearly at the time of entering school and of all job applicants. Severe penalties were prescribed for violators. Doctors were required to report all cases of infectious disease to the Ministry of Public Health; and all public places, such as schools and factories, were to be inspected at regular intervals.[36]

The organization of the public health service in Iran predated the rise of Reza Shah. The public health service was formed as a bureau within the Ministry of the Interior, remaining in the same administrative status until 1940, although its activities and services were steadily and effectively expanded throughout the reign of Reza Shah. In 1940 a separate Ministry of Health with equal cabinet rank was created. In addition to this central authority, municipal and local governments participated in public health activities. Many towns operated hospitals, clinics, and child welfare and maternity services; some government organizations, such as the State Railways, the Department of Mines, and the Ministry of Industry, had their own free health services and hospitals.[37] In 1939 civil employment for doctors and other medical personnel was made more desirable by the provision of adequate salaries and other privileges and incentives.[38]

Construction of hospitals in all the towns was pursued vigorously. The Reza Shahi Hospital in Mashad was set up and operated by German doctors (with German equipment) as a model municipal hospital. It was one of the most up to date in Iran.[39] The construction of a 1,000-bed teaching hospital adjacent to the Faculty of Medicine of the University of Tehran was the most ambitious undertaking of the government in this range of activity.

Charitable organizations, such as the Red Lion and Sun, orphanages, and the Organization for Care of Mothers and Children, are all products of the Pahlavi regime. With all the media of public information harnessed to the needs of the state, the press and radio were invaluable contributors in all matters pertaining to health and hygiene. Two other movements that were part of the program of Reza Shah—the feminist movement and the movement for promotion of sports—likewise carried out activities valuable to public health. The feminist newspaper, *Ayande-ye Iran,* played a major role in hygienic instruction and propaganda.[40]

The accomplishments of the Pahlavi regime in the field of public health would have been inconceivable without the direct and continuous aid of European experts and the advantages of Western education. Not only were the majority of Iranian physicians educated abroad, but ever since Reza Shah's assumption of power, large numbers of key personnel had been employed from Europe and America. From 1922 until 1941 seven Frenchmen, an American, a Pole, and a German were employed as professors by the Faculty of Medicine of the University of

Tehran for a total of thirty academic years. Two of these men—a Frenchman, Oberling, and the Pole, Melczarski—served as heads of the Faculty of Medicine and the School of Dentistry respectively. During the same period six Frenchmen, three Hungarians, two Germans, an Austrian, and a Belgian were employed in various specialist capacities by the Department of Health for a total of twenty-eight working years.[41]

Of the projects recommended by the League of Nations' report of 1925,[42] all were carried out by 1941, with one exception: the improvement of the water supply and the sewage disposal system. These two most glaring deficiencies of Iranian cities were the subject of much study and planning throughout the years of Reza Shah's rule. A project for the Tehran water system was ready for implementation when the events of 1941 postponed it for another fifteen years.

In evaluating the achievements of the Pahlavi period in matters of public health, it must be admitted that every effort within the power of the government was made. The accomplishments of Reza Shah's reign, when contrasted with the almost total lack of sanitary facilities and public health measures before his rise to power, cannot fail to impress the observer with the success of his regime. There remained a wide gap, however, between the government's Westernized approach to assuming responsibilities and providing sanitary facilities and the public's response to these new methods. A full realization of everything that the government was trying to achieve required nothing short of a complete transformation of the nation's socio-cultural traits. Whereas there were abundant signs that such a transformation was in fact taking place among educated classes in the cities, there were virtually no appreciable changes among the peasants and tribesmen who made up the large majority of the population. The prevalence of disease and a high rate of infant mortality continued as reminders of the lasting qualities of old superstitions.

Chapter Five

THE NEW JUDICIARY SYSTEM

Nowhere is the impact of Western civilization upon the institutions of Muslim Iran more apparent than in the reforms of her judicial system. In its young and vital days Islamic society was distinguished by its system of jurisprudence. That this system should give way to Western secular legal concepts is an unspoken admission of the inadequacy of the social institutions of Islam for our time.

Shi'ah Islam admits of two systems of law, the *shari'ah* and the *'urf*. Bearing in mind some fundamental peculiarities and differences, these terms may be translated as canon and secular law. Originally it was intended that the *shari'ah* courts should have jurisdiction in matters pertaining to personal status and civil law, and the *'urf* courts in cases involving the state. In practice, however, the unstable governments of Iran had defaulted nearly all judicial authority to the *shari'ah* courts. As a result, the *'urf* system had not developed and, before the constitutional era, consisted solely of the *divankhane-ye 'adliye* (Court of Justice) in Tehran. "It had no code, no regular organization, and no established administration."[1] The delineation of jurisdiction therefore was vague, and the dispensation of justice highly individual and decentralized.

If the *'urf* system was inoperative, the *shari'ah* system, based upon the *feqh* (Islamic jurisprudence), proved completely inadequate. The former chairman of the Faculty of Law of the University of Tehran, analyzing the causes of its failure, noted that:

> [*Shari'ah* law] had become too involved and too ambiguous. Consequently, few *mujtahids* were competent to interpret and administer it properly. . . . [Moreover,] the world

conditions had changed so much that the *feqh* was not adequate to cope with new needs. A good example of this inadequacy is to be found in the provisions of the *shari'ah* regarding marriage. They would be practical if all the spiritual precepts of Islam were adhered to sincerely. But since few people are true Muslims now, these provisions lead to many abuses of marriage.[2]

EARLY REFORMS

The first step to remedy the lack of civil courts and a secular legal system was, of course, made with the adoption of the Constitution itself—the Fundamental Law of 1906 and its Supplement of 1907. In 1907 four skeleton civil courts were created in Tehran: the Court of Property and Financial Claims, the Criminal Court, the Court of Appeals, and the *divan-e tamiz,* or the Supreme Court of Appeals, which existed nominally, but did not function. Since, however, there were no codes for any of these courts to administer, they followed the *shari'ah* procedure. This frequently led to disputed sentences, and appeals were made to the *mujtahids,* whose interpretations of the law not only often conflicted with the findings of the civil courts, but also differed among themselves. Therefore in 1908 a court was created to settle disagreements between the civil and the *shari'ah* courts.[3] Attempts were also made to codify laws; but this proved a difficult task, involving a hard struggle with the clergy.[4]

In 1910 the office of Attorney General was created, and finally in 1911 a bold step for the reorganization of the judiciary was taken. Upon the suggestion of Moshir ed-Dowle, then Prime Minister, the old Ministry of Justice was dissolved, and a new one was formed. A temporary judiciary committee was set up in the Majlis to consider experimental codes, and a committee of experts under the guidance of a French jurist, Adolph Perni, was charged with the task of formulating a civil code.[5] The experimental and temporary nature of these measures was emphasized in order to circumvent the opposition of the clergy, who insisted upon the constitutional guarantee embodied in the second article of the Supplement to the Fundamental Law.

This article specified that no laws which are contradictory to the *shari'ah* should be enacted. In 1915 a commercial code was promulgated on the same temporary basis, and thereafter no further radical steps were taken until the Reza Shah period.

The new civil courts of the constitutional era were faced with several great obstacles. The persons appointed to these courts were generally unfamiliar with the exact, and often lengthy, procedure prescribed by the new codes; furthermore, there was a great shortage of personnel with adequate legal training. As a result, most cases were relegated to the *shari'ah* courts, where they were delayed or misjudged owing to incompetence and lack of legal discipline. Moreover, the operations of the civil courts were hampered and complicated by the system of capitulations that put aliens outside the reach of Iranian law and permitted foreign consulates to interfere with the courts. Consequently, the new judiciary system had only partial effect in Tehran and virtually none in other parts of the country.[6]

THE JUDICIARY UNDER REZA SHAH

Reza Shah pledged himself to the reform of the judiciary system as soon as he became Prime Minister.[7] Characteristically, his interest in legal reforms was motivated by nationalistic considerations, for his first objective was to abolish the system of capitulations. But he was extremely sensitive to foreign criticism, and he realized that so long as Iran did not have a judicial system along Western lines, the abolition of capitulations might attract adverse publicity in Europe. He therefore proceeded as quickly as possible with his plans for reform. Experimental commercial and penal codes were introduced in 1924 and 1926.[8] The old Ministry of Justice was dissolved early in 1927, and on April 26 of the same year, new personnel, many of whom had received European education, took over the administration of the new Ministry of Justice from the former clerical officials. On this occasion, before a gathering of judges and lawyers in Gulistan Palace, Reza Shah made one of his characteristically short but revealing speeches: "The prestige of a nation depends upon the quality of its justice. I expect of you the most honorable conduct that will at once bring justice and prestige to our country."[9]

The new Ministry of Justice was charged with the preparation of codes of law. The man who carried the weight of this responsibility possessed the qualities required by the task. Davar, the Minister of Justice, was one of the chief young lieutenants of Reza Shah in his efforts to reform and Westernize Iran. A man of great ability and tact, Davar was of middle-class origin, had graduated in law at the University of Geneva, and became Minister of Justice while still a relatively young man. He has been called the chief member of the "brain trust" of the Reza Shah regime.[10] Early in 1928 a commission within the Ministry of Justice, headed by Davar, presented the Majlis with the first volume of the Civil Code, as well as a judicial reorganization bill establishing a hierarchy of courts.[11] The government was anxious to abolish the capitulations and acted promptly; on May 8, 1928, with little opportunity for debate, the code was approved. In effect this code was a secularization of the *shari'ah*. In the parts dealing with general subjects (for example, the first ten articles), it was a verbatim translation of the civil code of France.[12] But in matters of personal status it was a codification, simplification, and unification of the *shari'ah*.

The legal reforms did not stop with the abolition of capitulations. On November 25, 1928, on April 30, and November 3, 1929, and on April 17 and November 3, 1930, the Majlis passed bills empowering the Ministry of Justice to put into practice the newly proposed laws—as soon as they had been approved by the Judiciary Committee of the Majlis—for a temporary trial period. Then, after any shortcomings that came to light in practice had been corrected, the Ministry of Justice was to submit the bills to the whole body of the Majlis for permanent enactment into law.[13] The same practice was continued throughout the eighth session of the Majlis.[14] From 1928 until 1930 various laws regulating trust funds, damages, methods of testimony in court, individual claims against the state, the trial costs of aliens, the jurisdiction of *shari'ah* courts and their limitations, inheritance, and the use of court injunctions were promulgated as supplements to the Civil Code. Some of these laws proved impractical or unnecessary, and were repealed. In 1929 the Ministry of Justice followed the first volume of the Civil Code with two concluding volumes, but with the matter of the capitulations out of the way, the Majlis proved more reticent. Twice the bills were rejected.[15] It was not until January 26 and October 30, 1935, that the Majlis finally approved the second and third volumes of the Civil Code.[16]

In the meantime, fears of Communist conspiracy had led to the passage of a law on May 19, 1931, dealing with political and press offenses.[17] A novel feature of this law, although rarely invoked, was the provision of a jury for trials concerning such offenses.

In 1936 the reform of the judiciary system in Iran reached a turning point. So far, for the sake of prudence as well as experimentation, the government had emphasized the temporary nature of all its reforms. By 1936, however, Reza Shah had met every form of opposition from the clergy and had emerged from the contest in absolute triumph. There was, then, no more cause for prudence. In effect, the vital blow to the position of the clergy in the judiciary system had been dealt on March 17, 1932, when the Majlis enacted a law concerning the registration of documents and property.[18] (An experimental version of this law had been operative since 1929.) It required that the registration of legal documents, of ownership, and of other transactions concerning property be carried out in secular state courts only. This function had previously been the monopoly of the *shari'ah* courts and, together with the registration of marriages and divorces, had been the most important function of those courts. Furthermore, it was by far the largest source of legitimate revenue for the *mujtahids* and lower clergy. As a consequence of the law of 1932, many members of the clergy were forced to abandon the robe and seek secular employment.

Legislation completing the permanent secularization and Westernization of the judiciary system was enacted on December 27, 1936, when a law concerning the reorganization of the judiciary system and the employment of judges was passed by the entire body of the Majlis. In setting the following employment qualifications for judges, it eliminated many members of the clergy from the judiciary:

1. [Judges must hold] a degree from the Tehran Faculty of Law or a foreign university, attesting to three years or more of legal study.
2. Former judges of the Ministry of Justice who do not possess such a degree must pass special examinations in Iranian and foreign law in order to remain in the employ of the Ministry, and at any rate may not rise above the rank of six on a promotion scale of eleven ranks.[19]

It was clear from the beginning of Reza Shah's reforms that ultimately the *'ulama* would have to be removed from the judiciary system. But there is reason to believe that the final step taken in 1936 was motivated primarily by a desire to hasten that separation, and not by a consideration of the needs of the new system, and the effects that such legislation would have. Yet it was inevitable that since the judiciary system had been so greatly expanded, the sudden exclusion of a large proportion of former practitioners should have grave results. No less an authority than the Prime Minister of Iran in the final years of Reza Shah's regime has affirmed that "in 1936 a crisis arose in the judiciary system of Iran, because there were not enough educated and qualified personnel to fill the new and vast organization."[20]

From 1937 to 1939 various laws regulating the practice of attorneys and legal experts were enacted. In 1939 a law concerning bankruptcy was promulgated.[21] The final and permanent version of the Civil Code was being studied in the judiciary and legislative committees of the Majlis throughout its eleventh session; and on September 16, 1939, it was passed, in 789 articles, by the entire body of the Majlis.[22] This Civil Code differed specifically from the long series of provisional codes enacted since 1911 in that it allowed greater jurisdiction to lower courts; it increased the powers of the state attorneys and prosecutors; it provided, for the first time, special procedure for the trial of foreign nationals; and it introduced a scale of priorities designed to minimize hardship or loss due to court process. Although it is entitled the Civil Code, it applies also in commercial cases unless otherwise specified.[23] On June 23, 1940, 378 articles were added to the Civil Code, defining the rights of the state in such matters as inheritance and the probating of wills.[24]

The final version of the Penal Code, provisionally promulgated in 1926, was approved in 1940 by the twelfth session of the Majlis. The new code was drastically revised, using as a model the penal code of Fascist Italy.[25]

Both the Civil Code and the Penal Code reflect the influence of Western judiciary models. Thus, for example, article 5 of the Civil Code of 1939, which provides that "the court must pass judgment on each case in accordance with a specific article of the code and not based on generalities,"[26] and which is designed to prevent the judiciary branch from interfering with other branches of the government, is a direct copy of article 5 of the French civil code and article 127 of the French penal code. Article 130 of the Penal Code of 1940 is designed to prevent the executive from interfering in the affairs of the judiciary branch. This concept of the separation of powers reinforces article 89 of the Supplement to the Fundamental Law of 1907, and is in turn copied from article 107 of the Belgian Constitution. The organization and jurisdiction of the county courts (*bakhsh*) are modeled on those of similar institutions established in France in 1790. The office and the powers of the Attorney General duplicate those of the French Attorney General, indeed the French term *parquet* is used in referring to this office. The

Attorney General's duties are also defined in the French manner along the dual lines of *voie d'action* and *voie de réquisition*.[27] Further examples of exact imitations of the French system are to be found in the qualifications and ranks prescribed for attorneys at law and legal experts, in the laws covering forcible expropriation, and in the procedure laid down by law for defense, pronouncement of sentence, and appeal.[28]

Like the Civil and Penal Codes, the organization of the courts in Iran follows the French pattern. There are today four kinds of courts: *bakhsh* (county courts); *shahrestan* (regional courts); *ostan* (provincial courts); and *divan-e keshvar* (the Supreme Court). The first two are courts of first instance and the third and fourth, courts of appeal. The jurisdiction of the *bakhsh* courts is limited to disputes involving sums of not more than 20,000 rials, or entailing penalties of not more than two months' imprisonment or a fine of 1,200 rials. The *shahrestan* courts rule on all cases involving sums of 20,000 rials and more, as well as on all criminal offenses, whether major or minor. They also have appellate jurisdiction in cases appealed from *bakhsh* courts. The *ostan* courts do not judge a case, but review sentences passed by *bakhsh* and *shahrestan* courts. They either affirm the sentence or refer the case back for retrial. The *divan-e keshvar* merely affirms or denies the constitutionality and legality of a sentence. Only in trials of cabinet ministers does it sit as a court of first instance. Within this system there are specialized courts, such as penal courts, civil service courts, and military courts.[29]

No account of the process by which the judiciary system was Westernized is complete without mention of the various European professors of law and advisors to the Ministry of Justice who were employed by the Iranian government during the regime of Reza Shah. From 1922 until 1939 eight French and two Italian professors were engaged to teach at the Faculty of Law of the University of Tehran for a total of sixteen academic years. A top-ranking French advisor held a permanent position at the Ministry of Justice to assist in the codification of the laws.[30]

This in brief is the record of legal reforms carried out during the rule of Reza Shah—a revolutionary record that achieved no less than the Westernization of the judicial concepts, institutions, and practices of Iran.

THE SECULARIZATION OF THE LAW

In order to measure the true extent of Western impact upon the legal structure of Iran two factors should be considered: first, the conflict between the new law and the old, and the defeat of the old; and second, the effect of the new law upon the fiber of society. Whereas the first subject lends itself to examination and can be documented, the second, by its very nature, its proximity to us in time, and its lack of documentary evidence, is extremely hard to define. An attempt, however, can be made by studying those laws that affected the lives of the people most closely, in particular the laws pertaining to marriage, divorce, and family relations.

The conflict between the old and the new legal systems was resolved in an arbitrary fashion. Indeed, it is difficult to imagine its being resolved in any other way. The powerful clergy, backed as they were by the fanatical sentiments of the masses and safeguarded by the provisions of the Constitution, could be shorn of their authority only by strong measures possible under a totalitarian government such as the one established by Reza Shah. However, it should be noted that only one article of the Constitution was redefined in the course of the reforms of the judiciary system, and that was to allow the government a greater freedom in the rotation and removal of judges.[31] The specific *shari'ah* reservations remained, without exception, entirely unchanged. They were merely ignored. The legal texts of the Faculty of Law of the University of Tehran explained that:

In regard to differences that may appear between the secular and the *shari'ah* laws, the second article of the Supplement to the Fundamental Law specifies that at no time may the laws be contradictory to the *shari'ah*. But we know the Islamic *shari'ah* is not limited to *shi'ah feqh*. Furthermore, if we were to follow the *feqh* scrupulously today, we would soon reach an impasse. Therefore, we interpret the second article of the Supplement to the Fundamental Law to mean that new laws should not conflict with the *shari'ah* in principle. Otherwise that article would be impractical.

For example, articles 1041–43 of the Civil Code set an age requirement for marriage that is not compatible with the *shari'ah*, and yet it does not violate the liberal principles embodied in the *shari'ah*.[32]

In order to appreciate the degree of secularization achieved by the legal reforms of Reza Shah, one must examine articles 144 through 149 of the first Civil Code promulgated in 1911.

Article 144. Matters pertaining to the *shari'ah* are those delineated and prescribed by the laws of Islam.

Article 145. The state courts of law shall refer the following cases to the *shari'ah* courts of the *mujtahids*:

A. When the dispute is caused by ignorance of the provisions of the *shari'ah*.

B. Matters pertaining to marriage and divorce.

C. In absentia sentences involving *shari'ah* jurisdiction.

D. Cases involving the declaration of bankruptcy, the confiscation of the property of persons who refuse to pay their debts, and injunctions of restitution.

E. When the solution of the dispute is possible only by recourse to witnesses and/or by oath.

F. When legal writs issued by *shari'ah* courts are ambiguous, vague, or contradictory.

G. When the dispute pertains to the principles of *waqf*, will, or guardianship.

H. When the appointment of a trustee of *waqf*, a *shari'ah* supervisor, or a legal guardian is involved.

Article 146. When there is a dispute over whether a case falls under the *shari'ah* or the *'urf*, it may not be referred to a state court of law without the agreement of a competent *mujtahid*.

Article 147. If the courts of *shari'ah* insist that the dispute

involves a case decribed in article 4 of this law, namely,
that the state laws on the matter are non-existent, incom-
plete, or contradictory, the Ministry of Justice has no
right to examine the case, even if both parties to the
dispute agree to such an examination. In such cases the
dispute must be referred to the assembly of *mujtahids*.
Article 148. In all *shari'ah* cases except those described in
article 145 of this law, the state courts may exercise jurisdiction, if both parties agree to such jurisdiction. Otherwise they must be referred to *shari'ah* courts.
Article 149. The state courts may not hear appeals from the
verdicts of *shari'ah* courts. Such appeals must be referred
to the assembly of *mujtahids*.[33]

For nearly ten years after the rise of Reza Shah, the power
of the clergy was diminished by a process of attrition. In 1922
the state courts were given partial appellate jurisdiction over the
shari'ah courts, and this jurisdiction was further expanded in
1926.[34] One feature of the *shari'ah* was its sanction to pronounce
sentence on the strength of sworn witnesses alone. Large numbers of cases, when nothing but circumstantial evidence could
be found, were decided by *shari'ah* courts by the simple administration of the Koranic oath to a witness. This procedure, however, was considered incompatible with Western codes, and in
1929 the Majlis enacted a law forbidding it.[35] Finally on November 30, 1931, the Majlis approved a law redefining the status
and jurisdiction of the *shari'ah* courts as special courts.[36] Whereas article 144 of the code of 1911 had defined the jurisdiction of
the *shari'ah* courts as matters "delineated and prescribed by the
laws of Islam,"[37] article 2 of the new law stated that *"shari'ah*
courts are formed to judge such cases as are defined within their
jurisdiction by laws of the realm. No cases may be referred to
a *shari'ah* court without authorization from state courts and the
office of the Attorney General."[38]

The area of jurisdiction of the *shari'ah* courts was narrowed
and defined in article 7 of the law to include only (1) disputes
involving the principles of marriage and divorce, and (2) the
appointment of trustees and guardians. In the latter cases all
actions of the *shari'ah* courts were subject to the concurrence

and supervision of the Attorney General. Article 8 of the law forbade the *shari'ah* courts from pronouncing sentences. Their verdicts were to be sent to the state court that had referred the case to them, to be pronounced by that court. In case of appeal by the defendant, the verdict of the *shari'ah* court could be reviewed by the state court. The provisions of this law were made retroactive to January 5, 1929, in all cases pending before *shari'ah* courts (article 17), thereby removing a large number of cases from those courts.[39]

If the reorganization of the Ministry of Justice in 1936 removed the final vestiges of authority from the clergy in such a way as to make no provision for *shari'ah* courts, the Civil and Penal Codes of 1939 and 1940 finally left no room for *shari'ah* law at all. The deviations from the *shari'ah* patterns were all explained and justified from Western, secular, humanistic viewpoints. The Penal Code of 1926 set the trend for the disregard of *shari'ah* provisions. Although both corporal and capital punishment were retained, the instances for their use were drastically narrowed. Theft, for example, which in the *shari'ah* is punishable by cutting off an arm, was to be punished by light prison terms. Flagellation, although it remained on the statutes until 1936, was never resorted to in the final decade of Reza Shah's rule.[40] (However, it was revived in 1942.) The death sentence still remains in force; but no less a person than a former Attorney General of Iran, Shams ed-Din Amir-'Ala'i, devoted a lifetime to pleading for the abolition of capital punishment. His views[41] were based exclusively on Western secular thought and had no precedent in Islamic legal theories. He supported his arguments with quotations from Beccaria, Rousseau, Montesquieu, Durkheim, Zola, and other European writers. Finding more solace in the charity of the New Testament than in the severity of the Koran, he deplored and openly condemned the religious sanction of capital punishment.

In addition to its marked disregard of *shari'ah* provisions, the Penal Code of 1926 introduced a number of Western concepts into Iranian law for the first time. For example, whereas the *shari'ah* law is vague on the subject of insane criminals, articles 38–41 of the 1926 Code exempted the insane from punishment. Article 222 of the same law defined instances of theft not recognized as such by the *shari'ah*. Article 276 represented another Western innovation by defining instances of poor sanitation, cruelty to animals, and the use of obscene language, as well as traffic violations, as offenses against the law.[42]

LAWS RELATING TO MARRIAGE AND THE FAMILY

Despite the striking changes of the Reza Shah period, it would be erroneous to assume that the time-honored concepts of the *shari'ah*, which were at the heart of Iranian society and culture, were disregarded and replaced altogether. Although *shari'ah* principles have persisted less in criminal law than in civil law, the present laws of Iran are often a perplexing mismatch of the *shari'ah* and the Western secular codes.

Nowhere did the hold of the old *shari'ah* concepts prove more lasting than in laws pertaining to marriage, divorce, family relations, and crimes against morality. From 1926 to 1940 the laws concerning these matters were changed four times, each change constituting a further departure from the strict *shari'ah* principles, and yet each still preserving a modicum of the original concepts. A comparative study of these laws as they were codified, revised, and completed in the span of Reza Shah's regime provides a good example of the degree of compatibility on the one hand, and of the conflicts and contradictions on the other, between the *shari'ah* and the newly adopted laws. Above all, it demonstrates the all-too-frequent absurdities of their uneasy union.

Article 180 of the Penal Code of 1926 specifies that if a man kills his wife and/or her accomplice while in the act of adultery, he is exempt from punishment; if he kills his daughter or sister and/or their accomplices under the same circumstances, he is punishable by one to six months' imprisonment. No such license is allowed the wife, the daughter, or the sister under reverse circumstances. Articles 207 through 214 of the Penal Code of 1926 define the penalties for adultery, polyandry, homosexuality, statutory rape, rape, prostitution, and conspiracy to promote prostitution.[43]

To take another example, classification of family relations in terms of direct and indirect lines is not found in Islamic jurisprudence. It is European in origin, as may be seen, for example, in articles 735–38 of the French civil code, article 20 of the Swiss code, and articles 1589–90 of the German civil code; the corresponding article in the Civil Code of Iran, article 1032, is a combination of the *feqh* and European law. Nevertheless, in the matter of inheritance, as specified in article 862, the purely *shari'ah* classification is accepted, thereby creating a paradox.[44]

Marriage became secular in law, but for the most part the laws pertaining to marriage clearly followed the *shari'ah*.[45] They were not consistent, however, in their conformity with the *shari'ah* pattern: sometimes they followed it very closely, as in articles 1056–57 of the Civil Code, legalizing, and thus perpetuating, special and temporary marriages; and at other times they completely departed from it, as in articles 1041–43 of the same code, which set a legal age requirement for marriage.[46] Moreover, marriages and divorces were not recognized as legal unless they were registered in civil bureaus, and marriage certificates were issued by these bureaus only if all the requirements of the law were complied with.[47] This law, however, could not be strictly observed, since in many rural districts no official bureaus existed.

Articles 1062, 1064, and 1070 of the Civil Code require agreement of both sides as a prerequisite for marriage. In effect, these provisions are not enforced and, as yet, are not enforceable in the majority of cases. Marriages are still arranged for daughters, although more and more freedom of choice is being exercised among the upper classes in towns. Article 1035 of the Civil Code permits the breaking of an engagement, even after the arrangements for depositing the *mehr* (the prenuptial sum given by the groom to the bride) are completed. No such action is permitted by the *shari'ah*. Articles 1042–43 require the father's permission for marriage of daughters. No such permission is required for male children. Article 1060 of the Civil Code states that Iranian women may not marry aliens without the special permission of the government; this has no foundation in Islamic jurisprudence and was added for purely political reasons. Articles 1050 and 1051 forbid polyandry, but articles 942, 1046, 1048, and 1049 allow men four permanent wives and an unlimited number of temporary wives. This is a straight translation of the *shari'ah*.[48]

Articles 1150–56 specify the period that a woman must wait after divorce or death of her husband before she can marry again (130 days). This is based on the Koran (II, 234) and has counterparts in European codes also (articles 228, 296, and 306 of the French civil code; article 103 of the Swiss civil code; and article 1313 of the German civil code). But in the Iranian Civil Code there are some discrepancies arising from contradictions already existing in the *shari'ah*. Admittedly, the purpose of this period of waiting is to make certain that the woman is not pregnant. But there are no exemptions allowed for instances where absence of pregnancy is a verifiable fact (i.e., long separation from the husband). Also the waiting period for temporary wives is shorter than the period for permanent wives, thus defeating the rational purpose of the interval and legalizing the inferior social status of a temporary wife.[49]

Articles 1057–58 of the Civil Code specify all the *shari'ah* causes for divorce, based on the Koran (II, 229, 230). These include the provision for triple divorce, in which case the divorced couple may not remarry unless the woman enters into a consummated marriage with another man first. This of course is an anachronism and has led to many evil practices, such as the case of the *mohallel*, or the person who marries a triple-divorced woman, consummates the marriage, and then divorces her, for a fee, so that she may remarry her original husband.[50]

Article 1059 forbids the marriage of a Muslim woman to a non-Muslim, but a Muslim man is free to marry anyone so long as she is not an idolator (Koran: II, 220).

Articles 1075–77 legalize temporary marriage, but are full of contradictions and omissions in defining the length of such marriages, their *mehr*, support, and inheritance rights. This practice, although based on the Koran (IV, 28), is peculiar to *shi'ites* alone. The caliph 'Umar forbade it, and *sunnis* do not practice it.[51]

In regard to divorce, article 1133 of the Civil Code states that a "husband may divorce his wife at any time he wishes."[52] No Western code (with the possible exception of the early Soviet laws) allows such free rein for divorce. The Iranian Code establishes two basic differences between men and women in their right to seek divorce: (1) divorce is considered a natural right of the man, and he needs no conditions for it, whereas women need certain conditions, and (2) men need no cause for divorce, whereas women must have cause and must prove it in court.

In dealing with married couples, articles 1102–18 of the Civil Code[53] divide their rights and obligations into two categories, material and nonmaterial. The right of the wife to own property and have independent use of it is a feature of *shari'ah* law (preserved in article 1118 of the Civil Code) that has only recently been adopted in some Western countries. The material obligation of the husband and the right of the wife is defined as support. Support includes food, clothing, and home in accordance with the needs of the wife (Koran: II, 223). Only the permanent wife, however, has the right to receive support. The material obligation of the wife and the right of the husband is defined as submission. Submission is described as general and particular: in the general sense it means all the wifely duties; in the particular sense it means the husband's right of sexual gratification at times of his choosing.

The nonmaterial rights and obligations of marriage are defined thus: "The foundation of the family is based upon harmonious coexistence of husband and wife" (article 1104 of the Civil Code). But this harmonious coexistence does not preclude the dominant role of the husband (Koran: IV, 37, and II, 228; also article 160 of the Swiss civil code; article 213 of the French civil code; and article 1354 of the German civil code).

Article 1117 of the Civil Code says that the "husband may forbid his wife to accept a job that is degrading to him or her." This implies that otherwise the wife is free to accept a job without permission from her husband. In this respect the Iranian law is more liberal than, for instance, the Swiss law (article 167 of the civil code) and the French law (article 4 of the Code de Commerce).

In conformity with the *shari'ah,* the Civil Code of Iran states that legally children belong to the father, and in cases of separation, custody is the right of the father. Similarly, laws covering the right of inheritance, the use of name, and guardianship are all codified in conformity with the *shari'ah*.[54]

One of the more absurd compromises between the old laws and the new appears in the law requiring medical certificates before marriage, enacted by the Majlis on November 24, 1938.[55] According to this law, certificates attesting freedom from disease, issued by physicians designated by the Ministry of Justice, were required of all prospective brides and grooms. But, paradoxically enough, brides-to-be were exempted from furnishing certificates attesting freedom from diseases of the genital organs. This was obviously a concession to the prudence and sensitivity of women who did not wish to submit to an examination by a male physician.

By the end of the reign of Reza Shah the influence of the Western-inspired laws upon the lives of the people was considerable, but nowhere near the degree indicated by the statute books. The social and cultural patterns were changing among the urban population, but in the villages the age-old practices showed no signs of disappearing.

Chapter Six

EDUCATIONAL REFORMS

The educational values and practices of every society are the products of its cultural traditions. In time these values and practices may become so laden with tradition that they result in social stagnation. The educational system of Iran during the nineteenth century—if it may be called a system—was just such an agent of stagnation, as a brief glance at the traditions of Iranian education will show.

THE NINETEENTH-CENTURY LEGACY

Education in nineteenth-century Persia did not reflect the dynamic era of flourishing Islamic civilization. The eager spirit of intellectual curiosity and scientific inquiry, so characteristic of the lively days of Islam, had totally disappeared, leaving behind an empty shell of tradition. But since there had been a proportionate decline in every other aspect of society, the relative status of education remained unchanged. Education for those who have the aptitude seems to have been the guiding principle of Islamic society. Although the princely class and the landed and the mercantile gentry always had greater access to education, the privilege was never denied to the members of the lower classes, and in this way education paved a freeway across the usual class divisions. The educated Persian was a respected citizen who enjoyed social prestige and material benefits. In nineteenth-century Persia—just before the main impact with the West—this was still true.

By then, however, all the vigor had gone out of educational values and processes. After centuries of cultural, social, political, and economic decline, education had come to be the monopoly of narrow-minded and parasitical clergy. The school in its institutional sense did not exist. Elementary education was confined to the *maktab,* a single classroom, with one *akhund** as the teacher. He was totally free of any governmental or even professional control. There was no kind of professional hierarchy, and he did not have to meet any professional requirements. In the cities and towns the *akhund* often simply opened a *maktab* where the neighborhood needed and could support one. The tuition fees were not standard, and were arranged privately between the *akhund* and the parent. Greater munificence was expected from and provided by the wealthier parents, whereas it was not uncommon for a good-natured *akhund* to accept a bright pupil from a poor home either gratis or in return for household service. Those who did not relish the pace and the vicissitudes of urban life could move into villages, where sometimes a small stipend in crops from the landlord and usually payment in kind from the peasants provided the *akhund* with a modest but secure livelihood. Since this form of teaching supplied a major source of revenue as well as prestige for many lower-ranked members of the clergy, there were numerous *maktabs* in the country.

The *akhund* taught children of all ages. They usually began their education with him at the age of 7, and he continued to instruct them for as long as they were left in his care. But although a number of *akhunds* made generous terms for pupils from poor families, in rural areas and among the indigent urban classes poverty prevented the large majority of parents from availing themselves of this opportunity. Those children who were sent to the *maktab,* however, could not enter on the basis of wealth alone; they had also to show ability. According to the cultural traditions of Islamic Persia, some people are born

---

* This is the general Persian designation for a clergyman; it includes all ranks and, unlike *mujtahid* and *imam,* does not signify any particular function or authority.

gifted and others are not, and it is useless to educate the unfit.* Thus the highly selective process that operated, although to a large extent dictated by economic considerations, was also determined by the talent of the pupils. Furthermore, owing to pseudo-religious and socio-cultural restrictions, girls were excluded from any organized process.

These circumstances—educational discrimination against the poor, the less able, and girls—were responsible for an extremely high rate of illiteracy. The very fact that attempts were made during the twentieth century to introduce mass education (including education for girls)—quite apart from any consideration of the changes in the subjects taught and the methods of teaching them—must in itself be looked upon as the direct result of influences from the West. These attempts represent a drastic break with Islamic traditions, and they have been responsible for profound changes in the social and cultural patterns of the country.

The subjects taught in the *maktab* indicate the static nature of culture and society in nineteenth-century Persia. Ability to read and write, with particular attention to good penmanship, were the first objectives. The pupil then embarked on a simple but long process of memorization. The *shi'ah* catechism, a good deal of poetry, a standard Persian-Arabic dictionary in verse form, known as the *nisab,* some Arabic grammar, and vast portions of the Koran itself were assiduously memorized.† The generally accepted mark of distinction and attainment was the recitation of the entire Koran by heart. There was no set number of years for attending a *maktab*; when the pupil had learned what the *akhund* had to teach, he ceased to attend.

---

* The highly popular poetry and maxims of Sa'di, for example the saying "Education for the unfit is like placing a walnut upon a dome," may have fostered this notion.

† To satisfy the meager demands of commerce a semicoded, cumbersome method of bookkeeping known as *siyaq* was also sometimes taught in the *maktab.*

Beyond the *maktab* there were no institutions for general education. Secondary schooling was entirely on a private tutorial basis. Painstaking attention to calligraphy, a thorough study of classical literature, mastery of Arabic grammar, and, very occasionally, the rudiments of logic, mathematics, and music made up the sum of the subjects taught by private tutors at the pupils' homes. The tutor was usually a lay scribe rather than an *akhund*. Sometimes a scholar acquired a reputation for learning and wisdom (often through the gift of oratory), and eager students gathered at his home to hear him discourse. Unless a pupil intended to go into clerical life, this was the extent of education.

Not one of the magnificent medieval Islamic universities was left; Nishapur, Tabriz, and Baghdad but dimly remembered their past. The only institutions of higher learning were the seminaries (*madrasah*) in Qom and Isfahan, where the chief subjects of study were theological treatises, sectarian tracts, Arabic grammar, rhetoric, incantation, and jurisprudence (*shari'ah* and *feqh*); some logic, arithmetic, and astronomy were also taught (astronomy for the regulation of the calendar and the proper observance of the fast and prayers). Although the sole purpose of these seminaries, and the important ones in the *shi'ah* centers of Najaf and Kazemein in neighboring Mesopotamia, was to train young clergymen, it was not uncommon for students to receive the education and then not to pursue a clerical career, a tendency that increased toward the end of the nineteenth century.

Western-inspired reforms began sporadically and haphazardly early in the nineteenth century. The flow of Western ideas was accelerated in the second half of the century, and with the establishment of the Constitution elaborate plans were drafted to give the country a modern educational system. A modest beginning was made in the implementation of this program. But it remained for the regime of Reza Shah to give the reforms a new impetus and a regular tempo, and to create conditions in which such reorganization could be carried out.

The first attempts to introduce Western-type schools into Persia were made by foreign missionaries in the mid-nineteenth century. Attendance in these schools was at first limited to the Christian minorities; but soon an increasing number of openminded Muslims allowed their children to attend. In time some of them, such as the Presbyterian Mission School in Tehran, developed into institutions of national importance, educating a large number of the new generation of men of affairs who played such vital roles in the Westernizing campaigns of the Reza Shah era. By 1929 there were no less than fifty foreign schools in Iran, most of which were operated by religious missions; of these, twenty-five were American missionary schools.[1]

The founding of *Dar-ul-Fonun* in Tehran in 1851 represented a major landmark. This was the first Western-type school to be established by the Persian government. It corresponded to a French *lycée* in that it included secondary education as well as rudimentary higher education. Two more schools of this type (one of them being the School of Political Science, which was organized by the Ministry of Foreign Affairs for training diplomatic personnel) and two military colleges constituted the total of governmental achievement in education during the remaining half of the nineteenth century.

The government's first systematic attempt to create an organized educational structure for the nation was in 1898, when the Council for National Schools was founded. This body, comprised of prominent men of the day (many of whom had been to Europe), proceeded to establish ten state schools in the same year; similar schools were set up in the provinces soon afterwards. These new state schools were graded elementary schools competing with the *maktabs*; their curriculum was organized along similar lines—Persian, Arabic, and arithmetic —and there was an average of 14 teachers, 250 pupils, and 1 doctor per school.[2]

The next impetus came from the constitutional regime during its brief period of feverish activity.[3] In 1910 the second session of the Majlis created a ministry to deal with educational affairs, whose full title was the Ministry of Education, *Waqf*, and Fine Arts.[4] The same law that created this Ministry contained numerous modern innovations. It proclaimed boldly for compulsory elementary education. It called for the collection of educational statistics, professional training for teachers, the formation of adult education classes, and the publication of textbooks. Further, it required the Ministry to send students to Europe and to found libraries, historical and scientific institutions, and historical and technological museums. It demanded sanitary inspection of the schools. This law also called for a Consultative Board attached to the Ministry. One of the duties assigned to the Board was to find a "solution to the conflict between religious schools [*maktabs*] and state schools," a somewhat unrealistic commitment. However, the Fundamental Law of Education, passed by the same Majlis in 1911, left no doubt about the strength of clerical influence in the country, as the following extracts show:

> *Article 7.* Non-Muslim students have no right to request instruction in the tenets of their faith at the state schools.
> *Article 13.* Schools that are operated by *waqf* endowment are subject to the supervision of the Ministry of Education . . . insofar as such supervision is in accordance with the intentions of the donor of the endowment.
> *Article 14.* The Ministry of Education must forbid instruction and the use of books that are harmful to . . . the religion of students.
> *Article 17.* The curriculum of elementary and secondary schools must incorporate religious instruction, i.e., the *shi'ah* catechism.[5]

Clerical influence worked against the realization of many other ambitious provisions of this law. The articles pertaining to the licensing of schools, principals, and teachers, the uniform adoption of approved textbooks in the *maktab* as well as the state schools, the maintenance of hygienic standards in classrooms, the requirement that the *maktab* pupils take state examinations, and a quixotic ban on corporal punishment,[6] remained unrealized platitudes, although the fact that these clauses were included at all is a significant indication of the degree of Western influence.

The extensive planning and the organizational reforms of the constitutional era bore few practical fruits. Inertia brought on by clerical influence, political instability, scarcity and mismanagement of funds, and the lack of qualified teachers and administrators posed nearly insurmountable obstacles. The only real achievement of this period was the founding of nine more state elementary schools[7] and the sending of thirty students to Europe.[8] When Reza Shah appeared on the scene, there were no more than 10,000 students enrolled in the national (state and private non-religious) schools.[9]

In 1921 the fundamental reforms needed to create a modern educational structure still remained unrealized. It must be remembered that in the first years of power Reza Shah concentrated his energies on establishing internal security and reorganizing the army. But whereas these projects were carried out under his personal supervision, other areas of national activity, such as educational reform, although they also received attention, were left to lesser men. The structure of the Ministry of Education as laid out in the laws of 1910 and 1911 was largely retained; the main task was to infuse the new organization with life and strength. By 1921 the Ministry's control over the educational process was still negligible. It was the goal of the Reza Shah regime to expand the new state school system to meet the needs of the entire nation. The prerequisite for this scheme was the creation of an efficient, centralized Ministry that would have complete authority over all phases of education in the country.

The first legislative act of the new regime in the field of education was the creation of the High Council of Education in 1921. This was a policy-making, supervisory, consultative adjunct to the Ministry of Education, with authority to pass on the promotions of administrators and teachers.[10] Two of its duties, clearly set forth in its charter, were "[to give] serious consideration to the curriculums of schools in Europe" and, even more significant, "to prepare a curriculum for teacher training colleges for men and women"—the first project for the professional training of teachers in the country. Other tasks assigned to the Council were: to discuss the use of *waqf* endowments for the support of state schools, to pass on the qualifications of persons seeking to open private schools or to publish periodicals or newspapers, to establish a system of ranks and a plan of promotions for teachers in the state schools, to select students to be sent to Europe on government funds, to approve textbooks commissioned by the Ministry of Education, and to create a sub-committee of the Council to "discipline, reform, and supervise the teaching in *maktabs*."[11]

In 1921 the Ministry of Education drew up the first full program for elementary and secondary education to exist in Iran. It covered a twelve-year span, like most modern school systems, and the twelve years were divided into two six-year sections—the elementary and secondary levels. Uniform examinations were administered by the Ministry of Education to students of all national schools—state and private alike—at the end of the sixth, ninth, and twelfth grades. Official certificates were issued to the successful candidates.

The curriculum of the elementary schools consisted of Persian, Arabic (by 1930 eliminated from the elementary curriculum and confined to the secondary), penmanship, arithmetic, Persian history, Iranian and world geography, and physical education. Beginning in 1936 art and music were added to the curriculum.

The six-year course of the secondary schools was patterned after the French *lycée*. It was divided into two three-year "cycles." The curriculum of the secondary schools was greatly expanded: geometry, natural science, a foreign language (generally French), Arabic, world history, and hygiene were introduced in the first year (seventh grade); algebra, biology, physics, chemistry, geology, and mechanical drawing were added in the second and third years; and trigonometry, solid geometry, zoology, and elementary economics in the final three years. The courses of the twelfth year were separated into three divisions: pure science, natural science, and humanities. In the first division emphasis was put on mathematics, calculus, analytical geometry, and astronomy; elementary psychology and anatomy were taught in the second division; and logic, history of philosophy, Arabic literature, and literary analysis were taught in the third. The study of Persian itself was divided into separate courses of grammar, composition, and literature and literary history, raising the students' load in any given year during the six years of secondary schooling to as many as fifteen subjects.

The incorporation of the various scientific subjects into the curriculum was of course gradual. A shortage of texts and teachers precluded such an ambitious program as outlined above from taking effect during the first decade of the Reza Shah regime. Indeed the entire period from 1921 to 1941 must be considered a time of experimentation and gradual expansion of school curriculums, rather than of immediate achievement.

These were the beginnings of a modern educational structure in Iran, and they created new and urgent needs—trained teachers and administrators, textbooks, different teaching methods, and more school buildings. The most pressing need was undoubtedly for qualified teachers. As early as 1911 fifteen students were sent to Europe to study pedagogy. A teachers' college with separate divisions for men and women was established in Tehran in 1918. This was modeled on the French *école normale,* and French educators were brought in to supervise it; it was the only specialized teacher training institution in the country until 1934. In 1928, however, the Majlis appropriated funds for an annual dispatch of one hundred students to Europe and America, and specified that 35 per cent of the funds should be spent on the study of education.[12] In 1929 state scholarships were established for fifteen needy students each year at the Tehran Teachers College.[13]

Finally, the Teacher Training Act of March 1934 approached the problem on a large scale.[14] This Act envisaged the establishment of twenty-five teachers' colleges in five years, a goal that was exceeded in 1939; and in the final year of Reza Shah's regime there were thirty-six such colleges throughout the country.[15] The Act also provided preferential treatment in matters of tenure, promotion, and retirement benefits for teachers graduating from these colleges. In this respect the effects of the professionalization of teachers were felt beyond the field of education. A new, relatively secure, and respectable professional class, admirably placed for furthering the national goals of the regime, was created, and a corresponding change in social attitudes came about. Thus, for example, young graduate teachers not only drew considerably larger salaries but also enjoyed far greater prestige than the few venerable old-fashioned teachers and tutors of the previous era. Nowhere was this attitude more striking than in the classroom, where the young bow-tied teacher of physics commanded the close attention and respect of the students and often fulfilled their hero-image, while the calligraphy and Arabic classes of famous old craftsmen and scholars were scenes of mayhem and cruel practical jokes played on the teachers.

Next in urgency to the shortage of teachers was the need for modern textbooks. Before 1928 there were no uniform, official textbooks. In that year the Ministry of Education began the task of preparing and publishing textbooks.[16] In this field it is difficult to overestimate the influence of French texts and educational methods. In a subject such as Persian, primers and readers took their general pattern from French models; and in history, geography, and particularly the sciences, adaptations or even simple translations of French texts were made. Beginning in 1939, a new series of textbooks was published by the Ministry of Education, covering for the first time the entire range of the school curriculum from the elementary grades through the first "cycle" of the secondary level.

With the introduction of graduate teachers and modern textbooks, the group recitation-for-memorization method of the *maktab* was discarded. Reliance upon memorization, however, continued. With the rapid increase in the number of school children, and growing social pressure to take examinations, a vast portion of the student body was soon devoting its entire time to memorizing the material in the textbooks.[17] Nor was this superficial method of learning limited to students' study habits. An increasing number of teachers in the upper grades relied on the reading aloud of notes and texts in the classroom.

PRIVATE AND FOREIGN SCHOOLS

In addition to the growing number of new state schools, there was a limited number of private schools in the country. Generally these were run by indigenous religious minorities such as Baha'is, Zoroastrians, Jews, and Armenians, or by foreign Christian missionaries. The student body of the Jewish and Armenian schools was drawn exclusively from their own communities; but this was not true of the Baha'i and the Zoroastrian schools, or of the foreign-operated mission schools. Because of their contact with and aid from co-religionists abroad, these schools were in the vanguard of reform and Westernization. British-trained Parsees from India taught in the Zoroastrian schools; American Baha'is taught in the Baha'i schools for boys and were instrumental in organizing the Baha'i schools for girls. The Tehran Baha'i schools, covering elementary and secondary grades, enjoyed particular prestige during the two decades before and after the accession of Reza Shah, despite the official suppression and nonrecognition, the popular prejudice, and the clerical opposition that operated against the Baha'is. In fact a large number of the open-minded and influential families of Tehran enrolled their children in these schools. Reza Shah's eldest daughters and his eldest son (the present Shah) themselves received their early elementary schooling in the Tehran Baha'i schools.

Governmental policy toward these private schools was consistent with the nationalist-centralist outlook of the Reza Shah regime. The government was not opposed to the operation of these schools, and in some cases even subsidized them;[18] but, step by step, they were gradually brought under the full control of the Ministry of Education.

The foreign missionary-operated schools were the first to come under Ministry regulation. On September 5, 1928, the Ministry of Education issued an ordinance to regulate the American mission schools, which set the pattern for the regulation of all foreign schools open to Iranian students. According to this ordinance all American schools were required to carry out exclusively the official course of study prescribed by the Ministry of Education during the first four elementary grades, using the Persian language as the only medium of instruction. In the higher grades the full official requirements of Persian, Arabic, and Iranian history and geography were to be taught. No Bible instruction was to be given Muslim children, but ethics and "sayings of great prophets" were permitted.[19] In 1940 the nationalist policy of the Ministry of Education was so intensified that all foreign missionary educators were asked to leave the country. Their schools were taken over by the Ministry and operated as public state schools.

Governmental control of the indigenous private schools followed soon after. Their curriculum, textbooks, and examinations were made to conform with those of the state schools, and teachers were subject to approval by the Ministry of Education. Finally, in October of 1930, a status of official state recognition was bestowed upon those private schools that "qualified under the academic and moral standards of the Ministry."[20] In this manner all nonconformist private schools were legislated out of existence, since their certificates and diplomas had no value for employment purposes. An example of this coercive governmental policy was the closing of the Baha'i schools in October of 1934, because they observed a religious holiday not recognized by the state. The Armenian schools were closed in 1939 in an effort toward national assimilation of this minority group.

TECHNICAL EDUCATION

An important effect of Western influence upon education in Iran is to be seen in the introduction and growth of technical schools. In this respect the efforts of the Reza Shah regime followed a highly utilitarian pattern. Diverse technical schools and colleges were founded not by the Ministry of Education, but by the Ministries of Industry, Communications, Health, Roads, Agriculture, War, Finance, and Mines with the immediate purpose of training qualified personnel for their respective departments. Thus, for example, the Ministries of Health and Agriculture, with the aid of French professors, founded colleges of medicine and veterinary science. (These were later incorporated into the University of Tehran.) Similarly the Ministry of War founded a military academy in Tehran, and military preparatory schools in Tehran, Tabriz, Mashad, Isfahan, Shiraz, and Kermanshah.[21]

The first independent polytechnical school in Iran was founded in Tehran in 1922 by a group of German technicians with the aid of a generous subsidy from the Iranian government.[22] This Irano-German Industrial School remained the most popular technical school in the country during the entire period of Reza Shah. Significantly, in 1940, when all foreign-operated schools were taken over by the Ministry of Education and the foreign teachers expelled from the country, an exception was made for the German staff of this school.

Agreements reached with foreign concessionaires afforded the Reza Shah regime another means by which to obtain Western supervision for technical education. From 1923 onward every concession given to foreign interests included provisions for a special percentage of foreign advisors either to act in a consultative capacity at the local department of education or to assist Iranian citizens in the scientific and technical education needed to put the concession concerned into operation.[23]

Nor were the fine arts neglected. An Academy of Music and an Academy of Fine Arts were founded in the thirties. The emphasis in these two colleges was sharply differentiated: the Academy of Fine Arts concentrated upon reviving typically Persian arts and crafts, such as carpet design, miniature painting, book illumination, enamel and inlay work, titles, and pottery, whereas the Academy of Music became a channel for the rapid dissemination of Western influences.

THE UNIVERSITY OF TEHRAN

The foundation of a university was among the early goals of Reza Shah's Ministry of Education. Although the act establishing the University of Tehran was not passed until 1934, several institutions of higher learning—incorporated into the University upon its foundation—existed before that date. Several of these—the Tehran Teacher College, the colleges founded by the Ministries of Health and Agriculture, and the medical school—have already been mentioned, and there was also a faculty of law. The medical school had grown out of the old *Dar-ul-Fonun,* which had been conceived as a college in the mid-nineteenth century, but was classified as a secondary school after the reforms of the Reza Shah regime. The faculty of law, similarly, had grown out of the School of Political Science founded at the turn of the century.

The act establishing the University of Tehran was passed in May 1934, but the officially celebrated date is February 5, 1935, when Reza Shah himself laid the foundation stone of the new University.[24] This date is celebrated annually as a joint festival of education and tree planting.* In its founding charter the University was established as a relatively autonomous institution governed by a board composed of a president, a vice-president, the chairman of each department or faculty (the European nomenclature was in fact adopted), and a member-at-large from each faculty. But all the appointments, including that of the president, and the regulation of ranks, salaries, schedules of instruction, and number of chairs were made by the Ministry of Education.[25] (In the year following the abdication of Reza Shah, in a wave of sudden and general liberalization, the Majlis removed the University from the control of the Ministry and made it entirely independent.)

Originally, five faculties were intended: arts, science, medicine, law, and engineering. Later, existing colleges of theology, fine arts, and agriculture were incorporated as three additional faculties of the University.[26] Except in the school of medicine the University granted no doctorates until 1941. The course of studies in the school of medicine lasted six years, in the school of engineering four years, and in all others three years only.

The teaching staff of the University, with the exception of some old scholars of Arabic and Persian literature, had generally been trained in Europe (predominantly in France). There was also a considerable number of European professors.[27] The influence of French education and French methods was so pre-

---

* Since the new campus grounds were quite barren, on the same occasion of the laying of the foundation stone, the Shah also planted a sapling, as did a representative group of boy scouts. The publicity given to this ceremony left no doubt that more than the utilitarian aim of landscaping the new campus was intended. A campaign of conservation and reforestation was given an ideological content consistent with the national spirit of the regime. Ancient Iran had celebrated an annual tree-planting day, and the care of trees and general husbandry are supreme virtues in Zoroastrian writings. This combination of practical needs and ancient virtues was characteristic of the propagandists of the Reza Shah period.

ponderant that an open discrimination was often experienced
by graduates of British, and particularly American, universities, when they sought teaching positions at the University.

A large majority of the students of this first modern university in Iran were residents of Tehran, since residential facilities for students from the provinces were limited. In the
first decade of its existence the University of Tehran also attracted a few students from India, Afghanistan, Iraq, Turkey,
and the Soviet Union.[28] The students from the USSR usually
pursued studies in the fields of Persian and comparative Oriental literature.

The standards of the schools of medicine and engineering
were generally adequate to meet the needs of the country. In
the fields of social studies, however, the standards were very
low. The professor would read a lecture—often translated from
a French text—and the students would take verbatim notes. In
preparing for examination a memorization of these notes was
all that was necessary. The small departmental libraries were
usually empty of students. Traditions and standards of scholar-
ship, academic integrity and intellectual discipline, had been
nonexistent in Persia for so long that it was impossible for the
new University to avoid giving an impression of superficiality.
Furthermore, the uncritical acceptance of French theories and
methods, apparently without awareness of the atmosphere of
intellectual freedom and honesty that had given birth to those
theories and methods, was conducive to early calcification of
opinions. Such intellectual short-sightedness, coupled with the
attendant vices of exclusiveness, jealousy, social and personal
rivalries, and political ambitions, prevented the University from
attaining a high academic standing. The faculty of the University enjoyed considerable social prestige; but the students
and the alumni suffered under a stigma of social and professional inferiority, any degree or even record of attendance from
a European institution automatically carrying greater social,
economic, and psychological value.

Lastly, in the oppressive political atmosphere of the final years of the Reza Shah regime, the young University never had the opportunity to become a true nucleus of intellectual activity. An early tendency to Marxism among a group of professors and students was nipped in the bud,[29] and from then on, the University became the center of conformity from which the state expected—and received—nothing but servile adulation, propaganda support, and ideological justification.

STATE SUPPORT OF STUDY ABROAD

No single institution or group of people was more responsible for bringing Western influences into Iran than the students who had been educated in Europe and America. Because they were at an impressionable age and too young to have more than a scanty acquaintance with Persian cultural traditions, these students were particularly responsive to Western influence, and they eagerly absorbed everything Western. Upon their return to Iran high social prestige and responsible positions awaited them. The role of earlier Western-educated students in the general political and intellectual upheavals of the nineteenth and the early twentieth centuries has been noted. Once again, Reza Shah did not initiate a trend, but he altered its course and intensified it.

The first occasion that students were sent abroad was when the disastrous defeat of 1828 in the war with Russia induced Crown Prince ʿAbbas Mirza to dispatch a small group of young men to Europe to study military sciences. Since this was done at the personal initiative and state expense account of the Prince, his premature death left the students stranded, and the project was abandoned.

Similarly, the governments of the constitutional period had always spoken of sending students to Europe; but political instability and financial chaos had prevented all but a very few of such schemes from being realized.[30] Although a significant number of students had already gone to Europe before 1921, they were the privately supported sons of the ruling class. During the reign of Reza Shah state scholarships, given on the basis of competitive examinations, extended this privilege to deserving but poor students.* But, as we have seen, a regular program was not devised until 1928, when the Majlis appropriated funds for sending one hundred students to Europe every year. In 1932 provision was made for the first state-supported students to be sent to the United States.[31] Figures published in 1940 show that from 1922 to 1938, 396 students had returned to Iran from studying abroad, and another 452 were still abroad completing their studies. These figures comprise only the students sent under the auspices of the Ministry of Education. If the number of students sent by the Ministries of War, Roads, and various other government agencies, as well as private individuals, be added, the total for this period would be over 1,500.[32] A large majority of this group—no exact figures exist—were enrolled in French institutions of higher learning.[33] No statistics are available for the number of Iranian students trained at the American University of Beirut or Robert College in Constantinople, but the numbers, particularly at the former institution, were considerable.

It is impossible to overemphasize the role of the returning student in spreading Western influence in Iran. He brought about a revolution not only in the fields of intellectual activity and scientific, technical, administrative, and professional enterprise, but also in the less tangible but perhaps more significant areas of cultural traditions, social relations, and personal habits. The fact that when he came home he found himself a social lion was ample proof of the eager and indiscriminate admiration of his countrymen for everything Western. The proud family would often build a new room or a separate apartment, with Western sanitary facilities and Western furnishings,

---

* The reader must not overlook the various evils of nepotism, bribery, and favoritism that at all times were present in the selection of state-sponsored students. Nevertheless, many students who would never have had the opportunity before were now sent to Europe.

for the returning son. The vast number of friends and relatives would compete for the distinction of giving parties in his honor. At such occasions the hosts would outdo themselves, and not infrequently with comic results, in trying to defer to the Western tastes and habits of the guest. His example meant the adoption of Western modes in everything from dress to food to manners and even to the frequent use of European words, constructions, and pronunciation in Persian speech. The young man educated in Europe was much sought after on the marriage market; but he also did a great deal toward breaking down the old system of arranged marriages, with all the complicated preliminaries that went with it.

ADULT EDUCATION

Programs for adult education had been drafted by the various Ministries of Education ever since the early days of the constitutional period, but these projects had never been implemented. Reza Shah, however, realized that adult education would potentially provide his program of nationalism, reform, and modernization with a broader mass support, and in 1936 the Ministry of Education began to put its plans into operation.[34] Since the program of adult education affords a good field for observing the national policy of the regime and some of its modern aspects, and since it is also one of the few areas for which official figures are available, it repays careful attention.

At the beginning of the academic year 1936–37, 1,500 evening classes for adults (held in the buildings of elementary schools) were opened in all parts of the country.[35] Since these classes were attended by two shifts of students, the total number of classes taught was 3,000. The enthusiasm with which the program was greeted soon forced the Ministry to open an additional 97 classes, which brought the total cost of maintaining the program to more than 1,607,327 rials.[36] At the outset the classes fell into two categories, those for the totally illiterate, and those for the semi-literate. The Ministry noted that the purpose of the program was twofold: to combat illiteracy, and "to provide adults with useful individual and social training conducive to good citizenship."[37]

The two-year course of study was made up of 96 lessons each year, taught in three classes per week.[38] The lessons of the first year were divided as follows:

Lessons

1. Reading and writing of the alphabet and simple short sentences 6
2. Reading and writing of sentences and numerals, and addition and subtraction 18
3. Reading of selected pieces covering the following subjects: 72
   General topics, such as descriptions of the countryside, home life, etiquette, and the training of children 10
   The history and geography of Iran 10
   Educational and moral poems 13
   Civics 8
   Hygiene 12
   Ethics 12
   Composition 3
   Verses from the Koran on health and ethics* 4

The program of the second year covered the following subjects:

Lessons

1. General topics, ranging from the study of electricity, meteorology, and agricultural machinery to discussions of duty and the dignity of work 14
2. Arithmetic and geometry 11
3. Hygiene 11
4. Civics 11
5. The history and geography of Iran 32
6. Selections of prose and poetry 13
7. Ethics 4

With all the authority of the regime behind it, an extensive campaign was launched to promote these adult education classes. Numerous new books and pamphlets were published for this purpose alone. To encourage the students to read newspapers, the foremost Tehran daily paper, *Ettela'at,* ran a

---

* Although the source does not specify, these passages were studied in a Persian translation, an innovation frowned upon by the clerical elements.

column geared to the vocabulary level of the adult classes. Articles by students were published, and free copies of the paper were distributed to the classes all over the country for classroom instruction as well as reading during leisure hours.[39] Attendance at adult classes was made compulsory for all the illiterate or semi-literate employees of government offices. Associations were formed throughout the country to encourage participation, and students were given report cards as an incentive to diligence.[40] Finally, taking advantage of the fact that adult classes were taught in the evenings, outstanding students of the University of Tehran organized a series of lectures on various aspects of good citizenship. These young students were deeply imbued with the spirit of nationalism and hero worship, and the lectures were therefore an effective means of propaganda and indoctrination. The intensity of the campaign is demonstrated by the fact that in April and May of 1937 alone, 150 such lectures were given in the Tehran area.[41]

The success of elementary adult education led to the opening of twenty-two secondary schools for adults early in 1937. These were in operation six evenings a week from 7 until 10 P.M. The curriculum was exactly the same as that of regular day schools.[42] Although the main purpose of these night schools was to afford adults an opportunity to complete their secondary schooling, young people of school age, who for economic reasons could not attend day schools, were also admitted.

At the end of the first year of the experiment, 9,356 adults received certificates of literacy. By the end of the second year (June 1938), the expenditure for adult education had been nearly doubled, the total number of classes had risen to 1,700, the salaries of the teachers had been raised by 45 per cent, and a total of 124,000 adult students had been enrolled.[43] By the end of 1940, the number of classes had risen to 2,133, and the total of students enrolled stood at 157,197.[44] The following table[45] of breakdown of students in the adult classes, by age and occupation, for the year 1939 shows how deeply the program had penetrated.

Age		*Occupation*	
Under 18	43,218	Policemen	3,416
18–25	28,932	Civil servants	9,589
25–30	19,222	Traders	5,600
30–35	17,624	Construction laborers	10,645
35–40	16,832	Porters	3,135
40–55	9,079	Teahouse operators	1,444
over 55	2,796	Farmers and peasants	33,618
		Bakers	3,315
Total	137,703	Butchers	2,578
		Bath attendants	2,491
		Carpenters	3,419
		Drivers and mechanics	1,180
		Iron and coppersmiths	4,873
		Miscellaneous	52,300
		Total	137,703

Encouraged by the success of the adult education program, the Ministry of Education now assumed the responsibility for mass propaganda. A department of public enlightenment was established within the Ministry. This organization sponsored public lectures by well-known authorities and professional men on a wide range of topics, including ethics, history, hygiene, literature, social sciences, education, and "modernism, patriotism and loyalty to the sovereign and the remarkable improvements achieved in the country in recent years."[46] According to the Ministry figures, in its first year (1937) the organization sponsored 700 public lectures attended by 181,250 persons.[47] It must be remembered that it was not advisable for public figures and officials who had been invited to attend to decline the invitation.

PHYSICAL EDUCATION

The activities of the Ministry of Education during the period of Reza Shah marked a vast revival of sports. In 1933 a Council of Physical Training was set up in the Ministry of Education.[48] It not only organized regular interschool athletic events, but instituted nationwide annual championship games. Physical education, starting with Swedish callisthenics and later including gymnastics, track and field, volleyball, soccer, and basketball became part of the regular school curriculums.* Much was done to revive and popularize ancient traditional sports, such as riding, wrestling, and polo; other sports, such as tennis and ping-pong, were introduced by members of foreign diplomatic corps. Upon his return in 1936 from a Swiss school, the Crown Prince showed clearly that he had absorbed Westernism on the playing fields as well as in the classrooms of Europe. His intense interest in all sports greatly aided the cause of physical education, since he assumed the honorary presidency of all athletic associations as well as that of the Boy Scout movement.

The first scout troop in Iran was founded in 1925 and affiliated with the international body. In 1939 scouting was made compulsory for all school boys from the fifth through the ninth grades.[49] At this time, however, scouting was made into a paramilitary movement with much emphasis upon drill and physical fitness. The Boy Scout creed of preparedness was made subsidiary to worship of God, King, and Country. In all the propaganda and indoctrination, however, God was the nearly ignored member of this trinity. Beginning in 1939, all the boys in grades ten through twelve were required to spend four hours a week in military drill, weapon familiarization, and indoctrination courses. This was done with the aid of the army, which supplied training officers to schools.

GOALS AND ACHIEVEMENTS IN EDUCATION

At least two other significant modernizing roles of the new educational system—the education of women and the tacit suppression of the clergy—are not specifically touched upon here. Vast cultural and sociological considerations prohibit their inclusion within the limited frame of this work. The chief

* Soccer, which, following an international pattern, soon became the most popular sport, had a curious beginning in Iran. It was introduced in the twenties by the then existing Socialist party. Its first popular hero was known as Habib the Bolshevik.

steps for the advancement of education may therefore be summarized as the sending of hundreds of students to Europe and America, the improvement and expansion of elementary and secondary schools, the founding of the University of Tehran, the introduction of physical education and scouting in all schools, the erection of many modern school buildings, stadiums, and playgrounds, the foundation of teachers' colleges in the capital and the provinces, and the introduction of technical and adult education.

A review of the proposed budgets of the Iranian government from 1922 to 1941 reveals that an average annual increase of .75 per cent was allotted to the Ministry of Education. The average percentage of education in the total expenditure, however, was only 4 per cent.[50] This figure is particularly distressing when compared with the large sums spent on the expansion and equipment of the armed forces. Although, unfortunately, detailed and categorized figures are not available, certain general comparisons can be made to indicate the extent as well as the rate of growth in education. In 1922 the total number of schools of all kinds (state, private, and religious; elementary, secondary, and higher) in Iran was 612. No figures for the number of students and teachers are available for that year. In 1936 there were 4,901 schools, 257,051 students, and 11,370 teachers. By 1940 the number of schools had risen to 8,237, with 496,960 pupils and 13,646 teachers. In the same year 12,847 boys and 4,905 girls received their sixth-grade primary certificates, 645 boys and 451 girls their high school diplomas, 506 students graduated from the various teachers' colleges, and 411 from the University of Tehran. In 1922 only 15 students were graduated from the *Dar-ul-Fonun*, then considered an institution of higher learning.[51]

The principles and practices of the Reza Shah regime in the field of education reflect very clearly the general ideological cultural direction of Iran during this period. Free, rapid, and unquestioning borrowing of Western methods, all mobilized for a feverish assertion of nationalism, glorification of the past, statism, and autocratic centralism; defensive sensitivity in the face of criticism by foreigners; growing xenophobia too often springing from a feeling of inferiority, and an unhealthy, disdainful air of superiority over neighboring countries—these are the characteristics of the new educational system that developed in Iran between 1921 and 1941. Nor would it be untrue to characterize in the same manner the spirit of Arab nationalism now following in parallel course the experiences that Turkey and Iran underwent between the two world wars.

In summary, the ideals of the Iran of Reza Shah were: to be independent and strong in order to preserve her national entity; to promote prosperity by the scientific development of her natural resources and the cultivation of favorable international trade; to banish want, sickness, and misery so that a healthy Aryan nation, descendent of heroic ancestors, might measure up to the bold reliefs carved on the mountainsides at Behistun and Persepolis; and to hold a place of honor among the nations of the earth and contribute her best to the culture of the world. Finally, there was an increasing feeling that traditional Islamic beliefs and institutions were incompatible with a realization of the country's goals and were therefore expendable. In the words of a former minister of education:

> Any scheme of education that does not provide for the attainment of these ideals is doomed to failure, a failure that is all the more imminent since Persia's neighbors—Russia, with her Five Year Plan, Turkey, with her radical methods of Westernization, India, with her continuous unrest—are undergoing rapid changes and making progress which, because of propinquity and other circumstances, may exercise considerable influence on the land of the Lion and the Sun. . . .
>
> It follows that an educational program must be built upon the following aims: (1) to create in the minds of the people a living consciousness of the past by showing the great achievements of the race; . . . (2) to train boys and girls to become good citizens of modern Persia; . . . (4) to

teach the rural people and the tribes how to live, . . . make a home, . . . prepare food and clothing, . . . prevent disease; . . . (5) in secondary schools and . . . the university the gifted youth must be trained for leadership and service in the State. They must be given a vision of Persia's place, past and present in the world, with the ideals of leading the country in culture, science, technology, business, statesmanship, and government to such heights as befits a progressive State.[52]

Writing for Columbia Teachers College (and influenced by its teaching), the same author criticized the Iranian cultural tendencies of fatalism, diffidence, excessive individualism, contempt for industrial pursuits, aversion to manual work, and superstition; he called for more professional experts, trained teachers, books, equipment and new buildings, conversion to Latin script, the use of *waqf* funds for education, more health instruction, the abolition of all religious schools, and a vastly expanded vocational training; and he advocated acting upon the principle that learning "how to live may be more important than merely learning the rudiments of literacy."[53]

Eight years after the abdication of Reza Shah, a group of American observers evaluated Iran's educational system in these terms:

> . . . the basic point of failure has been its educational philosophy. We feel that the existing school system has accomplished with relative success the aims which consciously or unconsciously motivated its founders . . . that of producing a distinguished intellectual elite, and of establishing an instrument by which the thoughts and actions of the common people might be efficiently guided. It is, therefore, not as much a technical failure of the schools, as a changed social philosophy which makes the existing system anachronistic and unsatisfactory.
>
> The educational philosophy, and the technical details of the school system, are largely a copy of the traditional French system—characterized by extreme centralization of administration, authoritarian methodology, theoretical rather than practical studies, stereotyped and overloaded curricula, and a policy of eliminating rather than salvaging

students who do not meet the arbitrary and rather artificial standards of academic excellency.[54]

In evaluating the educational reforms and the degree of Western influence upon the new educational system of Iran, one must pay equal attention to the new things accomplished and the old things discarded. Without any doubt the strangle hold of the clergy upon the educational and intellectual life of the nation was loosened. But at the same time the very cultural identity that the ardent nationalists sought to preserve was steadily weakened by an aimless imitation of the more superficial aspects of Western civilization.

Chapter Seven

ECONOMIC DEVELOPMENT AND
MODERNIZATION

It is necessary at the outset to emphasize the nontechnical nature of this chapter. It is outside the competence of the author as well as the scope of this book to make a technical examination of the economic developments in Iran during the twenties and thirties.[1] It is hoped that by a brief survey attention may be drawn to the Western origins of the new economic developments, motivations for the adoption of Western techniques, the desire of Iranians for such innovations, problems arising from the imposition of Western techniques upon Iranian cultural patterns, and the resultant transformation of cultural values in modern Iran. These problems are dealt with in a descriptive, historical manner.[2]

Technological importations, and the consequent changes in the economic life of the country, were undoubtedly responsible for the most apparent aspects of the Westernization of Iran. During the regime of Reza Shah Pahlavi, the science and technology of the West were the only elements of Western civilization that were officially and freely imported into Iran. The national philosophy dictated that the cultural spirit and the ancient virtues of Iran were superior to anything that the West had to offer. By adopting the science and technology of the West, Iran would be able to surpass the West itself. This optimistic view was not shared by everyone in the country. A century of Great Power politics and economic exploitation had intensified an almost pathological fatalism and diffidence that was already characteristic of many Persians. Although it is customary in Iran to blame all the nation's difficulties on the interference of powerful neighbors, it cannot be denied that the anachronistic statecraft of a long succession of inept and irresponsible Qajar rulers had defaulted in providing the country with the minimal services and pre-conditions for economic health that are expected of any government. Nor were there any hopes of immediate improvement upon the accession of Reza Shah. Although in his first cabinet program submitted to the Majlis one may find reference to nearly all the economic steps undertaken during his regime, such as fiscal reform, tax reform, development of mines, construction of railroads, improvement of communications, and adoption of the metric system of weights and measures,[3] it was quite evident that the immediate problems of state solvency and financial order were to receive attention before any long-range economic development would be considered. It has been noted earlier that the all-important precondition of internal security received primary and effective attention from Reza Shah. It is necessary now to attempt a brief review of the various economic conditions in Iran and the manner in which Reza Shah's government dealt with them. The degree of Western influence in these steps will be self-evident.

FINANCIAL REFORMS

The ambitious programs of internal security, modernization of the armed forces, and economic growth required regular and expanding state revenue. The immediate problem was not a general raising of the national income, but an efficient marshalling of the existing resources into the state treasury. In 1921 the main sources of state revenue were three: state lands, internal taxes, and custom tariffs on foreign trade.

The patterns and problems of land ownership, attempts at land reform, and changes in the rural economy of Iran will be dealt with elsewhere in this chapter. Here attention is paid only to the policies involving the state lands, and for the expressed purpose of raising revenue.[4] The usual method of deriving income from these lands was to rent complete villages to private tenants, who then assumed the role of the landlord in relation to the peasants. In this manner a small portion of the land income filtered back to the state. In 1924 the Majlis authorized a study board to explore the best way of increasing state revenue. It was decided to sell large amounts of state land for immediate cash.[5] Most of the purchases were made by the large landlords of the adjacent lands. In 1933, when the Majlis passed a further law authorizing the unrestricted sale of state lands, this process was accelerated. Thus, much of the desirable state land in distant regions, which had in effect been controlled by local chiefs and large owner-tenants, was now turned over to them legally. And most of the more desirable state lands (those nearer the capital) became the private property of high army officers and adjacent large owners.[6] It must be borne in mind that the Majlis was always composed of large landowners. Once more in 1937, when the government created the Industrial and Agricultural Bank, the Majlis authorized the sale of the choicest remaining state lands near Tehran to provide capital for the new bank.[7]

The internal tax problems of Iran in 1921 were substantially the same as those of many countries with similar political, social, and economic backgrounds. The chief form of property consisted of agricultural land, and this was subject to a land tax; but this tax was in effect collected only from smaller owners. The political power of the large owners made any systematic collection unrealistic. The backward social and economic structure of the country made an income tax impossible. Various indirect taxes on consumers' goods were the most productive form of internal revenue.

The efforts of the new regime were bent not upon levying new taxes but upon devising a more efficient method of collecting the existing levies. Full authority for this task was granted to a group of thirteen American financial experts, headed by a certain Arthur Millspaugh, who arrived in Iran in the autumn of 1922.[8]

The chronic problem of the government involved not only evasion on the part of the taxpayer but graft on the part of the collector. The problems encountered in this field cannot be ascribed entirely to the nonreceptivity of an Eastern society to influences and attitudes of the West. This basic absence of financial responsibility to the government, and its consequence, the total amorality of tax evasion, are present in most societies—both when vestiges of feudal fragmentation of power are too numerous, and when the degree of absolutism is too great. Millspaugh's mission represented a peculiarly Anglo-Saxon approach; his measures, though remarkably successful, were bitterly resisted. It is most likely that, given equal conditions, he would have faced equally severe difficulties in many countries of southern Europe and South America. According to an "optimistic" American observer, this mission did in fact achieve qualified success in developing the potential honesty of the Persians, and some competent, zealous, and scrupulous officials were trained.[9] But this same zeal and severity was criticized by a close associate of Reza Shah, when he said:

> Local customs cannot be interfered with all at once. We have had to repress a rebellion only the other day because the Americans are unwilling, in Khuzistan, to permit the Arab chiefs to take their part of the taxes they collect from their people—a custom which is very old.[10]

After the departure of the Millspaugh mission in 1927 the pattern of taxation and tax collection was hardly changed at all. The seventh session of the Majlis in 1930 did introduce some tax legislation, but it did not amount to much. It included an abortive corporation tax, repealed in 1933; the abolition of tax payments in kind; and the introduction of a non-agricultural real-estate tax to be collected by municipalities.[11] Other new levies introduced, such as the sugar and tea tax of 1925, were not for the purpose of general revenue, but for specific industrialization projects and will be dealt with below. It was not until after the abdication of Reza Shah that income tax was imposed, when it was introduced by Millspaugh during his second financial mission to Iran in 1942.

Of the three mentioned sources of state revenue the most productive, as well as the most reliable, was the tariff on foreign trade. There were two reasons for this: tariff duties were the easiest form of revenue to collect, and the collectors were both scrupulous and efficient (Belgian officials who had been managing the Customs Department since 1911).[12] The fact that tariff duties, the most important source of the country's revenue, were subject to binding treaty limitations imposed by powerful neighbors indicates the degree of Iran's impotence at this period. After the disastrous defeat of 1827, Russia, by the treaty provisions of Turkmanchai (1828), enforced what was virtually a free-trade policy with regard to Russian imports into Iran. In effect Iran was forced to impose a duty of no more than 5 to 8 per cent on Russian imports. Britain and other European powers were quick to demand and receive similar privileges. As of 1921 Iran was bound by the Russo-Persian Tariff Agreement of 1902 and the Anglo-Persian Tariff Convention of 1920.[13]

The policy of Reza Shah's government in regard to tariffs was to continue having Belgian supervisors for the customs administration, and eventually to achieve tariff autonomy. In 1922, following the appointment of the Millspaugh mission, the Majlis renewed the contracts for a staff of twelve Belgian customs officials; these contracts were repeatedly renewed, and occasionally new ones added, throughout the whole of Reza Shah's reign.[14] However, not until 1928 did Iran declare her tariff autonomy.[15] Although extensive use was made of tariff revenue for industrial and technical development, and considerable tariff relief was given for the importation of machinery and capital goods, even the final Tariff Act of the Reza Shah regime, passed on July 13, 1941,[16] retained a decided revenue character, and no resort was made to infant-industry protective tariffs.

Creating order in the collection of state revenue was only a portion of the task assigned to foreign advisors. The Act employing Millspaugh defined his duties as no less than reform of the finances, centralization of the treasury, preparation of new financial legislation for the economic recovery of the country, and attraction of foreign capital.[17] It is no exaggeration to say that the powers of this mission were in every respect realized. A British observer once remarked that "Millspaugh administers Persia in much the same way that Cromer administered Egypt."[18] One reason for the success of this mission was its lack of ostentation. Its members conducted themselves as employees of the Iranian government. They even wore the national Persian *kolah*, the visorless short hat of Iran.[19]

The early success of Reza Shah in reforming the army, pacifying the tribes, and establishing internal security would not have been possible without the revenue provided by the Millspaugh organization. It is equally important to remember that Millspaugh's chances of success without the aid and protection of Reza Shah's authority and army would have been meager. The mutually beneficial relationship that existed between the Millspaugh mission and Reza Shah during the period 1922–25 deteriorated when Reza Shah attained absolute power and his demands for funds for the army at the expense of other projects became increasingly insistent. In 1927 the mission's services were terminated. They left Iran, but left behind the rudiments of a modernized financial administration. Nor were they the last Western financial experts to be employed during the reign of Reza Shah. A number of American, German, Belgian, and British advisers were employed by the Ministry of Finance from 1925 to 1941;[20] but none of these was given the wide powers accorded the Millspaugh mission.

The structure of the Ministry of Finance and its methods of

operation became increasingly Westernized under the influence of these foreign advisers as well as such European-trained ministers as Davar and Hazhir. This transformation was accompanied by an unfortunate accretion of bureaucratic waste. Also, what was once inefficient and simple became only slightly less inefficient but vastly more complex. The commercial codes enacted in 1925 and 1932[21] helped greatly to secularize contracts and modernize business activities. But a steady stream of departmental regulations and procedural dicta often took up the greater part of the time and energy at hand.

Another aspect of financial reform concerned banking operations. Until the foundation of the Bank Melli Iran in 1927, all banks in Iran were foreign concessions. The British and the Russian banks were, in effect, one of the agencies by which those governments influenced the economic life of Iran. The Bank Melli, at once a state bank and a commercial bank, was vested with the power to issue currency and regulate fiscal policy. Under the advisory management of German financial experts this bank soon became a chief factor in capital formation and investment for development. The Bank Melli also played a role in the formation of social policy. In 1939, for example, it initiated a savings account plan in which the rate of interest was in reverse ratio to the size of the account.[22] At the same time this was accompanied by a public campaign to encourage saving by the poorer classes and the opening of savings accounts for children.

The government's efforts to maintain the position of the rial were much less successful. During the first decade of Reza Shah's regime Iranian currency was based on silver. Owing to the continuous postwar decline of the price of silver in relation to gold on the world market in the twenties, as well as to a growing unfavorable balance of payment in Iran's foreign trade in the same period, the exchange value of the rial declined rapidly.[23] On March 19, 1930, the Gold Standard Act was passed[24] with hopes of checking the depreciation of the rial. But owing to the adoption of the conservative gold-specie standard, and the lack of sufficient resources to purchase an adequate supply of gold, implementation of this act was postponed, and silver was, in effect, not demonetized until 1936. The depreciation of the rial therefore continued.[25]

No general appraisal of the financial reforms undertaken during the regime of Reza Shah can escape the following conclusions: (1) The state possessed an increasing degree of central control over the financial affairs of the country. (2) Owing to the erratic exercise of this control, as well as the adverse effect of external conditions, governmental measures were not always beneficial. (3) The sheer volume of the government's financial activity grew vigorously.[26] (4) This growth was accompanied by growing bureaucratic paraphernalia. (5) As an inevitable outcome of conclusions 1, 3, and 4, the public morality of state officials was subjected to tests that grew in severity. Although no official records are available, there seems to be evidence that a degree of dedication and public responsibility—sometimes inspired by fear of a vigorous ruler—was achieved during the early years of Reza Shah's reign. But as the honesty and austerity of his soldierly temperament gave way before the temptations of absolute power, he began to acquire land and accumulate wealth by methods not short of extortion. It is not surprising that large-scale graft and corruption followed in his wake. In 1942 'Ali Dashti, a prominent deputy with parliamentary immunity, was prompted to muse somewhat introspectively, "In what country can you find today so many . . . embezzlers, all immune from punishment?"[27]

AGRICULTURAL REFORMS

Iran, like many of her neighboring Middle Eastern countries, has a predominantly agricultural economy.[28] Yet the agricultural sector of Iranian economy was least affected by the modernizing efforts of the Reza Shah regime. It is perhaps a characteristic aspect of modern, nascent nationalism in backward countries, particularly in the Middle East, that these countries invariably aspire to a prestige-giving program of industrialization without a commensurate modernization and reform of agriculture. True to its quasi-revolutionary nature, however, the early government of Reza Shah was vaguely aware of the importance of land reform. In fact, in 1924 a study board was planned to report on the feasibility of land-tenure reform, as well as modernization of agriculture.[29] An indication of the avid xenophilia of the time is to be found in an item on the agenda of this projected board, approved by the Majlis. It called for "Preparations for attracting foreign technicians and particularly agricultural experts and farmers to Iran; *as well as formulation of a plan—with due attention to political and racial considerations—to encourage foreign workers and farmers to settle in Iran.*"[30] Nothing came of the project, however, and there are no records of any report from this board. The vested interests of large landlords in the Majlis militated against the success of any such scheme.

No grasp of the agricultural problem of Iran is possible without a brief view of land ownership and tenure, as well as of the relationship between the landlord and the tenant.[31] There are three types of land ownership in Iran: private, state, and *waqf,* or religious endowments. The state lands and the *waqf* lands are nominally administered by the Ministries of Finance and Education, respectively, but in reality they are often "rented" and managed by the neighboring large landowners. Mention has been made of the state lands in connection with the problem of raising revenue.[32] The *waqf*[33] lands are generally located in the vicinity of shrines, and the largest concentration is in Khorasan.* The forms of *waqf* vary. Some are outright donations

* The tomb of the eighth *Imam* (Reza) in Mashad, the provincial capital of Khorasan, is the most sacred *shi'ah* shrine within Iran's borders.

to the shrine, and may be sold or exchanged by the trustees of the shrine; others are nontransferable and their use is restricted to an individual clergyman or a religious order. The latter kind of *waqf* may, in two or three generations, have hundreds of owners and/or beneficiaries.[34]

Private ownership[35] may be differentiated into three categories, depending on the size of the landholding: Large owners have outright title to one or more villages; medium owners have title to a part of a village, more than is necessary for their livelihood; and small holders, with their families, depend entirely on their land.

In large holdings, in addition to land and water, the owner usually owns the forest, pasture, range, and so on. If the source of water is a *qanat* (subterranean canals peculiar to Iran), he owns the *qanat*; if the village is irrigated by a river, he owns the "water rights." The type and locality of the land often determine its ownership. Large holdings occur in wide, level, connected valleys where the land-to-water ratio is heavily in favor of land. In these holdings social stratification is often extremely rigid; that is, there is a complete dichotomy between the peasants and the aristocratic absentee landlord.

Medium and small holdings usually occur in mountainous regions where the land-to-water ratio is in favor of water. They also are found where there is a greater multiplicity of crops and where there are various forms of agricultural activity, such as forestry, truck gardening, animal husbandry, bee cultivation, silkworm raising, and cottage craft. Proximity to towns and markets also tends to encourage medium and small holdings. Social stratification is less severe in medium and small holdings. Furthermore, in such holdings the rights to land, range, and other assets may belong to different individuals. In such cases the owner of the water is usually the most influential person in the area. If water is relatively scarce, the value of the land usually depreciates to a point at which small holders lose their distinction of ownership and become little more than hired farmers of the owner of the water.[36]

It may safely be stated that no willful step was taken in the first fifteen years of Reza Shah's reign to alter the pattern of land tenure, or to change the relationship between the owner and the tenant of agricultural land. This relationship was conspicuously ignored in the Civil Code of Iran, and the peasant was given no safeguards. Civil authority in rural Iran, although legally the joint responsibility of the central government and the landlord, is in practice often the sole prerogative of the landlord.[37] This state of affairs seriously impedes reform, mechanization, and the growth of agriculture in Iran.

In the late thirties, when priorities had already been given to industrialization, control of foreign trade, and construction of the Trans-Iranian Railway, the government began to pay some attention to the inefficient and archaic agricultural sector of the economy. Not much was said of land reform, and the emphasis was put upon land development. The Land Development Act of November 16, 1937, constitutes a legislative landmark in agricultural reform.[38] This was a broad but specific plan to encourage agricultural development. It made the optimal utilization of land a legal responsibility of the owner. Optimal utilization was defined as including the development of new means of irrigation, the reclamation of exhausted land, the scientific and hygienic maintenance of canals, the construction of rural roads, the establishment of health stations, the draining of swamps, and rural housing (article 1). The Act even went so far as to create the necessary machinery for the enforcement of its provisions (article 4). It called for making government credit available to needy owners, for the punishment of delinquent owners,[39] and for the awarding of prizes to owners with initiative (article 9). It also empowered the Ministry of Agriculture to formulate an over-all plan with specific goals and quotas for the agricultural development of the entire country.

The basic weakness of this law lay in the fact that it entrusted the whole project to the landlords. The authority for regional planning as well as enforcement was vested in councils made up of the landlords of the region (article 2). In order to understand the reason for the reluctance of the landlords to initiate any reforms one must be aware of the economic relations between landlord and tenant peasant. The latter pays rent that is fixed not in terms of money but as a portion of the gross yield. The proportion varies according to the custom of the particular area and depends upon which party owns the water, which owns the plow oxen, which supplies the seed, and so on. On the average, a rent of 50 per cent of the crop is collected.[40] This very large income of the landlord is partially responsible for his lack of incentive to invest in development. He is also sensitive to possible social and economic dislocations that might occur if significant improvements are made in the subsistence-level standard of living of the tenant peasant.

The Land Development Act of 1937 was thus delivered into the hands of those against whose practices it was aimed. It was as good as stillborn, although in fairness to a handful of progressive landlords it must be pointed out that when they attempted scientific and technological innovations they invariably met with peasant apathy and lack of cooperation. Under the existing share-cropping ratio peasants feared that most of the benefits from any additional effort or development would accrue to the landlord and not to them. A belated gesture was made on September 16, 1939, when the Majlis authorized the Ministries of Justice and Agriculture to examine the possibilities of reform in share-cropping ratios and to draw up a joint procedure for the settlement of disputes arising from the distribution of crops between landlords and peasants.[41] This was not implemented.

Clearly, then, there was no amelioration of the iniquitous land-tenure system during the reign of Reza Shah. Indeed, when the debilitating effects of the vast land acquisitions of the monarch himself, as well as the passing of large areas of state lands into the hands of high-ranking army officers, are taken into consideration, one is forced to conclude that an appreciable deterioration in the circumstances of this basic socio-economic problem had taken place.

This fundamental failure, however, should not obscure a number of positive steps taken by the government for the improvement and modernization of farming methods. As early as 1925 tariff exemptions were granted for the importation of agricultural machinery.[42] In 1930 the Department of Agriculture* took some worth-while steps toward the scientific care of forests, the promotion of export crops, soil reclamation, breed improvements, and pest control.[43] In the same year an agricultural bank was founded to facilitate credit for these projects and particularly to aid the expansion of industrial and export crops.[44] In 1932 a relatively large appropriation was made for an extensive forestry and conservation program,[45] a program that was sorely needed. Until recent times when the use of oil products (and to a small extent, electricity) has become widespread in the urban areas, the country's only source of fuel was wood and charcoal. In the absence of effective controls, and because of an apathetic social attitude, the meager forest resources of the country were indiscriminately plundered. In the Caspian Sea littoral, owing to abundant rainfall, a natural equilibrium was kept; but the magnificent oak forests of central and western Iran were rapidly disappearing.

The foundation of an agricultural college in Karaj (some twenty-five miles west of Tehran) in 1929, and an institute for veterinarian research, production of serums, and inoculation of livestock in nearby Hesarak in 1939, was a great stride toward the introduction of modern agricultural methods into the country.[46] Although few sons of the peasantry were ever found among the student body of the college at Karaj, and almost no

---

* A division of the newly organized Ministry of National Economy and elevated to an independent Ministry in 1940.

graduates actually returned to live and work on the land, this college did train a cadre of desk experts for the growing organization of the Department of Agriculture.

As in other areas of national activity, a number of foreign experts were hired for the modernization of farming methods. Beginning with an American agronomist and a German forestry expert in 1925,[47] the list grew over the years and included four French professors and one Austrian professor for the College of Agriculture, nine Chinese and two Dutch tea and bamboo experts, a Polish entomologist, a French tree surgeon, a Greek tobacco expert, and six French, German, Austrian, and Hungarian veterinarians.[48] In addition, a number of breed animals including Australian Merino sheep, Hereford, Brahmin, and Jersey cattle, Maryland and Leghorn poultry, and Hungarian draft horses were imported, and promising experiments were carried out in cross-breeding with domestic animals. Under the direction of some cavalry officers, an Institute of Equestrian Registration and Breed Improvement was organized, but its chief task turned out to be the purchase of horses and mules for the army.

Some work was done for the improvement of seeds and fruit trees, and a great deal of expansion and progress was accomplished in the production of sugar beets, tobacco, silk, and tea. The last three crops are grown primarily in the Caspian littoral. (The region produces all the tea and most of the silk and tobacco in Iran.) The reason for these energetic efforts was that Reza Shah had acquired title to nearly the entire province of Mazanderan and large areas of Gilan and Gorgan. Improvements carried out by the Department of Agriculture and at the expense of the state benefited his private treasury.

A beginning was made in the introduction of agricultural machinery. Turning first to the mechanization of the production phase (the mechanization of processing for market will be dealt with below), there are no data available for 1941; but in 1950 an American observer estimated that there were fewer

than 300 deep wells, only 900 tractors, 100 combines, 40 thresh-
ing machines, 100 discs, and 60 sowing drills and barrows in
operation in the whole of Iran.[49] A large majority of these
were located on the royal estates.

The great obstacles to the mechanization of agriculture are
threefold: physical, socio-economic, and cultural. The lack of
service and repair facilities, spare parts, and fuel in the country,
as well as long distances and poor connections with towns, con-
stitute the main physical obstacles. The socio-economic and
cultural obstacles are more complex. Although the urban Iranian has demonstrated a high degree of intelligence and adapt-
ability in mastering Western technology, the rural Iranian has
not shown a similar talent unless he has been sufficiently urban-
ized. Once in the cities, however, he does not wish to return to
the country.

The presence of a mechanical piece of equipment often has
a disquieting effect upon the peasant. The tenant who owns his
oxen, and therefore receives a higher share of the crops, is rightly
fearful of losing his distinction. In Iranian villages women have
the customary right to pick the grain left over in the fields after
the harvest. This may provide a peasant household with up to
six weeks' supply of bread,[50] and sometimes spells the difference
between subsistence and sinking deeper into debt. The mechanical harvester in its relative efficiency is irritating to the
peasants, for it leaves not enough behind. In some areas all
poultry, their care, and their products also belong, by custom,
to women.[51] The incubator threatens to deprive them of this
asset. But above all, the greatest difficulty in the introduction
of machinery arises out of the relationship between the mode
of production and the socio-economic pattern of land tenure.
In all their efforts for the promotion of agricultural mechanization the officials and modernizers of the Reza Shah period
displayed no evidence that they properly understood this relationship. Without a commensurate program of land-tenure reform the little mechanization that was introduced tipped the

already uneven scale further to the advantage of the landlord and thereby added to social tension in rural Iran.

No description of village life is intended here.[52] Suffice it to say that evidences of change in the mode of life—so marked in Tehran and among the upper classes of other towns—are only dimly apparent in a minority of close and accessible villages and totally lacking in the vast majority of the villages. Except for tea, sugar, cheap cotton goods, and lamps, generally no articles of foreign origin find their way into the villages. "Practically none of the benefits of modernization and change and economic growth have reached the peasant, but he has had to share its costs by direct and indirect taxation."[53] On the other hand, both population movement and social mobility were appreciably accelerated in rural Iran during the regime of Reza Shah. The responsibility for these phenomena, however, lay entirely outside the rural society. Such strong external forces as universal military training, the growth of factories, and the construction of railroads were responsible for the change. There was practically no change for those who remained in the village.

No account of the land and peasant problem in Iran would be complete without mention of the nomadic tribes that comprise nearly 2 million or 18 per cent of the country's rural population.[54] The Kurds, the Lurs, and the Qashqa'is make up the largest proportion of this population, but by no means do all the migrant tribes belong to these larger groups. In geographic order, but not according to size and importance, the following are the more prominent tribal groups: Shahsavan in the northwest, Kurd in the west-northwest, Lur in the west and west-center, Arab in the southwest, Qashqa'i in the south, Baluchi in the southeast, Turkoman in the northeast, and Bakhtiari in the center.

Because of the inability of the central government to cope with tribal rebellions there was no internal security in Iran after the end of the First World War. Brigandage, intimidation, and looting of towns were rampant. It was to this task of terminating tribal anarchy that Reza Shah addressed himself first. Having broken the armed resistance of the tribes, he was faced with the infinitely more difficult task of pacification and settlement. He was determined not to permit any recurrence of tribal disorder such as he had witnessed during his early years of power. He pursued an energetic program designed to settle the tribes permanently on the land. This was done by the forced prevention of seasonal migrations, the construction of mud huts in certain areas to replace the tents, and the distribution of state lands and free seed to encourage modes of agriculture other than herding.

Of all the tribes the Lurs were the slowest to submit. As late as 1931 there were serious uprisings in Luristan. It was on this area in particular that the government concentrated its attention in 1932. A number of bills for the transfer of state lands to tribesmen were passed.[55] Also a total of 750,000 rials was appropriated in the same year for various forms of development aid for the tribes of Luristan.[56] Unfortunately the authority for implementing these measures was given to the army and the gendarmerie, who embezzled funds sent for tribal settlement, treated the tribal population brutally, and systematically looted their means of livelihood. The plots of land earmarked for the tribesmen were forcibly "sold" to them by the local authorities. The most effective method of preventing disorder was found to be forcible retention of the chiefs in Tehran, where often they lived comfortably, but under close surveillance. Many children of these chiefs attended schools in Tehran or Europe and became as Westernized as other members of the urban upper classes.

The government of Reza Shah by dint of its strong central authority had the opportunity to do what previous weak governments had been powerless to accomplish: remove the causes of constant irritation, provocation, and conflict between the tribes and the rest of the nation. Instead, by brutal, selfish, and martial methods, the government added to those causes of conflict. A measure of this failure became abundantly clear immediately upon the collapse of the regime in August 1941, when the exiled chiefs left Tehran and returned to their tribes, there to lead full-scale uprisings and horrible fratricidal wars on government troops.

FOREIGN TRADE POLICY

A brief account of foreign trade policy during the reign of Reza Shah is helpful insofar as it demonstrates the role of foreign trade in the dissemination of Western influences in Iran.[57] From the beginning of the sixteenth century on, foreign trade served as an avenue of European influences into Iran. With the advent of the industrial revolution and economic imperialism in the nineteenth century, the importation of foreign goods into Iran was accelerated. In connection with problems of state revenue and the Great Power economic penetration, Iran's loss of tariff autonomy has already been noted.[58] The Anglo-Russian economic policy in Iran prior to the First World War resulted in the widespread use of foreign-manufactured goods and thereby created changes in the modes of consumption and standards of living; at the same time it prevented Iran from developing any new methods of production to meet the new patterns of consumption.[59] Iran's dependence upon Western goods is revealed both by the rising volume of imports before the outbreak of the First World War and by the nature of the imported products, which consisted almost entirely of consumers' goods such as cotton textiles, sugar, and tea.[60]

The foreign trade policy of Iran during the interwar period may be divided into two phases, the first lasting from 1919 through 1929 and the second from 1930 to 1940. The early period was characterized by continuing relatively free trade, and passivity in relation to external forces; the later period was marked by the introduction of government controls and, with a brief respite in 1934–35, increasingly active state strictures.[61] The new policies in 1930 were due primarily to external causes, namely, Iran's increasingly unfavorable balance of trade;[62] the alarming depreciation of the exchange value of the rial;[63] and the need for adjustment to the new Soviet trade policy as applied to Iran. The main causes for the trade deficits were the depreciation of the rial as well as drops in the prices of Iran's export commodities on the world market. Furthermore, owing to global political conditions, a large share of Iran's foreign trade prior to about 1925 was confined to the British Empire, an area with an unlimited capacity for exports to Iran but a very limited need for imports from that country.[64] The causes of depreciation of the rial were referred to earlier.[65]

In order to appreciate the influence of Soviet trade policy on Iran, first it must be understood that Russia's proximity to Iran and capacity for absorption of Iran's export commodities make her potentially Iran's natural trade partner.[66] Although the Revolution of 1917 and the subsequent events dislocated Russo-Iranian trade, by 1927 Russia had re-emerged as Iran's greatest buyer. The rich agricultural provinces of northern Iran depended upon the Russian market for the sale of their surplus grain, rice, tobacco, cotton, wool, hides, and fruit. These provinces, however, had relatively free access to the Russian market, so long as Russia did not choose to apply the terms of her state foreign trade monopoly to Iran. After this privilege was partially withdrawn in 1928 and completely denied in 1930, Iran resorted to establishing her own state foreign trade monopoly in 1931 in order to cope with the new problems.[67] Adjustment to Soviet trade policy, however, was only one of the reasons for the introduction of a state foreign trade monopoly. And the foreign trade monopoly measures were only one feature of the new state controls. The other feature was the establishment of foreign exchange control in February 1930.[68]

The short-range objective of these controls was to stem the fall of the rial and redress Iran's trade deficit. But more significant from the viewpoint of the adoption of Western technology were the long-range reasons for these controls. Beginning in 1930 the government embarked upon an active policy of stimulating economic growth. Foreign trade was, in a sense, "mobilized" for this goal. It was hoped that by state control of exchange and foreign trade Iran would achieve economic autarchy. It was expected that state control would produce a favorable balance of trade, maintain the position of the rial, expand exports, aid industrialization, stimulate efficiency, and bring about self-sufficiency. In short, the Act of 1930 meant the full adoption of the statist, neomercantilistic policies adopted in Turkey.

The establishment of a foreign trade monopoly did not mean actual government conduct of trade, but only government regulation by means of quantitative controls and the requirement of import and export licenses. By these means the government was able to bypass the tariff treaty obligations. These controls grew in severity and the degree to which they interfered with trade. The exchange control, by contrast, was removed briefly in 1934–35, only to be reimposed in 1936 with greater restrictions.[69] In addition to the foreign trade controls a number of other steps were taken to facilitate economic growth, among them the formation of the first chamber of commerce in 1930, legislation for the regulation of commercial insurance in 1937, and the creation of an independent Ministry of Commerce in the same year.[70]

The achievement of the Reza Shah governments in creating capital for growth investment by the control of foreign trade was impressive. Specific evidence, such as the construction of the Trans-Iranian Railway with the aid of the state monopoly on the importation of tea and sugar,[71] and the encouragement of importers of capital goods by means of tariff exemptions and tax relief, will be provided below.

It remains to mention certain undesirable results of Iran's foreign trade controls. (1) Owing to an official overvaluation of the rial, the country's agricultural exports suffered. (2) Because of the same unrealistic exchange policy, Iran was inevitably pushed in the direction of bilateral trading with soft currency countries, notably Germany and the Soviet Union. These two countries thoroughly dominated Iran's trade during the 1930's.[72] At first glance, this trend may seem beneficial to Iran, since both these countries were well suited to provide a ready market for Iran's exports and supply all of her import needs. But the fact that German and Soviet trade accounted for nearly all of Iran's trade whereas Iranian trade was an insignificant part of those two countries' trade resulted in unfair practices highly injurious to Iran.[73] The partial paralysis of Iran's factories and mechanical equipment during the war, owing to the unavailability of German repair parts, was another penalty for this narrow bilateralism. And, finally, (3) the severe government interference in trade activities resulted in certain dislocations in the country's economy, which in turn caused a steady rise in prices. Since this rise in prices was not accompanied by a commensurate rise in incomes, the consumers suffered.

In the light of the above facts it must be asked whether the motives for the controls were entirely sound, and whether the controls were the best way of fulfilling the government's goals.

THE DEVELOPMENT OF MODERN TRANSPORTATION AND COMMUNICATIONS

Because of her relatively large territory (628,000 square miles) and her rough terrain, Iran badly needs a modern system of transportation and communication. Surplus crops are wasted in some areas owing to the lack of adequate transport facilities, and the cultural consequences of relative isolation are even more pronounced than the economic.

When Reza Shah appeared on the scene in 1921, some pioneering efforts had been made in the field of transportation and communication. Nearly all such work, however, was done by foreign powers, either in the prewar period as part of their policy of economic imperialism, or during the First World War for immediate strategic purposes. Among these works were the Julfa-Tabriz, the Rasht-Pilé Bazar, and the Quetta-Zahedan railways; the Khosrowi-Qazvin, the Rasht-Qazvin, and the Bushehr-Shiraz roads; and the Baku-Enzeli and the lower Karun water transport systems; the construction of telegraph lines had been started in the second half of the nineteenth century.[74] The only railroad constructed in the interior of Iran before 1921 was a narrow-gauge line from Tehran to Shah 'Abd al-'Azim, a religious shrine five miles south of the city. This was built and operated by a Belgian concession.

The Reza Shah regime turned its attention to this vital task at an early date. In 1924 the government undertook a complete study of the country's transport problems. A list of priorities was drawn up and adopted.[75] The construction of a Trans-Iranian Railway was the master project of this program. Building a railroad in Iran was more than an economic measure. An ambition that had been frustrated for nearly seventy-five years was about to be fulfilled. A project almost continually under study but never carried out, railway construction was tantamount to progress, sovereignty, and national status. There were serious doubts, however, about Iran's ability to finance such an undertaking without outside capital. When attempts to secure a foreign loan failed,[76] Iran was forced to rely upon internal sources. The low level of income and the difficulties in the collection of internal taxes precluded any form of tax on income or direct taxation. Recourse was made to the field of foreign trade. In 1925 a government monopoly was established on imports of tea and sugar. The funds derived from the monopoly tariff were earmarked for railroad construction exclusively.[77] The Act governing the construction of the Tans-Iranian Railway was approved by the Majlis on February 9, 1926.[78]

Although the railroad was financed by domestic capital, the job of construction had to be entrusted to foreign engineers and experts. In selecting these technicians, Reza Shah was careful to employ Westerners of diversé nationality from countries that had no history of political or economic interest in Iran.[79] The early surveying and drafting operations were carried out by an American firm and a German firm; the construction was accomplished by a Scandinavian concern.[80] In all, approximately two hundred foreign engineers and experts were brought to Iran for the construction of the Trans-Iranian Railway.[81] This enterprise also provided an occasion for sending a large number of Iranian students to Europe to study various phases of railroad construction and operation.

In 1938 the task was completed amidst much national rejoicing, and for months the newspapers printed epic poetry in which Reza Shah replaced Rostam (the mythological hero of Iran), and the new railroad, his seven labors.[82] The total cost of the construction of this 1,394-kilometer line (about 850 miles) is estimated at 2,552,700,000 rials.[83] A large portion of the sum was raised by the tax on tea and sugar. The fact that this task was accomplished by the marshaling of domestic resources had a great psychological value for the regime of Reza Shah and its statist public philosophy. This should not obscure the fact, however, that from an economic viewpoint this method of financing had certain drawbacks. It was inflationary and it did not have secondary beneficial values. A similar tax on cotton goods might not have produced as much immediate revenue, but it would have acted as an infant-industry protective tariff as well.[84] Apart from financing methods, there were other shortcomings. Too much prominence was given to strategic considerations at the expense of economic ones. The railroad did not link Iran with any international rail system. It did not connect the Gulf with the Caspian's most populous ports. It bypassed some of the country's most active economic centers.* In fairness to the

---

* These strategic considerations were primarily conceived against possible Russian or British invasions. They were perversely vindicated during the Second World War, when the task of transporting supplies to Russia was made doubly difficult because of the inconveniently located railheads.

government of Reza Shah, however, it must be pointed out that trunk lines of the Trans-Iranian Railway were in the process of being extended in three new directions when the Second World War interfered.

Nor was the task of building and repairing highways overlooked. The main effort here went into improving and maintaining the existing roads. By European standards these roads were generally well planned, but their surface condition was very poor. In 1925 alone, the Majlis appropriated 9,170,000 rials for road construction and repair.[85] In 1926 registration and licensing of vehicles were introduced, all the revenue from these measures being earmarked for road construction.[86] And in 1930 an independent Ministry of Roads was created with wide powers and elaborate plans for expanding the country's highways.[87] Apart from attention to roads, several steps were taken to encourage the use of motor vehicles. These included tariff exemption for trucks and buses, as well as reduced registration and licensing fees.[88] But in 1941, were an American or a western European to have traveled by road to Iran, he would have found it difficult to believe that any attempt had been made at road improvement. The only paved road in the country extended less than twenty miles and was located on the Shah's estates in Mazanderan. Camels, horses, mules, and donkeys were always in the way of the motorist. The most imposing and the most expensive new road built during the Reza Shah period was an alpine shortcut across the Alborz range from Tehran to the royal domains on the Caspian.

Except for a few boats on the Caspian, on Lake Reza'iye (Urumia), and on the lower Karun river, Iran had no water transport. The boats, docks, and other facilities left by the Russians and the British were maintained, but the greatest accomplishment of the period in water transport was the construction and launching of a dredge in the Caspian port of Pahlavi (Enzeli) in 1940. The work was done by a German firm. Manufactured parts were brought from Germany and assembled in Pahlavi. Christened the *Mazanderan,* this was the first modern motorized "ship" ever launched in Iran. Several Danish and Dutch engineers were employed to plan and aid in the construction of port facilities.[89]

Air transportation came relatively early to Iran. In February 1926 the German air firm of Junkers was given the rights for establishing air passenger and mail service between Europe, Iran, and points farther east in Asia. Junkers was also permitted to operate mail and passenger service between cities in Iran. The contract called for the establishment of pilot training schools and major repair plants in Iran, as well as for Iranian aid in the aerial mapping of the country by Junkers.[90] By 1929 Junkers was already providing air service between Tehran and the cities of Pahlavi, Qasr Shirin, Bushehr, and Mashad.[91] In the 1930's the German airline, now operated by Lufthansa, was still the only foreign airline serving Iran. But in 1937 Iran herself purchased three mail and passenger aircraft and established a weekly service between Tehran and Baghdad. This service was operated by the Ministry of Post and Telegraph, and the planes were piloted by Iranian officers from the Iranian air force.

Postal communications were reformed and regularized with the aid of Belgian experts in 1923.[92] Similarly, telegraphic and radio facilities were expanded and improved with the help of experts from France and Switzerland.[93] Iran did not have a broadcasting station until 1940, but in the thirties Iranians could listen to broadcasts in Persian from Berlin and Ankara radios. There were few telephones in Iran in 1921. By 1941 dial phones were in operation in Tehran, and government offices and well-to-do citizens in the provinces also had telephones.

By 1941 the transportation and communication facilities in Iran had risen considerably above the standard of 1921. Nevertheless, they were still far from adequate for the size of the country. This inadequacy was perhaps the greatest physical obstacle in the path of economic development. What was done, however, had already helped to bring about great economic and social changes. There were visible signs of a breakdown of old loyalties, of the movement of rural population to cities and towns, and of the spread of Western modes and amenities of life. What was more important, from Reza Shah's point of view, was that the influence and authority of the central government became more effective everywhere.

INDUSTRIALIZATION AND DEVELOPMENT OF NATURAL RESOURCES

In the overwhelmingly agricultural economy of Iran before the time of Reza Shah, what little manufacturing existed, such as rug weaving and silk weaving, was done by hand. The nature of this mode of manufacture, as well as the manner of carrying out trade, had given the traditional society of Iran a corporate character. Organization, loyalty, responsibility, and civic virtue, as well as social and political action, were expressed through *asnaf* (professional and trade guilds). The efforts of Reza Shah for the industrialization of Iran, therefore, were of both economic consequence and deep social significance. His goal was not only to introduce mechanical industry but to substitute the cohesive force of the central state for the old corporate basis of society. It is in the light of this philosophy that the following survey of industrialization should be examined.[94]

The few factories that had been set up in Iran before 1921, among them a sugar refinery and a match factory, were shut down owing either to wartime disrepair or to inability to compete with imported commodities. Certain steps for the development of technical schools and workshops were taken as early as 1924, when several German technicians and engineers were employed for that purpose.[95] A technical school under the direction of German teachers was set up at this time; its German staff was later expanded,[96] and it remained in existence throughout the 1930's. The importation of capital goods also began to be encouraged as early as 1925, when such goods were exempted from tariff duties.[97]

In 1930 the efforts of the government for industrialization of the country were intensified. Private initiative in this field was encouraged. Despite a law for the surrender of all foreign exchange to the government, those who had an accumulation of exchange outside the country were permitted to import it in the form of "productive machinery that can increase Iran's export items or decrease the need for imports. These machines are exempted from import quotas and given preferential tariff rates."[98] A subsequent law granted five years of tax exemption to privately established factories.[99] Although some advantage was taken of these laws—particularly in creating the woolen textile industry in Isfahan—certain basic reasons militated against private entrepreneurial activity in Iran. Chief among these reasons were the lack of sufficient capital, the contentment of the landowning class with their luxurious standard of living, a tendency to hoard savings in silver or gold or invest them in real estate, and a lack of faith in any long-range political stability and in the willingness or the ability of the government to protect private investments.

It was obvious from the start, then, that industrialization could be initiated and undertaken only by direct state action. With Reza Shah's instinctive belief in the virtues and practicality of an omnipotent state it is doubtful that a different course would have been chosen even if an alternative had been available. The course of state activity in the economic affairs of Iran, however, cannot be identified as socialism. The egalitarian social implications of a socialist system were totally lacking. The approach is best described as state capitalism, if such a designation is defined to convey the over-all motive of general development and welfare of the country rather than profit. The regulations governing industrial relations promulgated by the Department of Industries and Mines* in 1936 leave no doubt as to the prominent role of the state in industrial affairs.[100]

* A division of the Ministry of National Economy, elevated to independent ministerial level in 1940.

These regulations favor neither the workers nor the owners of factories. They provide basic benefits for the workers, but they prohibit strikes and restrict their individual freedom.[101]

The list of state and private factories set up in Iran during the Reza Shah regime is impressive. Despite the psychological attraction of heavy industry, priority was given to light industry with a view to decreasing imports and increasing exports. It is not intended here to present complete data on the industrialization of Iran,[102] but to indicate the type of factories established and their role in the development of the Iranian economy. Cotton, woolen, and silk textiles were logical choices. Cotton textile factories were established in Mazanderan, Isfahan, and Tehran. The woolen industry was concentrated in Isfahan (which the local citizens proudly referred to as the Manchester of Iran). And a modern silk fabric factory was set up in Chalus, Mazanderan, which supplied the needs of the country and had a slight export surplus. Several yarn-spinning factories were also created; but the output was not sufficient to supply all the needs of the cotton mills, and the deficit had to be imported. Several large campaigns were conducted to encourage the use of local clothing. Uniforms for the army, the schools, and various institutions were all made of local materials.[103] Iranian textiles were far from perfect, and those who could afford imported materials continued to buy them. The importation of silk fabrics was altogether prohibited, creating a brisk contraband trade in such luxury items as stockings.

A most successful record was achieved in the field of sugar refining. As in many countries with low dietary levels, the consumption of sugar is very high in Iran. Apart from an unsuccessful attempt by a Belgian concern to operate a sugar refinery in Kahrizak (eight miles south of Tehran), no attempt was made to produce sugar locally before the time of Reza Shah. However, the climatic and soil conditions in Iran were found to be perfectly suited for growing sugar beets, and it was only natural that particular attention should be paid to this industry. In all, eight state-owned refineries were built in various parts of the country, and the old Kahrizak plant was reactivated. Domestically produced sugar rose from 2,419 metric tons in 1932/33 to 35,636 tons in 1940/41.[104] An effective program of government subsidy and aid encouraged the landlords in the vicinity of the refineries to grow beets. This was extremely profitable to the landowners; but it did not please the tenant farmers, who objected to the additional chores and the unfamiliar techniques that the cultivation of this new crop involved, and who resented tending a crop that could not be pilfered and eaten. Moreover, they were accustomed to receiving their share of the yield in kind, and the necessity for cash compensation in the case of sugar beets was a dubious advantage. If the landlord and his manager in the village were honest, cash offered the peasant new opportunities; but where the landlord or the manager had no scruples, the peasant had little hope of receiving a fair wage.

Various phases of processing, storing, and distributing other agricultural products were also improved by the importation of modern equipment. Large grain elevators (constructed by Russian experts), bakeries, plants for fruit drying and packing, rice cleaning, and meat canning, vegetable oil refineries, breweries, wineries, and distilleries, an excellent sardine-packing plant on the Persian Gulf (built by Danish experts),* and several other similar enterprises were created in different parts of the country. The increasing construction needs of Iran were partially satisfied by the construction of several cement factories. And a number of miscellaneous light-consumer-goods industries, such as soap, glass (with the aid of Italian engineers), paper, matches, and cigarettes, nearly all state-owned, were in operation by 1941.[105]

During the last two years of Reza Shah's reign much effort went into establishing an iron foundry and a steel mill in Iran.

---

* The valuable fishing rights in the Caspian were held by a Soviet concession known as *Iran Riyba*. As in the case of oil, the development of these fisheries was somewhat insulated from the rest of the Iranian economy.

The economic priority for this scheme was rationalized in terms of the needs of the railroad and construction operations. But the tenor of publicity given to the project left little doubt that it was also a supreme matter of national prestige. The preliminary plans were completed, and much of the machinery had been imported from Germany, when Reza Shah was forced to leave the country in 1941.[106]

The government agency responsible for operating the state-owned factories was the Department of Industry and Mines, a division of the Ministry of National Economy. Since this Ministry combined administrative, managerial, and technical operations, it was easily the most professional segment of the government. It was relatively free of older politicians, and it provided jobs for all young engineers who wished to work for the government. This meant nearly all the graduates of the local technical colleges and the engineers returning from Europe.

As might be expected, considerable attention was paid to the exploitation of Iran's mineral resources. Her most abundant and important mineral—oil—was the reason for the earliest arrival of Western technology in Iran.[107] The activities and investments of the D'Arcy concession of 1901, which came under the control of the British government during the First World War, made Iran one of the early major oil-producing areas of the world. But a combination of factors, including the sweeping terms of the concession, the relative impotence of the Iranian government in the pre–Reza Shah days, and a deliberate policy of exclusiveness pursued by the Anglo-Persian Oil Company (the British-controlled company, later renamed the Anglo-Iranian Oil Company, in charge of the exploitation of Iranian oil), gave the oil industry in Iran a certain extraterritorial aspect. The Anglo-Iranian Company was instrumental in abetting the process of Westernization in Iran—by paying royalties in foreign exchange, by providing cheap oil fuels for Iran's other industries, by the stimulating effect of its local expenditures, by employing a large Iranian labor force, and by training at least a few Iranians for high-ranking technical and managerial posts in the industry. From a psychological viewpoint, however, the presence of the company had a depressing influence upon the haughty, sensitive, nationalistic mood of the Iran of Reza Shah. When so much was made of Reza Shah's success in ridding Iran of foreign interests, the oil company was an unpleasant reality that was difficult to ignore. Nor did the company's unfortunate lapses in public relations help the situation. At a time when all Iranians were being exhorted to maximum efforts in a burst of economic activity and growth, the oil company failed to identify itself with these national aspirations. (It cannot be denied, though, that the health and social facilities provided by the company were a great contribution to the welfare of the industry's workers.) An offensive air of superiority, bred by long years of colonial tradition, kept the British officials aloof from all but a handful of "Anglicized" Iranians.

In 1932, when Iran desired greater revenue from its oil resources in order to facilitate the importation of industrial machinery, the issue was referred to the League of Nations, and Iran accused the company of unfair practices in calculating the annual royalty.[108] The League of Nations recommended that the articles of the concession be revised to calculate Iran's share in terms of fixed payments on quantity of production. But the resulting slight increase in royalties was still not favorable to Iran owing to a considerable rise in the price of oil in the late thirties.[109] The royalties paid to the government of Iran by the Anglo-Iranian Oil Company over the twenty-year period from 1919/20 to 1939/40 averaged £1,619,000 (from £469,000 in 1919/20 to £4,271,000 in 1939/40). The production, meanwhile, had increased from 1.11 million long tons in 1919/20 to 9.736 million long tons in 1939/40.[110] Judged by the more enlightened investment practices in underdeveloped countries today, these royalties were small. Payment of large royalties to countries with archaic social and political structures is often criticized because of the inefficient and inequitable uses made of these royalties. In the case of the Iran of Reza Shah, however, a strong central government, with a sufficiently formulated pol-

icy of development and growth, was not able to avail itself of
the country's most precious natural wealth. To be sure, the
regime's investment of what royalties it did receive was not
altogether admirable. On the one hand, the royalties were
well spent in hiring a multitude of foreign technicians and advisors; on the other, they were squandered on excessive amounts
of armaments.

Efforts were made for the exploitation of oil outside the
concession area of the Anglo-Iranian Oil Company. Several
contracts were actually signed with American, French, and other
independent oil companies, but owing to political pressure from
the Soviet Union or opposition from the Anglo-Iranian Oil
Company, none reached the working stage.[111] Also some valuable work was done in surveying and discovering other minerals.
Several concessions for the exploitation of coal, antimony, man-
ganese, salt, and oxide of iron were given to Iranian companies
or Iranian affiliates of foreign companies.[112] Nine German min-
eralogists and mining engineers were in the service of the Department of Industry and Mines,[113] and three German and two
French professors of mineralogy and geology were on the staff
of the University of Tehran.[114] The government policy regarding ownership of mineral rights was indefinite and vague until
1939. In that year an Act of the Majlis classified all mineral
resources, provided for legal claims and registration of ownership, and permitted private ownership of all mineral resources
except oil and precious metals.[115] Shortly after the passage of
this Act a comprehensive contract was signed with a Dutch exploration and mining company for large-scale exploration and
exploitation of minerals in vast areas of the country.[116] There
was some highly promising preliminary work, but the project
lapsed during the Second World War.

PUBLIC CONSTRUCTION AND URBAN DEVELOPMENT

Next to the Trans-Iranian Railway, the most spectacular
visual aspect of Westernization was the physical transformation
of Tehran, and to a lesser extent of the provincial cities. The

Tehran of 1941 bore no resemblance to the Tehran of 1921.[117] Not much was done, at first, with the old quarters of the city. An entirely new city grew to the north of the old. Well-planned and wide streets intersecting each other at right angles, some paved with cut granite, others with asphalt and concrete, were a glaring contrast to the labyrinthal lanes of the old quarters. Large and imposing public buildings, the exteriors of some being executed in Achaemenian and Sasanian styles, dotted the city. Spacious circles and squares, with fountains, landscaping, and statues of Reza Shah in every conceivable pose, added to the "European" aspect of the capital. Yet, in many respects, the conglomerate atmosphere created by old and new buildings, old and new styles of dress among the people, old-fashioned methods of merchandising in new shops and stores, gave Tehran the look of a massive unfinished tableau worked on by several artists.[118] Some progress was made, too, in providing the city with the amenities of modern life. In 1921 electricity was available only to a few wealthy citizens who owned their own electric generators. Electric lighting of the streets began in 1925, the year of Reza Shah's coronation, and municipal electricity for homes was made available in 1929.[119] Electrification of homes, however, was a slow process and, at first, limited to the wealthy residents of the new quarters. Nothing was done to modernize the water supply system. The picturesque *jubs,* the open water ducts in the streets, lined with trees and foliage, gave the city an individual and often refreshing appearance; but they were highly unsanitary.

The steps taken by municipal authorities, in Tehran and the provinces, to condemn property and renovate the old quarters often ran into clerical opposition during the early years of the regime. The clergy alleged the necessity of preserving inviolate the many *Imamzade* (tombs of alleged descendants of the *Imams*) throughout the country. Later in the thirties the clergy dared not voice their disapproval, and much work was accomplished.[120] A law passed in June of 1941 placed all *waqf* property within city limits under the jurisdiction of the municipalities, to be used for urban development.[121] This law was abrogated shortly after the abdication of Reza Shah.

The improvement of provincial towns was hampered by an undue concentration of authority in the Ministry of the Interior in Tehran. The local authorities depended upon appropriations from the capital. Also, much of the external Westernization was done to impress foreign observers, who usually visited only Tehran. Nevertheless, electrification, city planning, and the construction of imposing government buildings spread to all the provinces. The year 1935 witnessed unusual activity in provincial urban improvement; a total of 48 million rials were spent in that year for the modernization of various provincial towns.[122] The standard feature of these reconstruction plans was two wide streets intersecting at right angles. With remarkable lack of originality the two streets were invariably called Pahlavi and Shah Avenues.

To the Iranian who remembered the pre–Reza Shah conditions, the changes in his physical surroundings and particularly the speed with which these changes were accomplished were nothing short of miraculous. To the Westerner who visited Iran for the first time in 1941, it was a land somewhere between the East and a shabby West. To many Iranians who had studied or traveled in the West, the chasm between the material progress of the West and their own country was a source of frustration and defeatism.

CONCLUSION

There is a fable about a crow who was so impressed by the graceful gait of a partridge that he set himself to imitate it. After long months of practice he had not learned the way of the partridge, but he had forgotten the walk of a crow. At first glance, it seems that not much more can be said of the Westernization of Iran. The truth, of course, is more complex.

The impact of the West on Iran was felt on two planes, the material and the nonmaterial. In the early days of Westernization in Iran the two were not clearly differentiated; but with the intensification of nationalism, a sharp delineation appeared. During the reign of Reza Shah emphasis was put on adopting the technology and other material achievements of the West. But the ideology that inspired the ambitious program of material reforms was an intense form of nationalism, itself a product of the West. It was a nationalism at once inspired by the example of cohesive, autarchic European states and fanned by the frustrating experience of being coerced and exploited by those states. Whereas the early manifestations of nationalism gained popularity by being expressed in terms of religion, those of the Reza Shah period were inspired by the concept of an omnipotent state. The earlier phase was more spontaneous but less productive. As long as the aristocratic landowners ruled, and the powerful *shi'ah* clergy controlled and manipulated opinion and socio-political expression, much was said but little done for the material Westernization of Iran. How, then, was Reza Shah able to achieve such a record in the introduction of Western techniques into Iran?

Reza Shah drew his power from two sources: an aroused

spirit of nationalism, and strong, autocratic, centralized control. Although in many emerging underdeveloped societies these two sources of power have proved to be of equal influence, in Iran by far the greater motive force was the absolute state. We hear much today about the positive role of rampant nationalism in the Middle East, but nationalism was at best a secondary factor—less important even than the favorable international situation—in the building of Reza Shah's Iran.

A tacit realization of this can be discerned in various manifestations of the national mood. An inflated glorification of the past; a deprecation of foreigners that too easily betrays a sense of inferiority; an appetite for industrialization far beyond the bounds of economic rationale, not for the sake of efficiency and welfare but as a symbol of prestige and status; an indiscriminate imitation of the surface gloss of Western societies; and a burning desire to become a truly sovereign and consequential power—these are the predominant characteristics of the Iran of Reza Shah (as indeed they are, in varying degrees, of the whole of the Middle East). The resulting loss of the society's cultural traditions is lamented only by a few men of the older generation.

An increasing number of scholars and observers, in the West as well as in the East, are concerned with the implications of the impact of West on East. Some are content to analyze and diagnose; others permit themselves to hazard opinions and prognoses. Over the years the tenor of these appraisals has changed significantly. One notices an early air of approval and optimism gradually change to doubt and finally to pessimism. During the 1920's no serious attempt was made by outside observers to pass judgment on Reza Shah and his Westernization of Iran, and indeed any such appraisal would have been premature; inside the country approval was implicit among Iranian intellectuals, whose intense desire for rapid and complete Westernization has already been noted.[1]

In the early thirties Sir Arnold Wilson, British soldier, diplomat, and scholarly observer, published his book *Persia*. Draw-

ing on his years of service in that country and his familiarity
with the Persian scene, Wilson muses over both the past and the
future of Iran. He displays a deeply sympathetic appreciation
of a civilization that lived more in his romantic heart than in
reality. One feels that his benign views of the East are the result
more of his misgivings about the state of Western civilization
than of his full comprehension of Eastern society.

> Yet I dare predict that the simple but solid fabric of society
> in Persia, the oldest and hitherto the most stable of Islamic
> kingdoms, will be found in the day of trial to endure better
> than the more elaborate structures, less firmly founded in
> human nature, of Western states.[2]

He speaks confidently of the ability of the Persians to absorb
the technical skills of the West, and he presents a most hopeful
view of the nature and purpose of the national movement of
Reza Shah.

> The Persians bid fair to show themselves able, in a measure
> equalled by no other nation, to imbibe, without intoxica-
> tion, the strong wine of the West. . . . They are endeavor-
> ing to help themselves and others to recover a unity which
> is neither offensive nor defensive, but cultural, and thus
> independent of the changing phases of world economy. On
> such a foundation a new civilization may arise and, having
> arisen, may stand.[3]

Naive and overindulgent as these sentiments seem today in the
case of Reza Shah's Iran, they are hopefully echoed by many a
well-wisher of the new national movements of the Middle East.
It remains to be seen with what success Nasser and his movement
can keep the negative aspects of nationalism—the virulent, irrational, and frustrating elements that distorted the reforms of
Reza Shah and left Iran in a state of tension—out of his quest
for Arab unity. One may hope, but one dare not predict.

The American diplomat and author James Rives Childs,[4]
coming to Iran in the mid-thirties, was impressed by Reza
Shah's achievements in undermining the influence of the clergy
and by the degree of secularization in public affairs and social
relations. There was no doubt in his mind, apparently, that by

eradicating the influence of the clergy and adopting the "materialistic" civilization of the West, Iran could advance unhampered along the path of progress.[5] Nor was he alone in these views. Most prominent Iranians, including Issa Sadiq, at one time Minister of Education, agreed that the power of *mullas* was the chief obstacle to progress: "The work of Westernization, or progress, needs . . . [a centralized] government. Without it the worldly priests would become too powerful and the task that has been started might be endangered and postponed."[6] Similarly, there were a number of Iranians who were satisfied with the material benefits of Western civilization and thought them sufficient to meet the country's needs.[7]

On the whole, however, there was considerable misgiving among Iranian intellectuals about indiscriminate adoption of the materialism of the West. Kazemzade-Iranshahr and Taqizade in their numerous articles in periodicals, and Jamalzade in his popular short stories, spoke frequently of such a danger. It was Ahmad Kasravi, however, who emerged as the chief spokesman of these views. The appearance of his book *A'iyn* (The Creed) in 1932 created a stir in the intellectual circles of the time. Although this book contained many implicit criticisms of the reforms of Reza Shah, it was allowed to circulate because its central message was a condemnation of the materialism of the West. Furthermore, it was critical of traditional Islam and particularly of the *shi'ah* clergy in Iran. In a long succession of subsequent books and articles Kasravi developed these ideas at length.

The regime of Reza Shah could not, of course, permit the existence of a distinct and independent ideology; but Kasravi's differences with the official ideology were not serious, and the regime found them easy enough to ignore. He soon acquired a large following, mainly composed of professional men (including government officials) and students, who managed to give his ideology the attributes of a pseudo-fraternal organization. His popularity among the nationalist elements was particularly great after the abdication of Reza Shah. But with the re-emergence of religious influences in the public life of Iran, Kasravi and his followers were subjected to persecution, and Kasravi himself was assassinated. It is important, however, to keep in mind that the articulate urban Iranian, despite being roundly critical of Western materialism, displayed an endless appetite for all the Western comforts and amenities of life.

The official criticisms of the West and its materialism led certain superficial observers, particularly Muslims from India, to conclude that the movement of Reza Shah was in reality a Muslim revival. The views of Sirdar Ikbal 'Ali Shah[8] are representative of this group. He believed that the clash between Westernism and Islam produces a certain kind of phenomenon in the East, a movement that goes forward while looking backward, i.e., that achieves modernism and the material benefits of the West while reviving the social and scientific spirit of Islam. He even interpreted the Kemalist movement in Turkey in terms of this force. He used the argument, all too familiar to students of the Middle East today, that the people of the East must first learn the diabolic tactics of the West in order to oppose the West with its own weapons.[9] Essad-Bey, biographer and eulogist of Reza Shah, also considered him a great Muslim reformer and tried to trace all his reforms to the social principles of the Koran.[10]

However prevalent ideas of this general character may have been among the Muslims in India or in the Arab world, they did not find support among the Iranians of the Reza Shah period. Such views, comforting as they may be to a believing Muslim, do not take into account the deep sense of inferiority that the impact of the West created among the people of the Middle East. By the time Reza Shah came to power, there were certainly an increasing number of Iranians who were no longer confident of the superiority of Islam. Furthermore, the argument of fighting fire with fire involves a moral judgment that has contributed quite considerably to the moral degeneration of societies in the East. Still more important, these Muslim revivalists have been unable to reconcile Islamic social institutions with the exigencies of modern society. Despite voluminous theoretical discussions, no workable model of a modern society organized on the principles of Islam has been created.

During the Second World War the superficial nature of Iran's transformation, the shallowness of the reforms, and the increased complexity of the country's social, political, and intellectual problems became clear to many people. In the early years after the abdication of Reza Shah the general consensus seemed to be that his reforms were carried out at too rapid a pace. The strain of hasty Westernization upon the fabric of traditional society was held responsible for the state of flux and tension in Iran. The ideologists of the newly organized Tudeh party were the first Iranians to criticize Reza Shah's method of reforms on these grounds.[11]

Professor Ann K. S. Lambton in an article written in 1944[12] points out that Reza Shah's Westernization was too quick, that a proper synthesis of the West and Iran had not occurred. Much that was old was removed, and not enough that was new was put in its place. He had failed to create a situation in which the "unimpaired faculties of the people could find scope in effective and creative social action."[13] The American scholar Richard N. Frye is also of the opinion that the Shah forcibly revolutionized the social and religious life of his people, and that as a result the revolution took place mainly on the surface.[14]

The charge of hastiness in reforms was accompanied in the criticism of some scholars by a more penetrating diagnosis that Iran's difficulties arose from an improper understanding of the West. The desire to adopt the products of Western civilization—whether material or nonmaterial, industrialization or constitutionalism—can only lead to frustration unless the underlying social, institutional, and spiritual foundations of these products are also understood and adopted.[15]

Professor Lambton introduces still another factor, the corporate nature of Iranian society prior to the reforms of the constitutional era.[16] The sense of social purpose, she points out, was felt and expressed, collectively as well as individually, in terms of class and professional associations; this corporate structure was the product of centuries of development, and it constituted the framework for the political and social attitudes and behavior of Iranians. This system did indeed exist, and yet to give it too much weight is mistaken. The reader should not assume that the traditional society of nineteenth-century Iran abounded in virtue and vitality; nor should he oversimplify the causes of tensions that arise from borrowing Western institutions by attributing these tensions to a simple incompatibility of systems. It is true that the modern governmental system has caused the traditional systems to atrophy, and that their intended substitute—national spirit—has not helped to abate what a recent observer has termed "disunifying pressures" in modern Iran.[17] But, on the other hand, the traditional systems were not adequate for the nineteenth century or capable of sustaining national life in the twentieth.

The clash between traditional and modern is clearly seen in the adoption of Western political institutions. Professor Lambton points out the unhappy consequence of one such borrowing in the constitutional period:

> The adoption of constitutional government in 1906 implied a revolution in the conception of society and in the relation of the individual to society. In theory the government was accorded certain powers and denied others, but in practice the conception of a contractual basis of society, of a system of mutual duties and rights above and beyond the outward forms of government upon which the system rests in the West, continues to be foreign to Persian thought. All power is still regarded as irresponsible; the new forms of government have failed to provide a framework for a full and fruitful national life, and certain of its organs have usurped control over fields outside their own, the inevitable result of which is tyranny.[18]

This criticism is perfectly true, and some Iranian observers were the first to point out and clearly define this problem. One of the most popular *shabname* (illicitly distributed "night letters") of the period of constitutional crisis (1906–11) was a pamphlet called *Haqq-e Daf'-e Sharr va Qiyam bar Zedd-e Zolm* (The Right to Resist Evil and to Rise Against Tyranny),[19] which spoke in much the same terms as Professor Lambton. Writing in the periodical *Now Bahar* in 1922, Muhammad Taqi Bahar, a leading journalist, poet, scholar, and politician of modern Iran, spoke of the absence of a modern and viable political principle as the chief deficiency of the reforms. He attributed this to the social structure of Iran and the absence of a politically conscious and articulate middle class.[20] A most searching criticism of Iran's Westernization appeared in the five-volume theoretical work of Dr. Musa Javan, an Iranian jurist.[21] He also laid the blame for Iran's failures at the door of her ruling classes. He was well aware of the irresponsibility of power in Iran and of the need for developing a contractual relationship between the government and the governed:

> In European countries safeguards have been developed to protect the rights of the individuals. . . . In Iran no such safeguards exist and absolute tyranny is the rule. . . .
> In the Western sense government is cooperation in public service. . . . In Iran . . . it is a form of cooperation among corrupt elements. . . . Our best reform legislation, which could have led to social equity, has been subverted or left inoperative, [whereas] all harmful laws have been vigorously enforced.[22]

Implicit in the views of those critics (whether Western or Iranian) who point to the need for the people of the East to understand the spiritual, philosophical, social, and cultural foundations of Western civilization before they can successfully share in it, is a belief in the superiority and viability of Western civilization. Indeed, some critics clearly see the future happiness of the East in terms of her ability to adjust to the West, assuming that any future order in world society will of necessity be oriented in the West.[23] Even Arnold Toynbee, despite his charitable estimate of the potency and regenerative powers of

Islamic societies, cannot help assuming a uniqueness and finality in what he considers to be the generative force of Western civilization, Christianity.[24]

What has been overlooked by many Western observers is the ability of the people of the East to discern the deep rift between Western preaching and Western practice. There are many people in the East who understand and are impressed by the nonmaterial content of Western civilization, but there are even more who are suspicious of the West and doubt the sincerity of the Western nations. Among the Western observers Sir Hamilton Gibb has perhaps the best grasp of this fact.[25] He correctly points out that what first attracted the people of the East was the humanistic idealism of the West. Influenced by this idealism, they accepted the practical institutions of the West. But the West itself provided the most striking examples of departing from those ideals, and naturally the East is now suspicious. "At every level the contrast between the humanitarian ideals proclaimed by the West and its disregard of humanitarian values in action has produced a profound disbelief in the whole system of Western public and private morality."[26]

Professor Gibb urges the West to bring the moral and technical elements of its civilization into better balance, and to view the East with a more open mind. He calls upon the East to reform the institutions of its traditional culture to allow for expansion of scientific and technical knowledge, and to open its mind "toward the profounder formative elements in Western thought."[27] This is admirable advice. But do the nations of the East and of the West possess the spiritual and intellectual resources for such a task? And if they do, are they willing to use them? Professor Gibb cannot, as indeed no serious scholar can, banish a sense of doubt and dismay:

> Yet, for all that Muslim thinkers and Western scholars may do to lay new foundations for the bridge across which East and West may meet, the bridge itself cannot be built unless the Western nations resolutely and effectively solve their own problem. . . . In spite of our scientific and technical

achievements, the repulsion of the Muslim world from Western civilization can only be reinforced the more that the Western nations display their powerlessness to control the demonic forces within them.[28]

This realization of the destructive forces that vitiate Western civilization should not blind us to the fact that more pernicious, if less dramatic, "demonic forces" have been sapping the vitality of Islamic civilization as well.

In the case of modern Iran a combination of negative conditions has contributed to what has in effect been a century and a half of crisis and tension. The geography of Iran, in the absence of modern transportation and communication, makes the virtual isolation of the country's various communities inevitable. Her population has no homogeneity in respect to language, interests, and modes of existence. The unfortunate effects of a long and ugly period of foreign interference and imperialistic designs upon her national life cannot be overlooked. But chief among the sources of modern Iran's endemic crises is a moral degeneration that has permeated every rank and institution of her society, a degeneration that manifests itself in the self-seeking irresponsibility of her ruling classes, the duplicity and greed of her religious leaders, the unprincipled opportunism of her politicians, the rapacity of her landowners and tribal chiefs, and the bigotry and fatalism of her masses. Despite the intentions and endeavors of innumerable responsible men of good will, increasing signs of this decline can be seen in the banality of her contemporary culture, in the corruption that infests her public life, and in the inertia that perverts her efforts at reform.

The prevailing tendency among Iranians is to attribute this moral degeneration to the pernicious influence of foreign interference. And when we consider the innumerable occasions on which some national enterprise has been caused to founder because of foreign intervention, it is not possible to dismiss this charge out of hand. But the roots of the degeneration are at least four centuries old. Ever since the disintegration of the Safavid dynasty when inept monarchs chose to share their power with the assembly of *shi'ah* divines, the strangle hold of the clergy has paralyzed every source of cultural vitality and intellectual vigor in Iran. It was the peculiar talent of the clergy to dull the sting of misfortune with resignation, and when external forces demanded change, to keep the essential structure of Iranian society unchanged. By artificially preserving obsolete traditions, they managed to create the illusion of order. The charge of fatalism so readily leveled at the masses cannot be considered independently of the pervasive influence of the clergy.

Of equal importance as a source of Iran's moral degeneration was the behavior of her ruling classes. By the short-sightedness of their outlook, by the unjust exploitation of their subjects, and by their constant intrigues and costly feuds they forfeited every moral right to rule.

In an atmosphere of apathy and irresponsibility, there was no strength of purpose left in Iran to withstand the imperialistic designs of foreign powers. There is no surer sign of moral resignation among Iranians today than their self-acquitting plea of impotence in the face of foreigners.

This is the state of Islamic civilization in Iran today, a time when the impact of Western civilization is greater and on a larger scale than ever before; it is ironic that at such a moment Western civilization should itself have become vitiated. It seems that two civilizations that share much of their spiritual and historical heritage have become alien to their own foundations. Both societies have lost their equilibrium in terms of their own central values. And when they lost their balance they leaned in opposite directions: the West to a consuming preoccupation with the material world, and the East to a degrading disregard of the material world. To a historian this is particularly intriguing, since in their early days the Christian West was more spiritually inclined and the Muslim East more conscious of the material world. In their subsequent state of disequilibrium and extremism the spiritual vision of both civilizations has been largely clouded and lost. For the fatalistic otherworldliness of Islamic societies cannot be considered anything but a perversion of the true spirit of Islam.

The West's powerful impact upon the East may be interpreted as a result of the East's attempt to compensate for its own extreme backwardness in material achievements. But since the desire for compensation is in turn inspired by an equally extreme movement in the opposite direction, that is, by materialism, it does not, indeed it cannot, result in the restoration of equilibrium. The East traces the sources of the West's preponderant power, and what the West herself considers progress, to Western science, technology, and materialism. The people of the East wholeheartedly wish to borrow these attributes. Much good can and does come of this. The material backwardness of the East is morally degrading. Without the rudiments of physical welfare, it is not easy to speak of social, political, and spiritual welfare. The role of the science and technology of the West in alleviating the material needs and the appalling socioeconomic injustices in the East is a most beneficial one.

When the impact of West on East is viewed in this light, one may appreciate the positive aspects of the Westernization of Iran during the reign of Reza Shah. Many valuable material improvements were accomplished. This study has concerned itself with the magnitude of these accomplishments in certain social areas and institutions of Iran. Despite great shortcomings one cannot deny the usefulness of the scientific and technological improvements in the material life of the country.

But there is not much else that is specifically Western that can be beneficial to the people of the East. It is not that the people of the East are unreceptive to ideological influences from the West, but that these ideologies, conflicting and complex as they are, add to the drift and the flux of the East. In the case of the Muslim world, the impact of Western ideologies is particularly perplexing and divisive. In contemplating the ideological foundations of Western civilization, a thinking Muslim is inevitably faced with this choice: either to attribute the moral and humanitarian idealism of the West to Christianity, or to attribute it to the fountains of anthropocentric thought in the West, be they eighteenth-century rationalism, nineteenth-century positivism, Marxist socialism, or twentieth-century scientism.

If he decides in favor of Christianity, he quickly realizes that his own Muslim faith contains the same germs of humane idealism. In its message of social justice and its attempt to establish a City of God on earth, Islam is even more explicit than Christianity. He may stop there, revived in his faith and fortified by it. But he cannot escape the historical fact of the inability of both Christians and Muslims to maintain the purity and the vitality of their faiths during the past several centuries. Confident as he may be of his personal salvation, he sees both Christianity and Islam powerless to combat the evil and iniquity that he finds on every side.

If he gravitates to the materialistic, man-centered trends of Western thought, invariably he cannot resist the allure of one form or another of Marxist socialism, combining as it does the pseudo-scientific, rationalistic approach, the humane message of justice and equality, and the massive sanction of half the world.

All this may be true of the thinking Muslim. What of the impassioned multitude, too easily given to extremes of violence and torpor, to religious fanaticism and moral degeneration, to hero-worship and xenophobia? They are religious, but their religion does not help them to avoid the pitfalls of nationalistic egoism any more than it shields them from Communism. If they are frustrated in their nationalism, they will be even more receptive to Communism. To expect Islam, in its present low state of vitality, to resist Communism any better than Catholicism can withstand it in Italy, or for that matter than Orthodoxy did in Russia or Buddhism in China, is not realistic.

The answer, if there is to be one, must be universal. The problems of modern Iran are but part of a universal ailment. The fusion of the East and the West, in their present state of disequilibrium, is not going to solve all the problems. What is needed is nothing short of a rebirth of the spiritual values that once animated both the East and the West. But to be effective these values must be applicable, and understood in terms of the economic, social, and political needs of the modern world.

NOTES

INTRODUCTION

1. H. A. R. Gibb and Harold Bowen, *Islamic Society and the West: A Study of the Impact of Western Civilization on Moslem Culture in the Near East* (London, 1950), although dealing with Ottoman society in the eighteenth century, serves as an admirable model for such a study.

CHAPTER ONE

1. For a useful review of Iranian history see Donald N. Wilber, *Iran: Past and Present* (Princeton, 1950).

2. No adequate work on Safavid Persia is available in any language. A wealth of diverse primary sources, however, does exist, namely, court chronicles, contemporary histories, records in the Armenian church at Julfa, original diplomatic correspondence, Jesuit missionary reports in the Vatican Library, innumerable travelogues by merchants and emissaries, such as the Sherley brothers, Chardin, and Pietro della Valle, and records of the Portuguese trading posts and the Dutch and the English East India Companies.

3. An excellent description of life in Persia in the early nineteenth century, and of the initial reactions of the Persians to the West, can be found in James Morier, *The Adventures of Hajji Baba of Ispahan* (London, 1824).

4. For detailed accounts of this period see David Marshall Lang, *The Last Years of the Georgian Monarchy, 1658–1832* (New York, 1957).

5. Recent Soviet historians justify this expansionism on two grounds: the desire of the inhabitants for Russian protection, and the "civilizing" role of the Russian rule. See articles on Gulistan, Turkmanchai, Russo-Persian wars, etc., in the *Bolshaia Sovetskaia Entsiklopediia*, XIII, 251, and XLIII, 443–44.

6. For further details about this turbulent phase see George N. Curzon, Earl of Kedleston, *Persia and the Persian Question* (London, 1892).

7. For chronological data see L. P. Elwell-Sutton, *A Guide to Iranian Area Study* (Michigan, 1952).

8. For further details see V. Tria, *Kavkazskie sotsial'-demokraty v persidskoi revoliutsii* (Paris, 1910).

9. Yahya Dowlat-Abadi, *Hayat-e Yahya* [Autobiography] (Tehran, 1949), pp. 1–2.

10. *Ibid.*, p. 3.

11. See Ahmad Kasravi, *Tarikh-e Hejdah Sale-ye Azerbaijan* [Eighteen Years of Azerbaijanian History] (Tehran, 1939), I, 95–98.

12. George Lenczowski, *Russia and the West in Iran, 1918–1948: A Study in Big Power Rivalry* (Ithaca, N.Y., 1949), pp. 6–8. This remains the best work in English on the subject.

13. Sir Percy Loraine to Vincent Sheean, in Vincent Sheean, *The New Persia* (New York, 1927), p. 162.

14. Edward G. Browne's *The Press and Poetry of Modern Persia* (Cambridge, 1914) provides the best evidence of Iranian feeling at this time.

15. T. Cuyler Young, ed., *Near Eastern Culture and Society: A Symposium on the Meeting of East and West* (Princeton, 1951), p. 137.

16. For the best account of this movement see Edward G. Browne, *The Persian Revolution* (Cambridge, 1910). Of the several lengthy works in Persian none is completely reliable, although Ahmad Kasravi's six-volume *Tarikh-e Hejdah Sale-ye Azerbaijan* (Tehran, 1939–41) is valuable for its wealth of otherwise unavailable information.

17. Muhammad Taqi Bahar, *Tarikh-e Mokhtasar-e Ahzab-e Siyasi-ye Iran* [A Short History of Political Parties in Iran] (Tehran, 1942), p. 2.

18. Iran, *Qanun-e Asasi va Motammam-e An* [The Constitution of 1906 and its Supplement] (Tehran, n.d.), pp. 27–29. Hereafter referred to as Iran, *Constitution*.

19. Iran, *Constitution*, pp. 30–34, 50, 56.

20. *Ibid.*, pp. 30, 34.

21. *Ibid.*, pp. 32–33, 46.

22. Law of Registration of Documents, 1911, article 5, section 2; in the *Majmu'e-ye Qavanin-e Mowzu'eh va Mosavvabat-e Majlis* [Record of Parliamentary Legislation], first and second sessions, 1906–11 (Tehran, n.d.), pp. 290–91 (hereafter referred to as Q1-Q2).

23. Law of Military Conscription, 1914, article 5, section 2; in Q3-Q4 (1914–23), 42.

24. Law of Qualifications of Judges, 1923, article 1, section 2; *ibid.*, p. 101.

25. See Bahar, pp. 9–12.

26. *Ibid.*, pp. 130–34.

27. Editorial in *La Patrie-Vatan,* Tehran (February 5, 1876); cited in *Yadegar,* I, No. 7 (1945), pp. 15–16.

28. 'Abdollah Razi, "Be Nam-e Iran va Iranian: Enqelab-e Afkar" [In the Name of Iran and Iranians: a Revolution in Ideas], *Rastakhiz,* II, No. 10 (1925), pp. 1–7. Italics mine.

29. See *Rastakhiz* [Resurrection], II, No. 6 (1925), pp. 22–25. See also S. R. Shafaq, "Patriotic Poetry in Modern Iran," *The Middle East Journal,* VI (1952), pp. 417–28.

30. *Rastakhiz,* II, pp. 1–8.

31. For first-hand accounts of the early history of Babism, see Nabil, *The Dawn-Breakers* (New York, 1932).

32. For examples see Count Arthur de Gobineau, *Les Religions et*

les philosophies dans l'Asie centrale (Paris, 1865), Edward G. Browne, *A Year Amongst the Persians* (Cambridge, 1927), and Ernest Renan, *The Apostles* (Boston, 1898).

33. Marzieh Gail, *Persia and the Victorians* (London, 1951), p. 58.

34. H. St. J. B. Philby, *A Pilgrim in Arabia* (London, 1946), p. 182.

35. See Shoghi Effendi, *Pattern for Future Society* (Wilmette, Ill., 1944), pp. 1–2.

36. Mario Monterisi, *Iran, Manuali di Politica Internazionale*, No. 32 (Milano, 1941), pp. 138–39.

37. Mahmud Zarandi, *Chand So'al az Kasravi* [A Few Questions for Kasravi] (Tehran, 1944), p. 7.

CHAPTER TWO

1. On this point see W. Morgan Shuster, *The Strangling of Persia* (New York, 1920), p. 245.

2. See, e.g., Hafez Farmanfarmaian, "Fall of the Qajar Dynasty" (unpublished doctoral dissertation. Georgetown University, 1954).

3. For the origins of this unique organization, see F. Kazemzadeh, "The Origin and Early Development of the Persian Cossack Brigade," *The American Slavic and East European Review*, XV (1956), 351–63.

4. For further details see Browne, *The Persian Revolution*.

5. Q2 (1909–11), 592–97.   6. *Ibid.*, pp. 598–99.

7. *Ibid.*, pp. 599–603.

8. For details see Edward G. Browne, *The Persian Crisis of December 1911; How It Arose and Whither It May Lead Us* (Cambridge, 1912).

9. Q2, 603.   10. Q3 (1914), 53–55.   11. *Ibid.*, pp. 56–59.

12. For a detailed description see Christopher Sykes, *Wassmuss, The Persian Lawrence* (London, 1936).

13. For an eyewitness account of Iran during the First World War, see William E. R. Dickson, *East Persia, a Backwater of the Great War* (London, 1924.)

14. Numerous accounts of Iranian history between the end of the war and the rise of Reza Shah are available. For a scholarly treatment see Farmanfarmaian.

15. For a detailed description see Hosein Makki, *Tarikh-e Bist Sale-ye Iran* [Twenty Years of Iranian History] (Tehran, 1945–46). Although extremely biased, this work contains a wealth of eyewitness accounts.

16. For a full account of this mission see Shuster, *The Strangling of Persia*.

17. Iran, Majlis, *Osul-e Mohakemat-e Jaza'i* [Penal Code] (Tehran, 1947), p. 172

18. For these various appointments in 1910 and early 1911, see Q2, 265–77.

19. A few purported biographies, e.g., Essad-Bey, *Resa Schah: Feldherr, Kaiser, Reformator* (Vienna, 1936), are in reality accounts of his reforms. The biographical passages they contain are inaccurate, contradictory, and sketchy.

20. Ne'matollah Mehrkhah, ed., *Ketab-e Reza Shah* [Appreciations of Reza Shah] (Tehran, 1946), pp. 59, 79.

21. As quoted in 'Ali-Asghar Hekmat, *Parsi-ye Naghz* [Pure Persian] (Tehran, 1951), p. 464.

22. See Q4 (1921–23), 321–28.   23. *Ibid.*, pp. 331–33.

24. See Bahar [Political Parties], p. 363.

25. Q5 (1923–25), 253.   26. *Ibid.*, p. 254.

27. Iran, *Constitution*, p. 29.

28. *Ibid.*, pp. 29–30.

CHAPTER THREE

1. See Bahar [Political Parties], pp. 247–53.

2. For a general, analytical approach to the question of nationalism and Western influence, see Hans Kohn, *Western Civilization in the Near East* (New York, 1936).

3. Ahmad Kasravi, *Afsaran-e Ma* [Our Officers] (Tehran, 1944), pp. 28–29.

4. L. P. Elwell-Sutton, *Modern Iran* (London, 2d ed., 1944), p. 71.

5. *Ibid.*, pp. 71–72, 87.

6. *Ibid.*, p. 144.

7. "Horriyat-e Adyan" [Freedom of Religions], editorial in *Rastakhiz*, II, No. 1 (April 1925), p. 9.

8. For further descriptions of these men see A. H. Ehteshami, *Bazigaran-e Siyasat* [Political Figures] (Tehran, 1949), pp. 30–41, 140–46, 71–83, 99–108, 109–17, 9–14. (Page references correspond to the order in which they are named; my brief accounts are drawn from Ehteshami's study. Absence of more authoritative biographical data has necessitated but brief and cautious use of this none-too-reliable source.)

9. See Rezazade Shafaq, *Yadegar-e Mosaferat-e Suis* [Memoirs of a Swiss Journey] (Tehran, 1948), pp. 195–202.

10. Sir Arnold T. Wilson, *Persia* (London, 1932), p. 165.

11. *Ibid.*, p. 48.

12. Shafaq, p. 156.

13. See Kazemzade-Iranshahr, editorial in the *Iranshahr*, No. 7 (1922), pp. 162–64.

14. "Ahammiyat-e Mohit" [The Significance of Environment], in *Rastakhiz*, II, No. 6 (September 1925), pp. 2–3.

15. "Horriyat-e Adyan" [Freedom of Religions], *ibid.*, No. 1, p. 10.

16. "Owza'-e Iran va Rah-e Nejat" [The Condition of Iran and the Road to Salvation], *ibid.*, pp. 34–35.

CHAPTER FOUR

1. See Bahar [Political Parties], pp. 135–36. For further information about the development of the Iranian military forces from the

beginning of the seventeenth century until the year 1922, see Jahangir Qa'em-Maqami, *Tahavvolat-e Siyasi-ye Nezam-e Iran* [The Political Evolution of the Iranian Army] (Tehran, 1947).

2. See F. Kazemzadeh, "The Origin and Early Development of the Persian Cossack Brigade," *The American Slavic and East European Review*, XV (1956), 342–53.

3. *Ibid.*, p. 363.

4. For firsthand accounts see Sir Percy Sykes, *A History of Persia*, II (London, 1951).

5. See Abolqasem Lachini, ed., *Ahvalat va Dastkhatha-ye 'Abbas Mirza Qajar* [The Times and Papers of Abbas Mirza Qajar] (Tehran, 1947), pp. 16 ff.

6. Q4, 267.   7. Q5, 429–30.   8. *Ibid.*, 217–22.

9. Q10 (1935–37), 251–83.   10. Q11 (1937–39), 263–302.

11. Q5, 219; Q11, 275–76, 352–56.

12. See Q4–Q12. Budget figures appear at the end of each volume.

13. See below, p. 134.

14. See Musa Javan, *Mabani-ye Hoquq* [Foundations of Law], III (Tehran, 1950), 556–57.

15. Q4, 78, 88–94.

16. Q8 (1931–33), 358.   17. *Ibid.*, p. 359.

18. Q11, 304–50.   19. Q4, 220.

20. Q7 (1929–31), 166–72.   21. Q10, 119–20.

22. Shafaq [Swiss Journey], pp. 126–27.

23. Elwell-Sutton, *Modern Iran*, pp. 127–28.

24. Q1 (1906–9), 111–12.   25. Q2, 257.

26. *Ibid.*, pp. 285–86, 311–14; Q3, 36.

27. League of Nations, *Report on an Investigation Into the Sanitary Conditions in Persia*, undertaken on behalf of the Health Committee of the League of Nations at the request of the Persian Government by John Gilmour (Geneva, League of Nations Health Organization, 1925), p. 12. Hereafter cited as *Report on Sanitary Conditions*.

28. See *ibid.*, pp. 60–61, 31–32.

29. Q4, 224.

30. *Report on Sanitary Conditions*, pp. 26–27.

31. Q5, 253; Q7, 24–25; Q10, 285–87.

32. Q7, 198–99.

33. See *Report on Sanitary Conditions*, pp. 14–15.

34. Elwell-Sutton, *Modern Iran*, p. 129.

35. Q10, 599.

36. Q12 (1939–41), 180–86.

37. See Elwell-Sutton, *Modern Iran*, pp. 129–30.

38. Q11, 359–64.

39. See Elwell-Sutton, *Modern Iran*, p. 128.

40. See Rosalie Slaughter Morton, *A Doctor's Holiday in Iran* (New York, 1940), pp. 240–45.

41. See Q4, 222–23; Q7, 367–75, 380, 383; Q8, 512, 520–22; Q10, 501–20; Q11, 443; Q12, 482–94.

42. See *Report on Sanitary Conditions*, pp. 63–64.

CHAPTER FIVE

1. A. Matin-Daftari, *A'iyn-e Dadresi-ye Modoni va Bazargani* [Civil and Commercial Court Procedure] (Tehran, 1945), p. 8.

2. 'Ali Shayegan, *Hoquq-e Modoni-ye Iran* [The Civil Code of Iran] (Tehran, 1945), pp. 29–30.

3. Matin-Daftari [Court Procedure], pp. 8–10.

4. Shayegan [Civil Code], p. 30.

5. See *ibid.*; and also Matin-Daftari [Court Procedure], pp. 10–11.

6. *Ibid.*, pp. 8–17.

7. Q5, 429–30.   8. *Ibid.*, pp. 69–164.

9. As cited by A. Matin-Daftari, *La Suppression des capitulations en Perse* (Paris, 1930), pp. 179–80.

10. Issa Sadiq, *Modern Persia and her Educational System* (New York, 1931), pp. 24–25.

11. Matin-Daftari [Court Procedure], p. 12.

12. The *feqh* books used as the source for this code were *Sharh Lam'a*, *Sharayi'*, and *Makasib*, the three most authoritative *shi'ah* compilations. The French, the Belgian, and particularly the Swiss civil codes were the European models utilized by the drafting committee. See Shayegan [Civil Code], pp. 35–39.

13. Q7, 40–43.   14. Q8, 1–4.

15. Matin-Daftari [Court Procedure], pp. 13–14.

16. Shayegan [Civil Code], p. 36.

17. Q8, 67–71.   18. *Ibid.*, pp. 90–132.

19. Q10, 98–100.

20. Matin-Daftari [Court Procedure], p. 1.

21. *Ibid.*, p. 16.

22. Q11, 94–257.

23. Matin-Daftari [Court Procedure], p. 17.

24. Q12, 3–62.

25. See Shayegan [Civil Code], pp. 33–38.

26. Q11, 95.

27. See Matin-Daftari [Court Procedure], pp. 19; 23; 33–34; 161–62, 174.

28. *Ibid.*, pp. 194–244; 245–59; 296–301; 319–20; 459, 509.

29. See K. Tammadon, *Sazeman-e Modoni-ye Iran* [The Civil Structure of Iran] (Tehran, 1945), pp. 26–30.

30. See Q4, 222–23, 225; Q5, 300–301; Q7, 367, 370; Q8, 501; Q11, 443.

31. *Ibid.*, p. 132.

32. Shayegan [Civil Code], pp. 287–88.

33. Q2, 467–68.

34. Q4, 116–18; Q5, 62–65.

35. Q7, 86–88.   36. Q8, 154–60.   37. Q2, 467.

38. Q8, 154.   39. *Ibid.*, pp. 156–59.

40. Q4, 140.

41. See S. Amir-'Ala'i, *Mojazat-e E'dam* [Capital Punishment] (Tehran, n.d.).

42. Q5, 79–85, 131, 160.

43. *Ibid.*, pp. 120, 127–38.
44. See Shayegan [Civil Code], pp. 273–83.
45. The laws pertaining to marriage were those passed on August 14, 1931, and May 19, 1937. Other laws pertaining to marriage and the family are articles 1031–1179 and 1195–1206 of the Civil Code of 1939.
46. See Shayegan [Civil Code], pp. 273–83.
47. Q8, 133–34.
48. See Shayegan [Civil Code], pp. 295, 297–98.
49. *Ibid.*, pp. 315–16.
50. *Ibid.*, pp. 316–18.
51. *Ibid.*, p. 339.
52. *Ibid.*, p. 348.
53. See *ibid.*, pp. 373–74.
54. *Ibid.*, p. 377.
55. Q11, 61–62.

CHAPTER SIX

1. Sadiq, *Modern Persia and Her Educational System*, p. 53.
2. Elwell-Sutton, *Modern Iran*, p. 132.
3. See above, p. 33.
4. Q2, 251–55.   5. *Ibid.*, pp. 343–46.
6. *Ibid.*, articles 9–11, 16, 18, 26, and 28.
7. *Ibid.*, p. 321.
8. *Ibid.*, p. 579. Of this group fifteen were to study pedagogy, eight were enrolled in military academies, and the remaining seven were to pursue scientific and technical training.
9. Elwell-Sutton, *Modern Iran*, p. 133.
10. Q4, 65–67.
11. *Ibid.*, articles 12 and 14.
12. Q7, 189; Sadiq, pp. 77–78.
13. Q7, 193.
14. Q9 (1933–35), 14–27.
15. Elwell-Sutton, *Modern Iran*, p. 139.
16. Sadiq, p. 53.
17. *Cf.* Overseas Consultants, Inc., *Report on the Seven-Year Development Plan for the Plan Organization of the Imperial Government of Iran* (New York, 1949), I, 22.
18. Q7, 196–98.
19. See Sadiq, pp. 53–54.
20. Q7, 199–200.
21. Elwell-Sutton, *Modern Iran*, p. 141.
22. Q4, 270.   23. Q4, 163, 164, 177.
24. *Rahnema-ye Daneshgah-e Tehran* [The Bulletin of the University of Tehran] (Tehran, 1938), I, 55.
25. Q12, 209–15.
26. Elwell-Sutton, *Modern Iran*, p. 137.
27. *Ibid.*, p. 138.

28. *Ibid.*
29. See Bozorg 'Alavi, *Panjah va Se Nafar* [The Fifty-three] (Tehran?, 194?), pp. 3ff.
30. See above, p. 38.
31. Q8, 355.
32. Elwell-Sutton, *Modern Iran,* p. 138.
33. *Sadiq,* p. 39.
34. For the full text of the resolution of the Council of Ministers of June 6, 1936, see Iran, Ministry of Education, *Adult Education* (Tehran, 1938).
35. *Ibid.,* p. 1.
36. *Ibid.,* p. 2. In 1936 the official rate of exchange was $1.00 = 18 R's.
37. *Ibid.,* p. 4.
38. *Ibid.,* pp. 5–6.
39. *Ibid.,* pp. 18–20.
40. *Ibid.,* p. 4.
41. *Ibid.,* pp. 20–21.
42. *Ibid.,* p. 26.
43. *Ibid.,* p. 50.
44. Elwell-Sutton, *Modern Iran,* p. 143.
45. *Ibid.*
46. *Ibid.,* p. 48.
47. *Ibid.*
48. See Elwell-Sutton, *Modern Iran,* pp. 130–31.
49. *Ibid.,* p. 131.
50. Q4, 232–37, 251–54, 258–62; Q5, 319–20, 343.
51. See Elwell-Sutton, *Modern Iran,* pp. 141–42.
52. Sadiq, pp. 83–85.
53. *Ibid.,* pp. 85ff.
54. Overseas Consultants, Inc., *Report,* I, 20.

CHAPTER SEVEN

1. Various primary sources and secondary works dealing with economic problems of modern Iran are available to the interested reader. For reliable primary sources see Bank Melli Iran, *Annual Reports and Statements* (Tehran, 1928–   ), and Great Britain, Department of Overseas Trade, *Economic Conditions in Persia* (London, 1923–   ). For a general and comprehensive survey of the Iranian economy, see Overseas Consultants, Inc., *Report on the Seven-Year Development Plan of Iran.*

2. A more revealing sociological approach, along the lines suggested by Margaret Mead, ed., *Cultural Patterns and Technical Change* (Paris, 1953), is at present ruled out owing to the absence of basic field research.

3. Q5, 190–93, 429–30.

4. The absence of reliable statistical data prevents both qualitative and quantitative appraisal of the state lands. Gideon Hadary, "The Agrarian Reform Problem in Iran," *The Middle East Journal,* V

(1951), 181–96, estimates that the state owned 10 per cent of the claimed land. But this estimate was made in 1950, after large areas of state lands had passed into private hands during the reign of Reza Shah.

5. Q5, 433–35.

6. See Ansari, "Malekiyat-e Arzi dar Iran" [Land Ownership in Iran], *Mardom,* Year II, 5th period, No. 9 (Tehran, June 1948), pp. 91–97.

7. Q11, 2–3. (Bearing in mind that the purchasers of these lands were also the main beneficiaries of the Bank, one can appreciate the double investment value of this measure.)

8. Q4, 213–17.

9. See Sheean, *The New Persia,* pp. 83 ff.

10. Statement by Teymurtash, the Court Minister, as cited in Sheean, p. 138.

11. Q7, 30–39.

12. See above, p. 37.

13. For a history of Iran's tariff system see Hadi Khorassani, *Le Régime douanier de l'Iran* (Paris, 1937), chaps. 2 and 3.

14. Q4, 217–18, 225–26; Q5, 286, 287, 294–97; Q7, 383; Q8, 493–512.

15. See Khorassani, chap. 3.

16. Q12, 229–451.   17. Q4, 213–17.

18. Sheean, p. 83.

19. See the illustrations in Sheean, p. 128.

20. Q4, 227; Q5, 290–94; Q7, 383; Q8, 493–512; Q10, 501–20; Q11, 443.

21. Q5, 2–59; Q8, 221–334.   22. Q11, 28.

23. For an analytical study of this problem see Gholam Reza Moghadam, "Iran's Foreign Trade Policy and Economic Development in the Interwar Period" (unpublished doctoral dissertation, Stanford University, 1956), pp. 42, 62, 120–28.

24. Q7, 2–7.

25. See Moghadam, pp. 126–27.

26. Q5, 316–23; Q12, 528–33. The estimated total state revenue in 1924 was 236,864,250 rials. In 1941 it had risen to 3,613,768,718 rials.

27. From a speech given in the Majlis in 1942, as cited in A. C. Millspaugh, *Americans in Persia* (Washington, D.C., 1946), p. 54.

28. For a general survey of Iran's economy early in the regime of Reza Shah, see Moustafa Fateh, *The Economic Position of Persia* (London, 1926). For a detailed statistical survey of the country's economy after the Second World War, see Overseas Consultants, Inc., *Report.*

29. Q5, 433–35.

30. *Ibid.,* p. 435. Italics mine.

31. For an excellent study of this subject see A. K. S. Lampton, *Landlord and Peasant in Persia* (New York, 1953).

32. See above, pp. 113–14.

33. In 1950 it was estimated that *waqf* lands comprised 25 per cent of the claimed land in Iran. See Hadary, pp. 184–85.

34. See Ansari, *loc. cit.,* pp. 95–97.

35. An estimated 65 per cent of the total claimed land was owned privately in 1950. *Cf.* Hadary, pp. 184–85.

36. Ansari, *loc. cit.*, pp. 95–97.

37. Javan [Foundations of Law], III, 558.

38. For the full text see Q11, 4–8.

39. Left up to future directives of the Ministry of the Interior (see article 8, *ibid.*, p. 7) and never acted upon.

40. See United Nations, Department of Economic Affairs, *Land Reform* (New York, 1951), pp. 15–17.

41. Q11, 8–9.   42. Q5, 178–79.   43. Q7, 1–2.

44. *Ibid.*, pp. 12–15.   45. Q8, 608–10.

46. Q7, 380; Q11, 112.   47. Q5, 290–94.

48. Q7, 380–83; Q8, 501, 512–22; Q10, 501–20.

49. Hadary, *loc. cit.*, p. 183.

50. See Lyle J. Hayden, "Living Standards in Rural Iran: A Case Study," *The Middle East Journal*, III (1949), 140–50.

51. See Josephine Vogt, "A Study of Home and Family Life in Rural Iran" (unpublished study prepared for the Near East Foundation, New York, 1950), pp. 5–6

52. For reliable firsthand descriptions see Lambton; Hayden is also illuminating.

53. Hadary, *loc. cit.*, p. 181.   54. *Ibid.*, p. 185.

55. Q8, 702–3, 705–7.   56. *Ibid.*, pp. 224, 640, 659–60.

57. For a definitive study of Iranian foreign trade policy and an otherwise illuminating analysis of Iran's economic development during the interwar period, see Moghadam.   58. See above, pp. 116–17.

59. For actual cases of this form of Great Power Pressure and Exploitation, see Shuster, *The Strangling of Persia*. See also M. Navai, *Les Relations économiques irano-russes* (Paris, 1935).

60. See Moghadam, pp. 35–38, 50.   61. *Ibid.*, p. 36.

62. See *ibid.*, Table 10, p. 59.   63. See *ibid.*, Table 26, p. 120.

64. The exploitation and export of Iranian oil by a British-government-controlled company cannot, for reasons far beyond the scope of this study, be counted as an integral part of Iran's economy during the interwar period. For a discussion of this question see Moghadam, pp. 35–36.   65. See above, pp. 118–19.

66. Russia accounted for 74.7 per cent of Iran's total foreign trade in 1912. See Moghadam, Table 1, p. 39.

67. For the text of the Foreign Trade Monopoly Act, see Q8, 171–93. It was supplemented in 1932 and partially revised in 1936 and 1941.

68. Q7, 7–11. Thus Iran became one of the first countries to establish foreign exchange controls in the thirties.

69. Q10, 123–24.   70. Q7, 172–80; Q10, 63–73; Q11, 1.

71. See below, p. 133.

72. See Moghadam, Tables 40, 41, 42 on pp. 202, 204, 213.

73. For an appraisal of the German practices see Frank C. Child, "German Exchange Control, 1931–1938: A Study in Exploitation" (unpublished doctoral dissertation, Stanford University, 1954).

74. For the most comprehensive work on the roads and communi-

cations of Iran, see G. Fuerstenau, *Das Verkehrswesen Irans* (n.p., 1935).

75. Q5, 435.　　76. See Moghadam, p. 102.
77. Q5, 185–89.　　78. *Ibid.,* pp. 199–200.
79. See Monterisi, *Iran,* pp. 323–24.
80. Q8, 514–16.
81. Q7, 375–80; Q8, 512–22; Q10, 501–20; Q11, 443–62; Q12, 490–94.
82. See *Nakhostin Kongere-ye Nevisandegan-e Iran* [Report on the First Congress of Iranian Writers] (Tehran, 1947), pp. 36–38.
83. See *Bank Melli Iran Bulletin* (May–November, 1940), pp. 82–91. At the unrealistic official exchange rate of the time this was over $140 million.
84. See Moghadam, pp. 110–11.
85. Q5, 363, 367.　　86. *Ibid.,* pp. 175–78.
87. Q7, 1–2.　　88. Q5, 178–79; Q7, 28–29.
89. Q10, 502.　　90. Q5, 279–81.　　91. Q7, 221–22.
92. Q4, 227–28.　　93. Q7, 376; Q8, 519.
94. For useful accounts of industrialization in the Iran of Reza Shah, see 'Abdollah Malekpur, *Die Wirtschaftsverfassung Irans* (Berlin 1935); Angelo Polacco, *L'Iran di Reza Scia Pahlavi* (Venice, 1937); and K. Grunwald, "L'industrializzamento della Persia," *Oriente Moderno,* XVIII (1938), 102–8; as well as Overseas Consultants, Inc., *op. cit.*
95. Q5, 283–86, 301–2.　　96. Q11, 449–51.
97. Q5, 178–79.　　98. Q8, 195–96.
99. *Ibid.,* pp. 206–7.　　100. Q9, 483–504.
101. The strong resemblance of Reza Shah's economic policy to Mussolini's concepts of the corporate state is undeniable. This fact was not lost upon Italian observers, who provide a sympathetic view of these policies. For the best example of this see Polacco.
102. For full details see Overseas Consultants, Inc., *Report,* IV.
103. For the output of Iranian textile industries see *ibid.,* pp. 134–46.
104. See Moghadam, Table 43, p. 218.
105. See Overseas Consultants, Inc., *Report,* IV, 116ff.
106. In 1959 the Iranian government reopened negotiations with a German concern for setting up a steel mill in Iran.
107. For the political background and struggles over Iran's oil, see L. P. Elwell-Sutton, *Persian Oil: A Study in Power Politics* (London, 1955). For a survey of the economic and technological growth of the Iranian oil industry, see Anglo-Iranian Oil Company, *Fifty Years of Oil* (London, 1952).
108. League of Nations, *Memorandum from the Imperial Government of Persia* (Geneva, 1933), p. 4.
109. For the text of the new agreement concluded in 1933, see International Court of Justice, *Anglo-Iranian Oil Company Case, United Kingdom vs. Iran* (The Hague, 1952), pp. 258–70. For data on the rise of the price of oil, see International Monetary Fund, *International Financial Statistics* (Washington, 1955), p. 23.

110. See Moghadam, Tables 9 and 19, pp. 57, 82; Tables 8 and 18, pp. 55, 77.
111. Q10, 292–337.   112. Q8, 365–68.
113. Q7, 391; Q8, 518; Q10, 521, 523.   114. *Ibid.,* pp. 506–7.
115. For the full text of this law see Q11, 28–32.
116. *Ibid.,* pp. 366–92.
117. See Laurence Lockhart, *Famous Cities of Iran* (Brentford, England, 1939), pp. 11–13.
118. For an architect's view of the modernization of Tehran, see S. Abdalian, *La Région de Tehran* (Tehran, 194?), pp. 147–57.
119. Q7, 377.
120. A *mulla's* remarks in 1942 are indicative of the clerical reaction to Reza Shah: "We were afraid that Farangis [Europeans] would come and desecrate our graves, but our own government turned out to be worse than the heathen Farangi. What is left of our faith now?" Quoted by Ahmad Kasravi, *Emruz Che Bayad Kard* [Collection of Speeches] (Tabriz, 1942), p. 45.
121. Q12, 199–206.   122. Q10, 597–612.

CONCLUSION

1. See above, Chapter Three.
2. Arnold T. Wilson, *Persia* (London, 1932), p. ix.
3. *Ibid.,* pp. 379–80.
4. His book *The Pageant of Persia* (Indianapolis, 1936) was written under the pseudonym Henry Filmer.
5. See *ibid.,* pp. 360 ff.
6. Sadiq, *Modern Persia and Her Educational System,* p. 40. For other evidences of anti-clericalism see above, Chapter Three.
7. For the best examples see Fateh, *The Economic Position of Persia,* and Zabihollah Fasihi, *A'iyne-ye Sepas* [Appreciations of Reza Shah] (Tehran, 1950).
8. Sirdar Ikbal 'Ali Shah, *Eastward to Persia* (London, 1931?).
9. *Ibid.,* pp. 180–86
10. See Essad-Bey, *Resa Schah: Feldherr, Kaiser, Reformator,* pp. 205–12.
11. See Hezb Tudeh Iran, *Mamlekat-e bi Naqshe va bi Hadaf* [The Country Without Plans or Goals] (Tehran, 1952), pp. 8–10. It is interesting to note that the Soviet views of Reza Shah and his reforms had been critical from the start. Because of his role in the liquidation of the Soviet Republic of Gilan he was viewed with dislike. The role of a nationalist movement against imperialism generally assigned to Kemalism in Turkey was only reluctantly and infrequently ascribed by Soviet propaganda to Reza Shah's movement. He was accused of Fascism and of allying himself with the reactionary ruling class. For an early appraisal see M. Pavlovich and S. Iranskii, *Persiia v Bor'be za Nezavisimost'* (Moscow, 1925); for recent Soviet-Marxist views see I. M. Reisner and B. K. Rubtsova, eds., *Novaia*

Istoriia Stran Zarubezhnogo Vostoka, 2 vols. (Moscow, 1952), and M. S. Ivanov, *Ocherk Istorii Irana* (Moscow, 1952).

12. Ann K. S. Lambton, "Persia," *Journal of the Royal Central Asian Society*, XXXI, Part I (1944), 8–22.

13. *Ibid.*, p. 14.

14. Lewis V. Thomas and Richard N. Frye, *The United States and Turkey and Iran* (Cambridge, Mass., 1951), pp. 224–28.

15. See *ibid.*, pp. 224 ff.

16. See Ann K. S. Lambton, *Islamic Society in Persia* (London, 1954).

17. See Joseph M. Upton, *The History of Modern Iran: An Interpretation* (Cambridge, Mass., 1960). This is an illuminating attempt at providing some keys for understanding recent Iranian history.

18. Ann K. S. Lambton, "Impact of the West on Persia," *International Affairs*, XXXIII (1957), 25.

19. These anonymously published pamphlets supply no information about the place and date of publication.

20. See *Now Bahar*, No. 4 (October 16, 1922), pp. 61–63, as cited in Bahar [Political Parties], pp. 247–53.

21. See Javan [Foundations of Law].

22. *Ibid.*, III, 544–58.

23. See T. Cuyler Young, "The Problem of Westernization in Modern Iran," *The Middle East Journal*, II (1948), 47–59.

24. For a summary of Toynbee's views on Islam, see his *Civilization on Trial* (New York, 1948), chap. 10.

25. See H. A. R. Gibb in the concluding chapter of Young, ed., *Near Eastern Culture and Society*, pp. 221–39.

26. *Ibid.*, p. 233.   27. *Ibid.*, p. 234.   28. *Ibid.*, p. 239.

BIBLIOGRAPHY

GOVERNMENT AND INTERNATIONAL DOCUMENTS

Great Britain, Foreign Office. Agreement Between the United Kingdom and Persia Modifying the Commercial Convention of February 9, 1903, Treaty Series, 1920, No. 17. London, 1920.

Iran, Majlis Showra-ye Melli. A'iynname-ye Dakheli-ye Majlis Showra-ye Melli (Parliamentary Rules). Tehran, 1949.

———. Majmu'e-ye Qavanin-e Mowzu'eh va Mosavvabat-e Majlis (Record of Parliamentary Legislation), 1906–46, 14 vols., sessions 1–14 (1st–9th sessions), 2d ed. Tehran, 1938–47.

———. Mozakerat-e Majlis Showra-ye Melli (Parliamentary Debates), 1906–23, 4 vols., sessions 1–4, 2d ed. Tehran, 1946–51.

———. Osul-e Mohakemat-e Jaza'i (Penal Code). Tehran, 1947.

Iran, Ministry of Education. Adult Education in Iran: 1938–1939. Tehran, 1938.

Iran, Ministry of Foreign Affairs. Nashriye (Bulletin). Vols. I and II, Nos. 1–5. Tehran, 1949–50.

Iran, Qanun-e Asasi va Motammam-e An (The Constitution of 1906 and Its Supplement). Tehran, n.d.

Iran, Vezarat-e Farhang, Edare-ye Amuzesh-e 'Ali. Rahnema-ye Daneshgah-e Tehran (The Bulletin of the University of Tehran), 2 vols. Tehran, 1938.

International Court of Justice. Anglo-Iranian Oil Company Case, United Kingdom vs. Iran. The Hague, 1952.

International Monetary Fund. International Financial Statistics. Washington, D.C., April 1955.

League of Nations. Commission of Enquiry into the Production of Opium in Persia. Geneva, 1927.

———. Memorandum from the Imperial Government of Persia. Geneva, January 19, 1933.

———. Report on an Investigation into the Sanitary Conditions in Persia. Geneva, 1925.

United Nations, Department of Economic Affairs. Land Reform. New York, 1951.

GENERAL BOOKS AND ARTICLES

Abdalian, S. La Région de Tehran. Tehran, 194?.

Afschar, Mahmoud. La Politique européenne en Perse. Berlin, 1921.

'Alavi, Bozorg. Panjah va Se Nafar (The Fifty-three). [Tehran?, 194?.]

'Amid, Hoquq-e Modoni (Civil Rights). Tehran, n.d.

Aminian, Sohrab. Qanun-e Asasi ya Khunbaha-ye Iran (The Constitution, or the Lifeblood of Iran). Tehran, 1945.

Amir-'Ala'i, Shams ed-Din. Mojazat-e E'dam (Capital Punishment). Tehran, [194?].

Amirian, A. M. Condition politique, sociale et juridique de la Femme en Iran. Paris, 1938.

Anglo-Iranian Oil Company. Fifty Years of Oil. London, 1952.

Ansari. "Malekiyat-e Arzi dar Iran" (Land Ownership in Iran). *Mardom,* Year II, fifth period, No. 9 (June 1948), pp. 91–97.

Arbery, A. J., ed. The Legacy of Persia. Oxford, 1953.

Bahar, Muhammad Taqi. Tarikh-e Mokhtasar-e Ahzab-e Siyasi-e Iran: Enqeraz-e Qajariye (A Short History of Political Parties in Iran: The Fall of the Qajars). Tehran, 1942.

Balfour, James M. Recent Happenings in Persia. London, 1922.

Barimani, Lotf-'Ali. Asrar-e Amlak-e Shahanshahi (The Secrets of the Crown Lands). Tehran, 1945.

Bazhang, M. Areman-e Iran (The Destiny of Iran). Tehran, 1948.

Behruz, Zabihollah. Zaban-e Iran: Farsi ya 'Arabi? (The Language of Iran: Persian or Arabic?). Tehran, 1934.

Bell, Gertrude. Persian Pictures. 3d ed. London, 1947.

Browne, Edward Granville. A History of Persian Literature in Modern Times: A.D. 1500–1924. Cambridge, England, 1924.

———. The Persian Crisis of December 1911: How It Arose and Whither It May Lead Us. Cambridge, England, 1912.

———. The Persian Revolution. Cambridge, England, 1910.

———. The Press and Poetry of Modern Persia. Cambridge, England, 1914.

———. A Year Amongst the Persians. Cambridge, England, 1927.

Child, Frank C. German Exchange Control, 1931–1938: A Study in Exploitation. Unpublished doctoral dissertation, Stanford University, Stanford, California, 1954.

Childs, James Rives (pseudonym Henry Filmer). The Pageant of Persia. Indianapolis, 1936.

Coan, Fredrick G. Yesterdays in Persia and Kurdistan. Claremont, California, 1939.

Cook, Nilla Cram. "The Theatre and Ballet Arts of Iran." *Middle East Journal,* III (October 1949), 406–420.

Curzon, George N., Earl of Kedleston. Persia and the Persian Question. London, 1892.

Dickson, William Edmund Ritchie. East Persia, a Backwater of the Great War. London, 1924.

Donaldson, Bess Allen. The Wild Rue: A Study of Muhammadan Magic and Folklore in Iran. London, 1938.

Donaldson, Dwight M. The Shi'ite Religion: A History of Islam in Persia and Irak. London, 1933.

Dowlat-Abadi, Yahya. Hayat-e Yahya (Autobiography). Tehran, 1949.

Ehteshami, Abolhasan. Bazigaran-e Siyasat (Political Figures). Tehran, 1949.

Elgood, Cyril. A Medical History of Persia and the Eastern Caliphate from the Earliest Times Until the Year A.D. 1932. Cambridge, England, 1931.

Elwell-Sutton, L. P. A Guide to Iranian Area Study. Ann Arbor, Michigan, 1952.

——. Modern Iran. London, 1944.

——. Persian Oil: A Study in Power Politics. London, 1955.

Encyclopedia of Islam, The. 5 vols. London, 1938.

Esfandiary, H. A. "Education in Iran." *Middle Eastern Affairs,* II, Nos. 6–7 (June–July 1951), 225–28.

Esfehani, 'Abdolhosein. "Zan-e Sharqi va Ayande-ye Khanevade" (The Oriental Woman and the Future of the Family). *Rastakhiz,* II, No. 6 (September 1925), 9–16.

Essad-Bey. Resa Schah: Feldherr, Kaiser, Reformator. Vienna, 1936.

Farman, Hafez F. Iran: a Selected and Annotated Bibliography. Washington, D.C., 1951.

Farmanfarmaian, Hafez. "The Fall of the Qajar Dynasty." Unpublished doctoral dissertation, Georgetown University, 1954.

Fasihi, Zabihollah. A'iyne-ye Sepas (Appreciations of Reza Shah). Tehran, 1950.

Fateh, Moustafa. The Economic Position of Persia. London, 1926.

Fatemi, Nasrollah Saifpour. Diplomatic History of Persia 1917–1923: Anglo-Russian Power Politics in Iran. New York, 1952.

Ferguson, Margaret. Bid Time Return. London, 1941.

Field, Henry. Contributions to the Anthropology of Iran. Chicago, 1939.

Fraser, David. Persia and Turkey in Revolt. Edinburgh and London, 1910.

Frye, Richard N. Iran. New York, 1953.

——, ed. Islam and the West. The Hague, 1957.

Fuerstenau, G. Das Verkehrswesen Irans. N.p., 1935.

Furon, Raymond. L'Iran: Perse et Afghanistan. Paris, 1951.

Gail, Marzieh. Persia and the Victorians. London, 1951.

Gibb, H. A. R. Modern Trends in Islam. Chicago, 1947.

Gibb, H. A. R., and Bowen, Harold. Islamic Society and the West: A Study of the Impact of Western Civilization on Moslem Culture in the Near East. London, 1950.

Gobineau, Arthur Count de. Les Religions et les philosophies dans l'Asie centrale. 2 vols. Paris, 1865.

Groseclose, Elgin. Introduction to Iran. New York, 1947.

Grunwald, K. "L'industrializzamento della Persia." *Oriente Moderno*, XVIII (February 1938), 102–8.

Haas, William S. Iran. New York, 1946.

Hadary, Gideon. "The Agrarian Reform Problem in Iran." *The Middle East Journal*, V (Spring 1951), 181–96.

Hamzavi, A. H. "Iran's Future: Some Lessons from the Past." *Journal of the Royal Central Asian Society*, XXXI, Parts III and IV (July-October 1944), 273–80.

Haqq-e Daf'-e Sharr va Qiyam bar Zedd-e Zolm (The Right to Resist Evil and Rise Against Tyranny). N.p., n.d.

Hayden, Lyle J. "Living Standards in Rural Iran: A Case Study." *The Middle East Journal*, III (April 1949), 140–50.

Hekmat, 'Ali-Asghar. Parsi-ye Naghz (Pure Persian). Tehran, 1951.

Hesam-Mo'ezzi, Najafqoli. Tarikh-e Ravabet-e Siyasi-ye Iran ba Doniya (A History of the Diplomatic Relations of Iran with the World). 2 vols. Tehran, 1946–47.

Hezb Tudeh Iran. Mamlekat-e bi Naqshe va bi Hadaf (The Country Without Plans or Goals). Tehran, 1952.

Homayunfar, Ebrahim. Naft (Oil). Tehran, 1945.

Ikbal, Sirdar Ali Shah. Eastward to Persia. London, [1931?].

Iqbal, Muhammad. Iran. Madras, 1946.

Iran: Past and Present. Tehran, 1950.

Iran va Jang-e Farangestan (Iran and the European War). Berlin, 1915.

Ivanov, M. S. Babidskoye Vostaniya v Iranye: 1848–1852. Moscow, 1939.

———. Ocherk Istorii Irana. Moscow, 1952.

Javan, Musa. Mabani-ye Hoquq (Foundations of Law). 5 vols. Tehran, 1948–51.

Karimi, Bahman. Mirza Abolqasem Qa'em-Maqam. Tehran, [194?].

Kasravi, Ahmad. Afsaran-e Ma (Our Officers). Tehran, 1944.

———. Az Sazeman-e Melal-e Mottafeq Che Natije Khahad Bud? (What Can Be Expected from the United Nations Organization?). Tehran, 1945.

———. Dar Pasokh-e Bad-Khahan (Collection of Speeches). Tehran, 1944.

———. Dar Rah-e Siyasat (Collection of Speeches). Tehran, 1946.

———. Emruz Chare Chist? (Collection of Speeches). Tehran, 1945.

———. Emruz Che Bayad Kard? (Collection of Speeches). Tabriz, 1942.

———. Haji-haye Anbar-dar Che Dini Darand? (Collection of Speeches). Tehran, 1945.

————. Mashrute va Azadegan (Collection of Speeches). Tehran, 1947.

————. Peydayesh-e Amrika (Origins of America). Tehran, 1945.

————. Qanun-e Dadgari (Law of Judgment). Tehran, 1945.

————. Sarnevesht-e Iran Che Khahad Bud? (Collection of Speeches). Tehran, 1945.

————. Tarikh-e Hejdah Sale-ye Azerbaijan; Ya Dastan-e Mashrute-ye Iran (Eighteen Years of Azerbaijanian History; or the Story of the Constitutional Movement in Iran). 6 vols. Tehran, 1939–41.

————. Yekom-e Azar: 1323 (Collection of Speeches). Tehran, 1944.

Keeling, Cecil. Pictures from Persia. London, n.d.

Kermani, 'Abdolhosein. Haftad-o do Mellat (Seventy-two Nations). Berlin, 1925.

Khajenuri, Ebrahim. Bazigaran-e 'Asr-e Tala'i (The Heroes of the Golden Age). 2 vols. Tehran, 1941–42.

Khal'atbari, Arsalan. Aristokrasi-ye Iran (Iranian Aristocracy). Tehran, 1945.

Khal'atbari, Muhammad Vali. Sharh-e Zendegani (Autobiography). Tehran, 1949.

Khodayar-Mohebbi, Manuchehr. Sharik-e Mard (Man's Partner). Tehran, 1946.

Khorassani, Hadi. Le Régime douanier de l'Iran. Paris, 1937.

Kiyanuri. Mobarezat-e Tabaqati (Class Struggle). Tehran, 1948.

Kohn, Hans. A History of Nationalism in the East. London, 1929.

————. Nationalism and Imperialism in the Hither East. New York, 1932.

————. Western Civilization in the Near East. New York, 1936.

Lachini, Abolqasem, ed. Ahvalat va Dastkhatha-ye 'Abbas Mirza Qajar Nayebos-Saltane (The Times and Papers of Abbas Mirza). Tehran, 1947.

Lambton, Ann K. S. "Impact of the West on Persia." *International Affairs,* XXXIII (January 1957), 12–25.

————. Islamic Society in Persia. London, 1954.

————. Landlord and Peasant in Persia. New York, 1953.

————. "Persia." *Journal of the Royal Central Asian Society,* XXXI, Part I (January 1944), 8–22.

————. "Some Aspects of the Situation in Persia." *Asiatic Review,* XXXIX, No. 140 (October 1943), 420–25.

Lang, David Marshall. The Last Years of the Georgian Monarchy, 1658–1832. New York, 1957.

Lee, Lester A. The Reforms of Reza Shah: 1925–1941. Unpublished master's thesis, Stanford University, Stanford, California, 1950.

Lenczowski, George. Russia and the West in Iran, 1918–1948: A Study in Big Power Rivalry. Ithaca, N.Y., 1949.

Lerner, Daniel. The Passing of the Traditional Society: Modernizing the Middle East. Glencoe, Illinois, 1958.

Leseur, Emile. Diktatori va Soqut-e Seid Ziya'eddin (Dictatorship and the Fall of Seid Ziya'eddin). Tehran, 1943.

Lockhart, Laurence. Famous Cities of Iran. Brentford, England, 1939.

Mahmud, Mahmud. Tarikh-e Ravabet-e Siyasi-ye Iran va Engelis dar Qarn-e Nuzdahom (History of the Anglo-Iranian Diplomatic Relations in the Nineteenth Century). 3 vols. Tehran, 1949–50.

Makki, Hosein. Ketab-e Siyah (The Black Paper). Tehran, 1951.

———. Tarikh-e Bist Sale-ye Iran (Twenty Years of Iranian History). 3 vols. Tehran, 1945–46.

Malekpur, 'Abdollah. Die Wirtschaftsverfassung Irans. Berlin, 1935.

Malekzade, Mehdi. Tarikh-e Enqelab-e Mashruityat-e Iran (A History of the Constitutional Revolution in Iran). 3 vols. Tehran, 1949–51.

Malkom Khan, Mirza. Majmu'e-ye Asar (Collected Works). Tehran, 1948.

Manshur-Gorgani, M. 'A. Siyasat-e Dowlat-e Showravi dar Iran az 1296 to 1306 (Soviet Policy in Iran from 1917 to 1927). Tehran, 1948.

———. Siyasat-e Engelis dar Khalij-e Fars va Jaba'er-e Bahrein (British Policy in the Persian Gulf and the Bahrain Islands). Tehran, 1946.

Manuchehriyan, Mehrangiz. Enteqad-e Qavanin-e Asasi va Modoni va Keifari-ye Iran az Nazar-e Hoquq-e Zan (A Feminist Critique of the Civil and Penal Codes of Iran). Tehran, 1949.

Massé, Henri. Croyances et coutumes Persanes: suivies de contes et chansons populaires. 2 vols. Paris, 1938.

Matin-Daftari, Ahmad. A'iyn-e Dadresi-ye Modoni va Bazargani (Civil and Commercial Court Procedure). Tehran, 1945.

———. Dekhalat-e Mostaqim-e Dowlat dar Eqtesad-e Keshvar (The Direct Intervention of the State in the Economy of the Country). Tehran, 1945.

———. La Suppression des capitulations en Perse: L'Ancien régime et le statut actuel des étrangers dans l'Empire du Lion et Soleil. Paris, 1930.

Mead, Margaret, ed. Cultural Patterns and Technical Change. Paris, 1953.

Mehdevi, Anne Sinclair. Persian Adventure. New York, 1953.

Mehrkhah, Ne'matollah, ed. Ketab-e Reza Shah (Appreciations of Reza Shah). Tehran, 1946.

Melzig, Herbert. Resa Shah, der Aufstieg Irans und die Grossmachte. Stuttgart, 1936.

Messina, G. Un Viaggio nell'Iran. Rome, 1937.

The Middle East, 1948. London, 1948.

The Middle East, 1950. London, 1950.

Millspaugh, Arthur C. American in Persia. Washington, D.C., 1946.

Mirza Muhammad Kalantar-e Fars. Ruzname (Diary). Tehran, 1946.

Mo'ayyad-Amini, Davud. Farar-e Muhammad 'Ali Shah (The Escape of Muhammad Ali Shah). Tehran, 1945.

Moazzami, Abdollah. Essai sur la condition des étrangers en Iran. Paris, 1937.

Moghadam, Gholam Reza. Iran's Foreign Trade Policy and Economic Development in the Interwar Period. Unpublished doctoral dissertation, Stanford University, Stanford, California, 1956.

Mojtahedi, Mehdi. Rejal-e Azerbaijan dar 'Asr-e Mashrutiyat (The Leaders of Azerbaijan during the Constitutional Period). Tehran, 1948.

Montazam. Mellat va Melliyat (Nation and Nationality). Tehran, 1948.

Monterisi, Mario. Iran. Manuali di Politica Internazionale, No. 32. Milan, 1941.

Moqayyad (pseudonym). Konjkaviha-ye Zendan (Reflections in Prison). Tehran, [194?].

Morton, Rosalie Slaughter. A Doctor's Holiday in Iran. New York, 1940.

Mostafavi, Rahmat. "Fiction in Contemporary Persian Literature," *Middle Eastern Affairs*, II, No. 8–9 (August–September 1951), 273–79.

Mostowfi, 'Abdollah. Sharh-e Zendegani-ye Man ya Tarikh-e Ejtema'i va Edari-ye Dowre-ye Qajariyye (My Life, or a Social Administrative History of the Qajar Period). 4 vols. Tehran, 1945.

Naamani, Israel T. "Iran and Her Problems," *Middle Eastern Affairs*, II, No. 6–7 (June–July 1951), 203–12.

Nabil. The Dawn-Breakers. New York, 1932.

Najmi, Naser. 'Abbas Mirza. Tehran, 1947.

Nakhostin Kongere-ye Nevisandegan-e Iran (Report on the First Congress of Iranian Writers). Tehran, 1947.

Navai, M. Les Relations économiques irano-russes. Paris, 1935.

Overseas Consultants, Inc. Report on the Seven-Year Development Plan for the Plan Organization of the Imperial Government of Iran. 5 vols. New York, 1949.

Parviz, 'Abbas. Tarikh-e Iran (A History of Iran). Tehran, [193?].
———. Tarikh-e Iran ba'd az Islam ta 'Asr-e Hazer (A History of Iran from the Muslim Conquest to the Present). Tehran, [1938?].

Pavlovich, M., and Iranskii, S. Persiia v Bor'be za Nezavisimost'. Moscow, 1925.

Payne, Grace Visher. The Unveiling. Philadelphia, 1950.

Payne, Robert. Journey to Persia. London, 1951.

Pernot, Maurice. L'Inquiétude de l'Orient en Asie Musulmane. 2 vols. Paris, 1927.

Philby, H. St. J. B. A Pilgrim in Arabia. London, 1946.

Polacco, Angelo. L'Iran di Reza Scia Pahlavi. Venice, 1937.

Qa'em-Maqami, Jahangir. Tahavvolat-e Siyasi-ye Nezam-e Iran (The Political Evolution of the Iranian Army). Tehran, 1947.

Qasemzade. Hoquq-e Asasi (Fundamental Rights). Tehran, 1947.

Rajput, A. B. Iran Today. Lahore, 1946.

Razi, 'Abdollah. "Be Nam-e Iran va Iranian: Enqelab dar Afkar." (A Revolution in Ideas). *Rastakhiz*, II, No. 1 (April 1925), 1–7.

Reisner, I. M., and Rubtsova, B. K., eds. Novaia istoriia stran zarubezhnogo vostoka. 2 vols. Moscow, 1952.

Rice, C. Colliver. Persian Women and Their Ways. London, 1923.

Roberts, N. S. Iran: Economic and Commercial Conditions. London, 1948.

Rosen, Friedrich. Oriental Memories of a German Diplomatist. London, 1930.

Ross, Sir E. Denison. The Persians. Oxford, 1931.

Saba, M. Bibliographie française de l'Iran. Paris, 1936.

Sadiq, Issa. Modern Persia and Her Educational System. New York, 1931.

Sadr, Kazem. Tarikh-e Siyasat-e Khareji-ye Iran (A History of Iran's Foreign Policy). Tehran, 1943.

Sadr-Hashemi, Muhammad. Tarikh-e Jara'ed va Majellat-e Iran (A History of Press and Periodicals in Iran). 3 vols. Isfahan, 1948–50.

Sa'ed, Muhammad. L'Iran. Rome, 1937.

Saghaphi, Mirza Mahmoud Khan. In the Imperial Shadow. New York, 1928.

Sa'idi, Seid Hadi. Islam va Sosiyalizm (Islam and Socialism). Tehran, 1947.

Sakha'i Mahmud. Mosaddeq va Rastakhiz-e Mellat (Mosaddeq and the Awakening of the Nation). Tehran, 1952.

Sangelaji, Muhammad, Kolliyat-e 'Uqud va Iqa'at (Fundamentals of Contracts in Shari'ah). Tehran, 1945.

Shafaq, Rezazade. "Drama in Contemporary Iran." *Middle Eastern Affairs*, IV, No. 1 (January 1953), 11–15.

———. "Patriotic Poetry in Modern Iran." *The Middle East Journal*, VI, No. 4 (Autumn, 1952), 417–28.

———. Yadegar-e Mosaferat-e Suis (Memoirs of a Swiss Journey). Tehran, 1948.

Sheean, Vincent. The New Persia. New York, 1927.

Shahriyari, Parviz. Ahmad Kasravi. Tehran, 1946.

Shayegan, 'Ali. Hoquq-e Modoni-ye Iran (The Civil Code of Iran). Tehran, 1945.

Shoghi Effendi. Pattern for Future Society. Wilmette, Ill., 1944.

Shuster, W. Morgan. The Strangling of Persia: Story of the European Diplomacy and Oriental Intrigue that Resulted in the Denationalization of Twelve Million Mohammedans—A Personal Narrative. New York, 1920.

Singer, Caroline, and Baldridge, Cyrus Le Roy. Half the World is Isfahan. New York, 1936.

Soltanzade, Reza. Kar va Pishe va Pul (Work, Skill, and Money). Tehran, 1944.

Sotude, Hasan. Tarikh-e Diplomasi (A History of Diplomacy). Tehran?, [194?].

Soviet Imperialism: Iran, 1919–1949. N.p., [1950?].

Speer, Robert E. Report on India and Persia of the Deputation Sent by the Board of Foreign Missions of the Presbyterian Church in the U.S.A. to Visit These Fields in 1921–1922. New York, 1922.

Stark, Freya. Beyond Euphrates: Autobiography 1928–1933. London, 1951.

———. The Valleys of the Assassins and Other Persian Travels. London, 1934.

Sykes, Christopher. Wassmuss, the Persian Lawrence. London, 1936.

Sykes, Ella Constance. Persia and its People. London, 1910.

Sykes, Sir Percy Molesworth. The Glory of the Shia World: The Tale of a Pilgrimage. London, 1910.

———. A History of Persia. 2 vols. London, 1951.

———. Ten Thousand Miles in Persia; or Eight Years in Iran. London, 1902.

Tabari, Ehsan. "Bar-resi-ye Sharayet-e Zohur va Marahel-e Roshd va Mobareze va Khasa'es-e Tarikhi-ye Hezb-e Tude-ye Iran" (Research in the Origins of the Tudeh Party). *Mardom,* Year I, fifth period, No. 8 (May 1947), pp. 1–13.

———. "Sadeq Hedayat: Shakhsiyat-e u, Afkar-e u, Jay-e u dar Hayat-e Adabi va Ejtema'i-ye Mo'aser" (A Socio-Literary Appraisal of Sadeq Hedayat). *Mardom,* Year I, fifth period, No. 10 (July 1947), pp. 42–47.

Tamaddon, Khalil. Sazeman-e Modoni-ye Iran (The Civil Structure of Iran). Tehran, 1945.

Tavakkoli, Ahmad. Ravabet-e Siyasi-ye Iran ba Afghanestan (Irano-Afghan Diplomatic Relations). Tehran, 1948.

Tehrani, Alexander. Iran. Berlin, 1943.

Tehrani-Afshari, Hasan. Mirza Kuchek Khan. Tehran, 1941.

Thomas, Lewis V., and Frye, Richard N. The United States and Turkey and Iran. Cambridge, Mass., 1951.

Tria, V. Kavkazkie Sotsial'-demokratii v persidskoi revoliutsii. Paris, 1910.

Upton, Joseph M. The History of Modern Iran: An Interpretation. Cambridge, Mass., 1960.

Vahid-Dastgerdi, Hasan. Rahavard-e Vahid (Memoirs). Tehran, 1928.

Vogt, Josephine. A Study of Home and Family Life in Rural Iran. MS. New York, 1950.

Waughburton, Richard. Innocence and Design. London, 1935.

Warriner, Doreen. Land and Poverty in the Middle East. London, 1948.

Weil, Gotthold. "Arnold Toynbee's Conception of the Future of Islam." *Middle Eastern Affairs,* II, No. 1 (January 1951), 3–16.

Wilber, Donald N. Iran: Past and Present. Princeton, N.J., 1950.

Wilson, Sir Arnold Talbot. A Bibliography of Persia. Oxford, 1930.

———. Persia. London, 1932.

———. Southwest Persia, a Political Officer's Diary, 1907–1914. London, 1941.

Yaddashtha-ye Serri-ye Reza Shah (The Secret Memoirs of Reza Shah). Tehran, [194?].

Young, T. Cuyler, ed. Near Eastern Culture and Society: A Symposium on the Meeting of East and West. Princeton, N.J., 1951.

———. "The Problem of Westernization in Modern Iran." *The Middle East Journal,* II (January 1948), 47–59.

———. "The Social Support of Current Iranian Policy." *The Middle East Journal,* VI (Spring 1952), 125–43.

Zarandi, Mahmud. Chand So'al az Kasravi (A Few Questions for Kasravi). Tehran, 1944.

Zolmajdein, Zeinal'abedin. Feqh va Tejarat (Feqh and Commerce). Tehran, 1947.

PERIODICALS

Bank Melli Iran Bulletin, 1933–59. Tehran.

Cahiers de l'Orient contemporain, 1945–51. Paris.

Ettela'at Mahane, 1948–50. Tehran.

Journal of the Royal Central Asian Society, 1925–59. London.

Mardom, 1946–48. Tehran.

Middle Eastern Affairs, 1950–59. New York.

Middle East Journal, The, 1947–59. Washington, D.C.

Muslim World, 1921–50. Hartford, Connecticut.

Oriente Moderno, 1921–59. Rome.

Parcham, 1943. Tehran.

Rastakhiz (Resurrection), 1925. Cairo.

Razm, 1948–49. Tehran.

Revue des études Islamiques, 1927–59. Paris.

Yadegar, 1945–46. Tehran.

INDEX

INDEX